D1588868

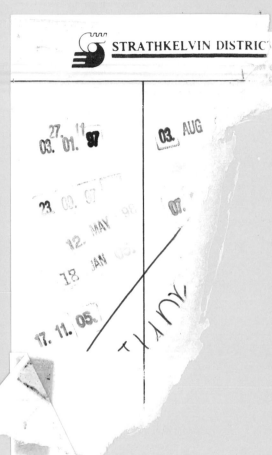

STRATHKELVIN DISTRICT

on or before

27
03. 01. 97

03. AUG

23. 09. 97

12. MAY

07.

18. JAN

17. 11. 05.

of F/odj

THE WINNER'S
GUIDE TO GAMES

Gyles Brandreth

GUINNESS PUBLISHING

LB 1776

COATBRIDGE LIBRARY
ACADEMY STREET
Tel. No. 24150

Copyright © Gyles Brandreth 1992

The right of Gyles Brandreth to be identified as the Author of this work has
been asserted in accordance with the Copyright, Design & Patents Act 1988.

Published in Great Britain by Guinness Publishing Ltd, 33 London Road,
Enfield, Middlesex

All rights reserved. No part of this publication may be reproduced, stored
in a retrieval system, or transmitted in any form or by any means, electronic,
mechanical, photocopying, recording or otherwise without prior permission in
writing of the publisher.

Designed by John Mitchell

Typeset in Garamond by Ace Filmsetting Ltd, Frome, Somerset

Printed and bound in Great Britain by the Bath Press, Bath

'Guinness' is a registered trademark of Guinness Publishing Ltd

A catalogue record for this book is available from the British Library

ISBN 0–85112–508–5

CONTENTS

INTRODUCTION

CARD GAMES

DOMINO GAMES

DICE GAMES

BOARD GAMES

PENCIL AND PAPER GAMES

INDEX OF GAMES

INTRODUCTION

Welcome to *The Winner's Guide to Games*. As the title suggests, my aim has been to provide a comprehensive compendium of many of the world's best indoor games together with advice on how you can play those games successfully. With each game, as well as providing a brief introduction to its origins and outlining the basic rules, I have given a 'guesstimate' as to the time required for an average game and a 'complexity rating' showing how easy or difficult I reckon the game will be to master. One star is for the most elementary, four stars for the most challenging.

While the rules offered for each game are the most widely and generally accepted ones (and where there are variations on rules these are indicated), the winning strategies proposed (more modestly and more accurately described as 'Tips' within the text) are simply based on my own observation and experience, together with that of games-playing friends. Of these, I must make a special mention of Tony Brett Young, without whose collaboration the book would not have been possible.

Of course, the best way to improve your play at any game is to practise, to play regularly but not 'automatically'. By that I mean that the player intent on improving his or her performance will constantly observe how he or she is playing and so aim to improve their performance rather than repeat their mistakes.

In my own family I am proud to say we have been indoor games enthusiasts for generations. A century ago, in New York, my great-great-grandfather published *Brandreth's Puzzle Book*, a compendium of his favourite games, pastimes and brainteasers. The book was really intended to promote the sales of Brandreth's Pills – 'a medicine that acts directly on the stomach, bowels and liver, and through them purifies the blood: they cure rheumatism, headache, biliousness, constipation, dyspepsia and liver complaint' – but having been to Sing Sing, the unlikely location of the Brandreth Pill factory, and tasted both the medicine and read the book, I am inclined to think my forebears were better games players than they were pharmacists.

My own parents met over a Monopoly board. In the winter of 1936 my father bought the then brand new board game and took the box back to his lodgings in Gower Street, London, where he asked his landlady if she fancied a game. She didn't, but she said that the Canadian lady and her daughter at the end of the landing might – and they did. Forty years later, when that Monopoly tyro and the Canadian lady's daughter were celebrating their Ruby Wedding Anniversary, I was in New York doing my best to uphold the family honour by coming third in the World Monopoly Championships. (Naturally, had I had this book to hand at the time, I should have come first!)

While I owe my very existence to the invention of Monopoly, I owe my enduring love of words to the invention of Scrabble. I have been playing Scrabble since the 1950s and founded the British National Scrabble Championships in 1971. Not only is it the world's best-selling word game, it is also the world's best word game.

While Monopoly and Scrabble are relatively new games, many of the games featured in this book have been popular for thousands of years. There is nothing new in people playing games. Indeed, playing games is an important part of life. As the German historian and philosopher, Johan Huizinga, puts it in his book, *Homo Ludens*, one of the few serious studies of the place of play in culture, 'play adorns life, amplifies it and is to that extent a necessity, both for the individual – as a life function – and for society by reason of the meaning it contains, its significance, its expressive value, its spiritual and social associations, in short, as a cultural function. The expression of it satisfies all kinds of cultural needs.'

That's a somewhat grandiloquent way of saying: Games are good for you. Enjoy!

CARD GAMES

The origin of playing cards is unknown. The Chinese developed a form of cards, and these may have reached Europe during the Crusades, or the China trade. It has also been suggested that playing cards in Europe may have had quite a separate European origin. The first record of them dates from the late 14th century when they appeared in virtually their present form.

IT'S A FACT...
The word 'card' comes from the Latin word 'charta', meaning a sheet of paper.

CARD TERMINOLOGY

The deck or pack: The standard international deck consists of 52 cards divided into four suits of 13 cards each. Decks also usually contain two jokers, sometimes used as wild cards.

The suits: These are called spades, clubs, hearts and diamonds with each card displaying the appropriate symbol, hearts and diamonds in red and clubs and spades in black.

The cards: Every card in a suit is of a different denomination. The ace is the '1' but is often the most powerful card of the suit. The next nine are numbered '2' to '10', and the other three are 'court' or 'face' cards – the jack (or knave), queen and king.

Order or cards: Depending on the game, this can be 2 (low), 3, 4, 5, 6, 7, 8, 9, 10, jack, queen, king, ace (high) or ace (low), 2, 3, 4, 5, 6, 7, 8, 9, 10, jack, queen, king (high). In either order, a card beats any card below it.

Trumps: In games in which tricks are taken, certain cards are made trump cards, or trumps. If so, any trump card ranks above the cards of any other card. Usually, all the cards of one suit are the trump cards. In some games however, only some cards of one suit are the trump cards. In other games, there are other trump cards as well as the trump suit.

Tricks: In some games, a trick signifies one round of cards during the play. It also means the cards themselves when they are gathered together.

A contract: An undertaking to reach an objective after bidding higher than anyone else.

Discards: Unwanted cards thrown out from a player's hand.

A meld: In certain games, this is a scoring combination. It could be three or more cards of the same denomination, or three or more cards in consecutive order of rank and of the same suit.

Lead: To play the first card in a deal or to a trick.

Long: A hand with more than the average number of cards in a particular suit.
Pass: To refrain from bidding.
Plain suit: One that is not trumps.
Sequence: A set of cards in numerical sequence such as ace, 2, 3, 4.
Stock: Undealt cards from the pack.
Wild card: One that may represent any card its holder wishes.

BRIDGE

Bridge has the pre-eminence among card games that Chess has among board games. It is the name given to the modern card game of Contract Bridge, and also to the earlier games of Auction Bridge and Bridge Whist. Contract Bridge takes longer to learn than other card games, but the effort in becoming proficient at the game is repaid many times over.

COMPLEXITY RATING:	★ ★ ★
NUMBER OF PLAYERS:	4
EQUIPMENT:	Standard pack of 52 cards
TIME REQUIRED:	1½ to 3 hours

Origins: Bridge (or more formally, Contract Bridge) has evolved from Whist (qv) during the past century. The game of Biritch or Russian Whist, introduced in about 1880, was a version of Whist in which the dealer could nominate the trump suit. Bridge Whist, introduced in 1896, gave the dealer the option of letting his partner nominate the trump suit. Contract Bridge was given its present form in 1925 by an American millionaire, Harold S Vanderbilt, and made especially popular by the promotion of Ely Cuthbertson, who also introduced the first standard bidding system.

Aim of the game: Bridge is a partnership game for four players, and each partnership aims to win a 'rubber' by scoring the most points in the best of three games. A game is won by scoring 100 points, earned by taking tricks that have been contracted for.

Basic rules: The cards rank from ace high to 2 low. For the purposes of bidding (though not in play) the suits are also ranked in order: spades (highest), hearts, diamonds, clubs (lowest).

An easy way to remember this is to think of them as ascending in value in alphabetical order: c, d, h, s. Spades and hearts are described as major suits and diamonds and clubs as minor suits.

TIP

To assist in deciding the worth of your hand, the high cards in your hand are valued by using a simple points count: ace = 4 points; king = 3; queen = 2; and jack = 1 point. This gives a total of 10 points in each suit, 40 in the whole pack and 10 in an average hand.

•

The game starts with a draw for partners and first deal. The pack is spread out face down with each player drawing a card. The players drawing the two highest play as partners against the other two, and the one drawing the highest card has first deal. Partners sit opposite each other, and are usually referred to as North–South and East–West. The cards are then dealt, one at a time and face down, to give each player 13 cards.

The game consists of two parts – the bidding (or auction) and the play. The play consists of 13 tricks, and in the bidding each side tries to estimate the number of tricks they think they can win with their combined hands. A bid is a declaration by one side that they will attempt to win a certain number of tricks with a certain nominated trump suit.

TIP

There are many systems and conventions which govern bidding in Bridge. A convention is a single bid which gives a particular message about a hand, while a system follows agreed principles which allow partnerships to reach the best contract for their hands. A particular convention may be used in a number of systems, and a particular system can use different conventions for the same result. The simplest convention, used by many social players, is the two-club system. If you are a beginner, it is advisable to start with this system. There are many books which describe this and other conventions and systems in detail. You should master them, particularly if playing regularly with another partner. However, even if you are playing with a new partner, it is necessary to find a common ground of systems and conventions.

•

TIP

Your bid will be governed by the strength of your hand, and what you can learn about your partner's hand through the bidding process. Tricks are won with trump cards, high cards (ace, king, queen and jack) and 'long' cards (those where you have more than the average number, ie four or more). Long cards in the trump suits are eventually unbeatable.

•

TIP

The strength of the hand does not depend entirely on high cards. The way in which the cards are divided between the suits is also important. For example:

i)	spades	: J 9 3	ii)	spades	: 7
	hearts	: A 8 6 2		hearts	: A K 9 7 4 3
	diamonds	: Q 4 3		diamonds	: K J 2
	clubs	: K Q 7		clubs	: 9 4 3

Hand (i) has a total of 12 points and hand (ii) only 11 but (ii) is the stronger hand because hearts is a much longer suit than any of the others.

•

TIP

The opening bid is particularly important to the side making it. The minimum requirements for an opening bid of one in a suit are:
13 points if you have no suit longer than four cards
12 points if you have a five-card suit
11 points if you have a six-card suit or two five-card suits.

•

The highest bid becomes the contract. In the subsequent play the side making the highest bid will attempt to fulfil this contract winning at least the declared number of tricks, while the opposing side will try to stop them – it does not matter what they themselves have bid.

The bidding begins when every player has had an opportunity to study the cards in his hand. Beginning with the dealer, each player in turn may pass, bid, double or redouble.

To pass, a player says "No bid". This does not prevent him from making a subsequent bid when his turn comes round again in the bidding. If all players pass, the hands are thrown in to the centre of the table and shuffled. A new hand is dealt by the next dealer.

TIP

The better the players, the more frequent the hands will be thrown in. Better to throw in two hands which would have made quite a good trick-winning combination than a call which is not justified.

•

A bid is a declaration that a player's side will win a certain number of tricks with a nominated trump suit (or with no trumps). Since there are 13 tricks to be taken, the side winning the majority of tricks must win 7 or more. The first 6 tricks won are known as 'the book' and tricks won in excess of that number are known as 'odd tricks'.

Bids are made in terms of odd tricks. So, for example, a bid of one club is a bid to win 7 tricks with clubs as trumps suit, and two no trumps is a bid to win 8 tricks with no trump suit.

Each bid must be higher than the previous one. That is, it must be for a higher number of tricks or for the same number of tricks but with a higher-ranking suit as trumps. A no-trump bid ranks above a bid in any suit. The possible bids in ascending order therefore are: one club, one diamond, one heart, one spade, one no trump, two clubs, two diamonds and so on.

The guiding principle is to bid on length. If you are bidding a suit, you are proposing it as trumps, and you will struggle if your opponents have more trumps than you. Bid your longest suit therefore when you have more than one suit to choose from. It is length rather than strength that counts in selecting a trump suit.

If you have two suits with the same number of cards, open your bidding with the higher-ranking one.

When you have a small number of cards in one suit, and they are high value, take particular notice of your partner's bid to see if most of your high cards are in suits with fewer cards, and through bidding you should be able to establish the strength of his hand.

When you open the bidding in a suit, you are obliged to bid again if your partner replies in another suit. In other words, an opening bid guarantees a rebid, but unless you take care when opening, you may be in trouble when it comes to finding a rebid.

If you have a hand count of 13 or more, you should not pass, even if your distribution is very even and you have no long suit. For example, if you have:

spades : *Q 9 6*	*diamonds* : *K 7 2*
hearts : *10 8 5 3*	*clubs* : *A K 6*

perhaps the best course is to open one club, even though you have only three cards in the suit. You have kept the bidding as low as you can, and you could then rebid with one no trump if you get a response of one diamond or one spade. If your partner replies with one heart, you would raise to two hearts.

•

As a general rule, do not open with one no trump unless you have a strong hand with a point count of 15 or better. Some people will open with less, or even more, but this is something you should agree with your partner. You should of course have a reasonably balanced hand.

•

GENERAL TIP
Before opening with a bid of one in any suit, plan your rebid.

•

When bidding has opened, it is important to know how to respond. A player can respond on a hand worth as little as 6 providing he has something worthwhile to add to the opening bid. Several possibilities are open to him: he can pass; he can bid 1 no trump; he can raise the bid in the same suit; or he can make a bid in another suit.

If you have less than 6 in your high cards, you should pass.

•

If you have 6 to 9 points, but are unable to support your partner's suit with four or more, you could bid 1 no trump, although this indicates weakness. If you have a balanced hand, and are reasonably strong in your partner's suit, you could reply with 2 no trumps to show 11 to 12 points, or 3 no trumps to indicate 13 to 15.

•

If your partner has bid a major suit, and you can support it with four trumps or more you can raise the bid, depending on its strength. You show the full value of your hand by the level to which you raise. If you are thinking of raising your partner's suit, it is very helpful to be short in a side suit. If you have only three cards in your partner's suit, you could still raise the bid, provided your trumps include an honour card, and the hand is not too weak. There is not the same need to raise when your partner bids a minor suit. To take the game, you need 11 tricks, and that will normally require a combined points count of 28 or more. It would be better to respond with a bid in a major suit if you have one. Your partner may be able to support this bid, or to bid no trumps, and a target of 9 or 10 tricks will be easier to reach than 11.

•

If you cannot follow the suit already bid by your partner, you can bid a new suit at the one-level with as little as 6 points. With 8 or 9 points it is necessary to have a strong suit of five cards or longer. Your partner should bid again when you respond in a new suit. If he passes, this could result in a missed game if your hand is in the upper range.

•

If you are responding in a new suit, the best choice can be made by following three rules:

i)   when you have suits of unequal length, you should bid the longest suit

ii)   when you have two five-card or longer suits, bid the one which is higher-ranking

iii)   when you have only four-card suits, you should make the lowest bid.

•

If you have a hand of 16 points or more, and your partner opens the bidding, you can indicate your strong position by bidding one more than necessary in a new suit – three diamonds in response to one spade, for example.

•

Bidding is sometimes finished in the first round. But with many hands it takes a second or even third round to complete. The second round needs more precision than the first.

When possible, the opener's rebid should be appropriate to his strength and distribution.

•

Instead of making a bid, a player may make a call of double or redouble. A call of double can be made only after an opponent's bid, and signifies that a player is confident of being able to prevent the opposing side from winning the number of tricks bid. A call of redouble can be made only if the previous call was a double from an opponent, and signifies that a player is confident that his partner's last bid which has been doubled, can be successful.

Doubling or redoubling doubles or quadruples the points or penalties for success or failure if the bid becomes the contract. A bid that has been doubled or redoubled can be overcalled by a higher bid in the normal way.

For example, the bidding might proceed: two clubs, double, redouble, two hearts – and the double and redouble are therefore cancelled.

It is often better to redouble when there is a risk of going down by one trick than on a firm contract because the redouble of a certainty may mean the opposition is provoked into further bidding.

•

The contract is established when the last and highest bid (whether doubled or redoubled) has been followed by three consecutive passes. The player on the contracting side who first nominated the trump suit of the contract is the 'declarer', and he will play his own and his partner's hand.

THE PLAY

The opening lead is made by the player to the left of the declarer. As soon as the opening lead has been made, the declarer's partner lays his cards face upwards on the table, with each suit in a separate column of overlapping cards in rank order. The declarer's partner takes no further part in the play, and his hand – the dummy – is played by the declarer.

The cards are played to each trick in clockwise order, and normal rules of trick-taking apply. A player must follow suit if he can, otherwise he must play a trump or discard a card of any other suit as he pleases. A trick is won by the highest-ranking card of the suit that was led, or by the highest-ranking trump if any were played. The winner of each trick leads to the next.

If the declarer wins a trick from his own hand he must lead to the next trick from his own hand; if he wins a hand from the dummy he must lead to the next trick from the dummy. All tricks won by one side must be kept in one place and arranged to show clearly the number of tricks won so far.

Playing the hand is, if anything, even more important than the bidding. A bad bid can sometimes be retrieved by spectacular play, but correct bidding counts for nothing if the caller cannot make the tricks he should.

•

In your opening leads, remember the bidding and try to place the high cards in the various hands. If your partner has bid, lead the highest of his suit. If you hold a suit with ace and king which have not been mentioned in the bidding, lead the king, then your partner's suit. He will then know how to get back into your hand when he needs to. Lead the king also from a suit headed by king and queen. Avoid leading from a suit headed by a 'tenace', ie two cards in a suit where the player does not have the intervening card (for example, ace and queen). The best 'blind' lead against a suit call of six or seven is a trump.

•

You should always remember the saying: 'Lead through strength up to weakness.'

•

A good defensive lead is a card which the declarer must trump in his own hand, therefore weakening his trump suit. Beginners often lead a card from dummy and trump it in their own hand. This is nearly always a bad move as their small trumps will make in any case. On the other hand, every effort should be made to make use of trumps in the dummy.

•

In playing a no-trump hand, you should play out from long suits rather than from short ones, even if the short ones have high honour cards. In defending against no-trumps, do not switch your lead from suit to suit. Instead you should be patient and follow one.

•

The basic principles of trick-play are similar to any other Whist-type game. Perhaps the main difference with Bridge is that you know much more about the cards from the start, through bidding, and through seeing the dummy. It is helpful for beginners to gain a good knowledge of whist before taking up Bridge seriously.

•

GENERAL TIP

The literature of the game is extensive, and it is easy to find books on Bridge by acknowledged experts on the game. It is essential to read two or three to start with to develop your knowledge and expertise of the game.

•

SCORING

The scoring in Bridge strongly affects the game's strategy, and must be mastered. Scoring is done on a sheet divided into two columns. It is customary for both sides to keep score to provide a double check. A horizontal line divides the columns into an upper half and a lower half, and points may be scored 'above the line' or 'below the line'. Only points scored below the line count towards the game. A game is won by the first side to reach or exceed 100 points below the line. A rubber is won by the first side to win two games. A side with one game won is said to be 'vulnerable'.

Trick points can only be scored by the declarer's side, if the contract succeeds. Only the odd tricks contracted for can be scored below the line. Overtricks – those won in excess of the contract – are scored above the line.

A successful contract to win 12 tricks is called a little slam, while a successful contract to win all 13 tricks is called a grand slam. There are bonus points for winning a slam, and for winning a doubled or redoubled contract. These bonus points are scored above the line. If the declarer 'goes down' (ie, if the contract does not succeed) the opposing side score points above the line for each 'undertrick' (ie, each trick by which the declarer falls short of the contract).

Regardless of whether the contract succeeds or fails, either side may score points above the line for honours – the five highest-ranking cards in the trump suit, ace to 10, or, in a no trumps contract, the four aces. Points are scored for having been dealt honours in one's hand, and thus represent an element of pure chance.

When a game is won, a line is drawn below the trick scores for both sides. Trick points for the next game, starting again from zero, are scored below this line. At the end of a rubber the winning side scores a bonus above the line of 700 premium points if the opposing side has not won a game, or 500 premium points if the opposing side has won a game. All the points above and below the line are then totalled for each side.

The difference between the two scores represents the value of the rubber. The difference is rounded to the nearest 100 (50 and above become 100) and divided by 100. For example 860 becomes 900, to give 9.

Each player of the winning partnership is then given a score of plus 9, and each of the opponents a score of minus 9. In subsequent rubbers, with different partnerships, the same procedure is followed. The player with the highest plus score at the end is the overall winner.

Details of scoring are shown in the table opposite:

Contract succeeds:

Points scored below the line for each odd trick bid and won

	undoubled	doubled	redoubled
In minor suits (clubs or diamonds)	20	40	80
In major suits (hearts or spades)	30	60	120
No trumps – first odd trick	40	80	160
No trumps – subsequent tricks	30	60	120

Contract succeeds:

Points scored above the line by declarer

	Not vulnerable	Vulnerable
Per overtrick, if undoubled	(Trick value, as above)	
Per overtrick, if doubled	100	200
Per overtrick, if redoubled	200	400
Bonus for doubled or redoubled contract	50	50
Little slam	500	750
Grand slam	1,000	1,500

Contract fails:

Points scored above the line by Defenders

	Not vulnerable	Vulnerable
If undoubled, for each undertrick	50	100
If doubled, for 1st undertrick	100	200
If doubled, for subsequent undertricks	200	300
If redoubled, for 1st undertrick	200	400
If redoubled, for subsequent undertricks	400	600

Honours:

Points scored above the line

For all 5 trump honours in one hand	150
For any 4 trump honours in one hand	100
For 4 aces in one hand in no trump contract	150

Rubber and Game Points

For winning rubber, if opponents have won no game	700
For winning rubber, if opponents have won one game	500
Unfinished rubber: for having won one game	300
Unfinished rubber: for having part score in unfinished game	50

GENERAL TIPS

Although many advice books have been written about Bridge, it is essential to have actual experience of play. You should have a number of rubbers among players of any standard to get a basis of the general procedure. However, from then on you should always try to play with good players.

Bridge is much more precise, and depends on mathematics more than other card games. You should memorise the principles right from the start, but do not be daunted by this. It is worth learning them for the enjoyment you will have.

•

IT'S A FACT...
More than 5,000 books have been published on Bridge, and those still in print sell 1 million copies every year.

WHIST

Whist has given rise to a whole range of games including Contract Bridge and Solo Whist. However the original game is still enormously popular in many countries. The rules are comparatively simple, but skill is needed to become a very good player, and anyone planning to take up bridge should learn whist by way of a helpful introduction.

COMPLEXITY RATING:	★ ★ ★
NUMBER OF PLAYERS:	4
EQUIPMENT:	**Standard pack of 52 cards**
TIME REQUIRED:	**20 to 30 minutes per game**

Origins: Whist appears to have evolved in the early 16th century in England, played originally by poorer and uneducated sections of the community. It came from several other games, especially triumph, a name which eventually became 'trump'. Early in the eighteenth century whist became popular with the aristocrats who frequented London's coffee houses. In 1742, the first book devoted solely to the game, Hoyle's 'Short Treatise on Whist' was published and became a bestseller.

It then became extremely popular in fashionable society, spreading to Europe and America, and remaining the most popular of card games for about a century and a half. As strategy became more highly-developed, players turned to bridge, which required greater scope for reasoning. Whist still has a strong following in Great Britain and parts of North America, but its former popularity has gone.

Aim of the game: Whist is a four-handed partnership game in which points are scored for tricks and honours. In English Whist, the first side to score five points wins the game, and a rubber is the best of three games. (In American whist, a seven-point game is used.) The object of play is to win a majority of the 13 tricks. The cards rank from ace high to two low.

Partners sit opposite one another, and the pack is cut to decide first deal. Thereafter each player deals in turn. Thirteen cards are dealt, one at a time and face down, to each player, except that the last card (the dealer's) is dealt face up to establish the trump suit.

Each player picks up the cards dealt to him, and arranges them into suits. The player to the left of the dealer leads to the first trick. The other players in turn must follow suit if they can, otherwise they may play a trump or discard a card of another suit as they wish. The trick is won by the player of the highest trump card, or if no trump card was played, by the player with the highest card of the suit which was led. The winner of each trick leads to the next, and so on until all thirteen tricks have been played.

Each side tries to win tricks in the suit in which, as a partnership, they hold most cards. To indicate this to your partner, you should lead it at the earliest opportunity, or discard a low card from it when unable to follow suit to the card which has been led. You should then try to establish the suit by forcing any high cards your opponents hold so that they cannot win when a number of cards of that suit are led. Having established it, you must try to eliminate trumps from the play so that your opponents cannot beat the established suit by playing a trump to a non-trump suit.

•

If you are leading, you have a clear advantage because you have a free choice of what to lead, and this tells your partner about what you have in your hand. You should therefore play your best suit to tell your partner which one you think you could win with. Your partner would then normally lead the same suit as soon as he has the chance, unless of course he feels he could do even better with the cards he holds. You can therefore convey to your partner whether you have a strong or weak hand by a careful choice of the card you lead. This is done by established signals, many of which have been adopted for Bridge.

•

If you are playing second to the trick, it is generally a good idea to play low unless you are certain of winning the trick or have only two of the suit which has been led. If you are the third person you should normally play a high card in an attempt to win the trick, unless you are certain that your partner's lead is unbeatable. As the fourth player you are in the best position, and can play as you see fit. If your partner has not already taken the trick, you should try to do so if you can. However, if he has taken it, you can throw away your most useless card.

•

The signals which have been devised are not 'rules' – they are helpful suggestions as to how you should play hands of various kinds, and have been accepted by most good players. It also means that you can give your partner some idea of what you are holding in your hand. This is very helpful in the early stages of the game.

They can be summarised in this way: If you have four or more non-trump cards in a suit, lead with a card from your best (ie the one with most cards) suit. If you have two suits with the same number of cards, play from the one with the highest cards. If your top cards in the opening suit follow any of these patterns, lead to the first and second tricks like this:

AS THE FIRST PLAYER

Plain suit cards	First lead	Second lead
Ace, king, queen, jack	king	jack
Ace, king, queen	king	queen
Ace, king, and others	king	ace
Ace, king only	ace	king
King, queen, jack and one low card	king	jack
King, queen, jack and more than one other card	jack	king, if five; queen, if more than five
Ace and four or more low cards	ace	fourth best of those left
King, queen and others	king	if king wins, fourth best of those left
Ace, queen, jack with or without one low one	king	queen
Ace, queen, jack with two or more	ace	jack
King, jack, ten, nine	nine	king, if ace queen falls
King, jack, ten	ten	
Queen, jack, ten, nine	queen	nine
Queen, jack, and a low card	queen	
Queen, jack, and two or more	fourth best	

Trumps may be led if you hold five or more, with these signals:

Holding	First lead	Second lead
Ace, king, queen, jack	jack	queen
Ace, king, queen	queen	king

Holding		
Ace, king and five others	king	ace
Ace, king and fewer than five low cards	fourth best	

AS THE SECOND PLAYER

Holding	Card led	Play, second hand
Ace, king, queen	low	queen
Ace, king, jack	low	king
Ace, king, and others	low	king
Ace, queen, ten and so on	low	queen
Ace, queen, ten and so on	jack	ace
In trumps	low	ten
Ace, queen, and low	low	low
Ace, jack, ten and so on	low	low
In trumps	low	ten
Ace and low	low	low
King, queen, jack and so on	low	jack
King, queen and so on	low	queen
Queen, jack, and low	low	jack
Ace and low	queen	ace
King and others low	queen	low
King and one other	low	low
Queen and one other	low	low
Queen and one other	jack or ten	queen

If you are the third player, and the opponent to your right plays a higher card than the one your partner has led in a suit in which you have the ace and queen, it is quite acceptable to try to win the trick with the queen. You hope, of course, that your partner, and not the fourth player, has the king. Such an attempt to win a trick with an inferior card is called a finesse. If the queen wins, the finesse succeeds against the king and your ace and queen win two tricks instead of one. This is called a finesse speculative.

•

There is another kind, the finesse obligatory. An example of this is when you hold a king, ten, seven and three of a suit. You lead the three, and your partner might play the queen taking the trick. He then leads a small card of the suit. Because the queen has won, you know that the ace is not held by the opponent on your right. You also know that your partner does not hold the jack, and when he leads a small card of the suit, you know he does not hold the ace. If the player on your left has the ace and jack, it does not matter whether you play the king or ten. If the player on your right holds the jack, your ten will draw out the ace, and you still have the king.

The finesse is always a risk, and you should not use it if you are likely to lose more than you would gain by winning with it. It can be used in all trick-taking card games.

Apart from when you are trying to win a trick, you should always play the lowest card you can of the suit which has been led. If you have just two cards left in the suit, you can alert your partner of this by playing the higher card first, and the lower one in the subsequent trick. In the same way, if you play what seems to be an unnecessarily high card before a lower one in the same suit, this is a signal to your partner that you want him to lead trumps at his first opportunity.

•

A game is won by the first side to score five points. The side winning the majority of tricks (ie seven or more) scores one point for each trick won in excess of six. Points are also scored for honours – the ace, king, queen and jack of trumps. A side dealt all four honours scores four points, or three points if dealt any three of them. However points for honours cannot be scored by a side already holding four points towards the game at the beginning of the deal. Nor can a side score honours points if the opposing side has already scored sufficient points from tricks to give them the game.

If a player revokes (ie fails to follow suit when he could have done so) the penalty is three points which his opponents may either add to their own score, or deduct from the score of the revoking side. Partners cannot win the game in any hand in which one or the other revokes.

A rubber is the best of three games, and the value of a rubber is determined by game points (not to be confused with points from tricks and honours). The side winning a game scores one game point if the opposing side has three or four points, two game points if the opposing side has one or two points, or three game points if the opposing side has not scored at all in this game. In addition, the winners of a rubber get two extra game points. The value of the rubber is the difference between the game points scored by the winners and the losers, and therefore may range from one to eight game points.

VARIATIONS OF WHIST

Bid Whist: In this game, instead of turning up a card for trumps, each player can bid how many tricks he believes he can take with his partner if he nominates trumps. No suit is nominated, just the odd number of tricks. When a bid is followed by three passes, the successful bidder nominates trumps and play starts.

If the contract is successful, the bidder's partnership scores 1 point for every odd trick achieved. If it is not successful, the opponents score 1 point for every odd trick they take and the score of the bidder's side is reduced by the number bid, eg a bid of 3 odd tricks costs them 3 points if lost.

Bismark: This is a three-hand version of whist in which each player deals four times, so that the game lasts 12 deals. The dealer receives 20 cards, but throws out four of them face down on the table. The other players receive 16 each. There is a different procedure at each deal. In deal 1, no trumps are played. The dealer scores 1 point for each trick he wins above eight, while each opponent scores 1 point for each trick above four. In deal 2, a trump card is established by turning up the last card. Scoring is the same as before. In deal 3, the dealer selects the trump suit, but play and scoring is the same. Deal 4 has no trumps, and players try to avoid winning tricks. The dealer scores 1 point for every trick he takes below four, and each opponent scores 1 point for every trick fewer than six.

SOLO WHIST

Solo whist is considered by many people to be the equal of bridge in terms of skill and complexity, but superior in terms of enjoyment because it is more flexible.

COMPLEXITY RATING:	★ ★ ★ ★
NUMBER OF PLAYERS:	4
EQUIPMENT:	Standard pack of 52 cards
TIME REQUIRED:	20 to 30 minutes

Origins: Solo whist has obscure origins, but it could be derived from a game called German solo, which comes in turn from ombre. As played today it combines the best features of nap and whist. Solo is probably derived from the fact that, as a result of the calling, the subsequent play usually takes the form of one against three.

Aim of the game: Each player tries to contract and to fulfil a bid.

Basic rules: Cards rank from ace high to 2 low. The players cut for first deal, and all cards are dealt face down, with the exception of the last card (to the dealer) which is dealt face up, and indicates trumps.

Each player in turn from the dealer's left may make a bid, or pass without making a bid. A player whose bid is overcalled by another player may subsequently make an even higher bid, but a player who has passed once is not allowed to make a subsequent bid.

A player whose bid is followed by three subsequent passes then has to win the declared number of tricks. If he is successful the other players pay him, otherwise he has to pay them – the stakes depending on the value of the bid.

The bids are ranked in the following order:

a) *Proposal and acceptance*, or 'prop' and 'cop'. A player who calls 'I propose' (more often 'prop') declares that in partnership with any other player who accepts he will win at least eight tricks with the trump suit indicated by the deal. Unless there has been an intervening higher bid, any subsequent player may become the partner by calling 'I accept' (or more commonly ('cop'). These two players team up for the hand unless there is a higher bid.

A player calling 'prop' gives a clear indication that he has at least four good tricks in his hand.

•

When you and your partner sit side by side, you should not finesse in one of his leads if he is sitting to your right. If your partner and an opponent play after you, you should win the trick with the highest of a sequence, ie holding the king and queen, put on the king or your partner will think the king is against you.

•

As a general rule for props and cops, trumps should be used to draw trumps in order to establish plain suit.

•

Never force your partner to trump if you have a weak hand of trumps.

•

b) *Solo.* A bid to win at least five tricks playing alone against the other three players, with the trump suit indicated by the deal.

The first person to bid is in a good position to make a strong bid because he has the lead and can therefore choose the attack. If he has a reasonable hand, he should prop, because if everyone passes he has the opportunity to convert his bid to a solo, because of the obvious weakness of the opposition hands.

•

If you are the dealer, you are in a good position to bid, because by the time it is your turn, you will have an idea of the strength of the opposition. Three passes, for example, allow you to bid solo on rather weaker cards than you might do as second or third bidder.

If you are the player opposite the dealer, the second person to bid, you are in the worst position to make a positive bid because you will be playing second to the first trick, and because you do not know what the third person and dealer might bid.

•

As a general rule, you should have a good hand of strong trumps rather than high cards in plain suits.

•

c) *Misere.* A bid to lose every trick, playing with no trump suit.

It is very difficult to win misere unless you have a good selection of two suits, with a substantial share of the lowest cards including the two or three and four.

•

The worst-placed player to bid misere is the first player after the dealer as most good misere hands need to be led up to, and not from. Therefore the dealer, and then the third player are best placed to be successful in playing for misere.

•

If you have to start against a misere, you should lead from your weakest suit, and lead a medium card if you have one, say a six or seven. You should certainly not lead a two, unless it is a single card, and even then it is not always a good idea.

•

d) *Abundance.* A bid to win at least nine tricks, with the trumps suit to be declared by the bidder himself. The trump suit is not named at the time of the bid. In some schools the player, if this is the highest bid, declares the trump suit after the other players have passed and before the first trick is played. In other schools the first trick is played with the trump suit indicated by the deal, and the abundance bidder's choice of trump only takes effect for the second and subsequent tricks.

Abundance is a rare achievement, and is extremely difficult unless you hold the bulk of one suit with ace and king or ace and queen for as your best, the

jack and five or six others. You also need a couple of other aces or ace and king of another suit.

•

e) *Royal Abundance.* A bid to win at least nine tricks, with the trump suit indicated by the deal.

f) *Misere ouverte (or spread).* A bid to lose every trick, playing with no trump suit, and with the bidder's cards exposed face up on the table after the first trick has been played.

g) *Abundance declared.* A bid to win all thirteen tricks, playing with no trump suit, but with the bidder having the privilege of leading to the first trick.

If all the players pass without making a bid the hands are thrown in and the deal passes to the next player. If a player makes a prop bid and the other players all pass he may, if he wishes, make a higher bid – otherwise the hands are thrown in. The one exception to the rule that a player may not bid after having passed is that the player to the left of the dealer (but no other player) may, after passing initially, accept a prop bid from another player.

The normal rules of trick-taking apply, with the lead to the first trick being made by the player to the left of the dealer (except in the case of an abundance declared bid) and the winner of each trick leading to the next.

Each deal counts as a separate game. Stakes are paid individually by the other players to the highest bidder if he succeeds in winning the required number of tricks. Otherwise he pays each of them individually. The actual stakes, of course, are a matter of agreement by the players but the relative values of the bids are normally as follows:

Prop and cop	2 units (1 for each partner)
Solo	2 units
Misere	3 units
Abundance (or royal)	4 units
Royal Abundance	4 units
Misere ouverte	6 units
Abundance declared	8 units

The usual practice is for the stakes to depend solely on whether or not the bid is successful, but some players also include bonuses overtricks and penalties for overtricks (often ¼ or ½ unit per trick).

GENERAL TIP

Solo Whist requires great skill, but you must also be prepared to take moderate risks if you can see that the run of cards is in favour of the person who calls.

•

Your discards should be from your weakest and shortest suits. You should not leave a king unguarded.

When you have a plain suit with lots of cards headed by ace, king and queen, it is sometimes a good idea to tell your partner by first discarding the ace. In other cases, your first discard should be from your weakest suit.

While it is usually a good idea to return your partner's suit, you should be careful to remember the saying that you should play through the strong hand up to the weak one.

VARIATIONS OF SOLO WHIST
Three-hand Solo:
There are several three-hand versions of Solo, but none is as good as the four-hand variety. Perhaps the best are:

40-card Solo: Take out all the twos, threes, and four from the pack, and then deal 13 cards to each player. The last card is turned up for trumps, but is not used during the game.

There is not proposal/acceptance, but if each player passes, the turn-up is turned down and players may bid abundance of six tricks.

Seventeens: Each player receives 17 cards and the last is turned up for trumps. Each player then discards four cards face down, and play goes ahead as before but without proposal/acceptance.

ECARTE

Ecarte is one of the family of games developed from Triomphe, and is related to Euchre. It is simple to learn, but has plenty of variety. It is often played for a stake, but can be played purely for enjoyment.

COMPLEXITY RATING:	★ ★ ★
NUMBER OF PLAYERS:	**2**
EQUIPMENT:	**Short pack of 32 cards; counters**
TIME REQUIRED:	**15 to 20 minutes**

Origins: Ecarte is an old French game which became popular early last century. It reached England in about 1820, but is less popular than it used to be. Its name is from the French 'discarded'.

Aim of the game: Each player tries to take tricks and to score points. The game is won by the first player to score 5 points. Scoring is kept with counters. Each player starts with five on his left hand side, and for every point scored he transfers one to his right.

Basic rules: The cards in descending order of rank are king, queen, jack, ace, 10, 9, 8 and 7. Note the unusual position of the ace.

Players cut for the deal with the highest card dealing first (the cards rank as in play). Each player deals in turns, and five cards are dealt face down to both players.

The remainder of the pack is placed face down to form a stock, and the top card of the stock is turned over and placed face up alongside to establish the trump suit. If this card happens to be a king, the dealer scores 1 point.

The non-dealer may start by leading to the first trick, and if he does he must win it, or be penalised. However, before leading, he may propose an exchange of cards. To do this he says 'cards' or 'propose', and the dealer may either accept or refuse. If the dealer refuses, the hands have to be played out as they stand. If the dealer does not then win, he is penalised. If however he accepts, the non-dealer discards any number of cards (from one to five) face down and draws an equal number from the top of the stock. The dealer then does the same.

The non-dealer may then, if he wishes, propose another exchange of cards which the dealer may accept or refuse. This continues until the non-dealer chooses to lead, or until the dealer refuses a proposal or until the stock is exhausted. The turned-up trump remains untouched. After the exchange, but before play, either player holding the king of trumps declares it to score 1 point.

The non-dealer leads first, and each player follows suit if he can, and may trump if he cannot. A player must always take a trick if possible, and the winner of a trick leads on to the next trick.

Although the rules of following which insist that a player wins a trick if possible might appear to limit the amount of skill involved, this is certainly not the case. Judgment is needed to decide when to exchange cards and when to play. A non-dealer has two advantages: the lead, and the likelihood that the odds are against the dealer holding more trumps. if you have three or more trumps and king, you should play without proposing. On the other hand, if you propose and are accepted, you should discard all cards which are not trumps or kings and therefore exchange at least three.

•

There are certain hands which are more likely to win than to lose, and should be played without proposing. Generally they are:

trumps held	*non-trumps include*
3+	*any*
2	*king and a void suit*
	queen and one of the same suit
	any three of a suit

trumps held	non-trumps include
1	king, queen or jack of one suit
	queen and two of the same suit
	queen and another in two suits
0	any four court cards better than four jacks

You would normally lead the best card of your best suit and continue until trumped. However if you hold the king of trumps, or the queen if the king has been turned up, it is safe to propose if you are not certain how strong your hand is, and can continue to do so. The dealer cannot win all five tricks (the 'vole'), and there is always the possibility that you might do so.

•

The scoring is as follows:

a) If any cards were exchanged, the winner of the hand scores 1 point for winning three or four tricks ('point' or 'the trick'), or 2 points if he wins all five.

b) If the non-dealer loses after failing to propose or if the dealer loses after refusing the first proposal then the winner scores 2 points regardless of the number of tricks won.

c) A player holding the king of trumps scores 1 point if he declares it immediately before playing his first card.

If a player has refused to exchange and does not make at least three tricks, his opponent scores an extra point if he makes point. There is no penalty however if the opponent scores vole.

Whether you decide to propose can also depend on the current score. If the dealer is leading with 3 points, do not play without proposing, because if you lose the deal, he scores 2 for the game. If he has 4 you should stay with a weak hand unless you have the king of trumps, or it is turned up. If you invite an exchange of cards, there is the possibility of him drawing the king to score a point for the game.

•

If you are the dealer, your opponent will usually make a proposal if he holds weaker cards. You should always refuse on a holding of three trumps of another suit. However, it could be worth accepting proposals with the king of trumps or the queen if the king is turned up.

•

FOUR-HAND EUCHRE

Euchre is a game with several variations, the most popular version being the four-hand partnership.

COMPLEXITY RATING:	★ ★ ★
NUMBER OF PLAYERS:	4
EQUIPMENT:	**Short pack of 32 cards**
TIME REQUIRED:	**Each game generally lasts 15 to 20 minutes**

Origins: Euchre, like Ecarte, is derived from the old game of Triomphe. It originated in the United States, and dates back to at least the 1800s. Its greatest popularity is in the north-eastern United States and Canada, and was the most popular card game there before Bridge took over. It also has a strong following in the West Country of England.

Aim of the game: Each partnership tries to win most games.

Basic rules: Four people play in partnerships of two with each player sitting opposite his partner. The 32-card deck is a standard pack with the 6s, 5s, 4s, 3s and 2s removed. The highest trump is the jack called the right bower. The other jack of the same colour, the left bower, is also regarded as a trump and ranks second. For example, if diamonds are trumps the jack of diamonds is the right bower and the jack of hearts is the left. Therefore in the trump suit there are nine cards. They rank right bower, left bower, A, K, Q, 10, 9, 8 and 7. The other suit which is the same colour as trumps has seven cards ranking A, K, Q, 10, 9, 8 and 7. In each of the remaining suits there are eight cards, ranking A, K, Q, J, 10, 9, 8 and 7.

The deal is decided by draw, and from then on, it passes to the left. Each player is dealt five cards, in batches of two and three (or three and two). The next card is turned face up to set the trump suit. However, this does not become trumps unless it is accepted by one of the players. Play begins with the person on the left of the dealer, and in turn each player has the choice of passing or accepting the trump suit. If one of the dealer's opponents accepts he says: 'Order it up,' while the dealer's partner accepts by saying 'I assist.' Whichever partnership does accept is required to win at least three tricks to take the hand. If they are beaten, they are 'euchred'.

If the turned-up card is accepted as trumps, the dealer has the privilege of discarding one of the cards he was dealt, and 'taking up' the turned-up card to become part of his hand.

If you are the dealer, you have a double advantage because you have a certain trump in the turned-up card, and another probable by the law of averages. This will make the other players slightly more cautious in the hand.

•

If you are the player on the left of the dealer, you should not normally order it up unless you hold three probable tricks. Even if you have two bowers, you would be well advised to pass, because if the dealer takes it up you will probably be euchred, and if he does not, you will then have first choice of another trump suit and can nominate the suit of the same colour.

•

If you are the dealer's partner, you would usually 'assist' on the strength of strong side suits such as two non-trump aces.

•

If you are the dealer's opponent on the right, you should have a good three tricks in your hand if you are to order up because it is obvious that your partner, in passing, does not have a particularly strong hand.

•

To reiterate, you can expect about six trumps to be in play. The person who makes trumps would normally hold at least three, leaving an average of one for each other player. If the trump is ordered up, opponents must expect to find two trumps in the dealer's hand. The odds are about 7 to 3 against any hand's being dealt a card of each suit, but about 2 to 1 against the opening side being able to trump the first lead of a side suit.

•

Once one player has accepted, play begins. If all four players refuse, the face-up card is placed at the bottom of the pack. There is then a second round in which each player in turn has the chance to nominate the trump suit or to pass.

If the first trump is rejected, the player to the left of the dealer and his partner should generally try to nominate the suit of the same colour as the card which has just been turned down. The reason for this is that since both the dealer and his partner rejected it, they obviously have no bower in the same colour. The opponent on the dealer's right should not make the trump however unless he is strong enough to go alone.

•

If all players pass again, the hands are thrown in and the cards are dealt by the next dealer.

The player who decides the trump suit, whether by accepting or nominating, becomes the 'maker'. He has the option of playing the hand without his partner (to aim for a higher score), in which case he says: 'I play alone.' His partner then lays his cards face down on the table, and remains out of the game, although he still shares in the stakes. If the maker is playing alone, then the opening lead is made by the player to his left. Otherwise, the opening lead is made by the player to the left of the dealer. The usual rules of trick-taking apply, as in Whist.

You should go it alone if you have three certain tricks, such as the three top trumps, or five cards which are strong trumps or aces.

•

If the maker and his partner win all five tricks, this constitutes a march, and scores two points. If the maker is playing alone, he scores four points for a march. If the maker and his partner win four or three tricks (called 'the point'), they score one point; if they win fewer than three tricks they are 'euchred', and their opponents score two points.

The first partnership to score a previously agreed number of points (usually 5, 7 or 10) wins the game. Scoring is normally carried out by using a 3 and a 4 from the unused cards as markers, with the number of exposed pips representing the current score.

EUCHRE VARIATIONS

Three-hand Euchre: In this version of the game, played with 32 cards, the maker always plays alone and the other two players form a temporary partnership against him. The maker scores 1 for the point and 3 for the march. His opponents score 2 points if he is euchred. Otherwise, the rules of the four-hand game apply.

Two-hand Euchre: This is similar to the four-hand game except that it is played with a short pack of 24 cards (all cards from 2 to 9 are removed). There are no partnerships, and the maker always plays alone. Scoring is 1 for the point, 2 for the march and 2 for the euchre.

Call-ace Euchre: This is played by 4, 5 or 6 players with a short pack of 32 cards. Trumps are chosen in any of the ways described for the four-hand game. The maker may then opt to play alone, or he may select a partner by naming any suit. The player holding the highest card of that suit in play becomes the maker's partner. As a result, at the start of play, the maker does not know the identity of his partner. Nor can any of the other players be sure whether or not he is the maker's partner – unless he happens to hold the ace of the nominated suit. Even then he does not announce the fact. The identity of the maker's partner only becomes known as the cards are played. It may turn out to be the case that the maker is playing alone, if he himself holds the highest card of the nominated suit. Scoring is as in the four-handed game, except that each player individually scores for point, march or euchre.

FIVE HUNDRED

Five Hundred is similar to Euchre, but with elements of Bridge and Whist.

COMPLEXITY RATING:	★ ★ ★
NUMBER OF PLAYERS:	3
EQUIPMENT:	**Short pack of 32 cards, plus joker**
TIME REQUIRED:	**20 to 30 minutes per deal**

Origins: Five Hundred dates from the early part of this century when it was created to try to improve Euchre by introducing a bidding system comparable with the new game of Bridge. It continued to be popular in America for about ten years but was overtaken initially by Auction Bridge and then by Contract Bridge. A form of Five Hundred is still extremely popular in Australia. That variety uses 11, 12s and two red 13s to make a pack of 63 including the joker, and is played as a four-hand partnership game.

Aim of the game: Each player tries to make a contract by bidding, and then plays to win enough tricks to complete it. Points are won for tricks won with a total target of 500 points. If two players reach the total in the same deal, the player who actually reaches 500 first wins.

Basic rules: In the trump suit cards rank, from highest to lowest, joker, right bower, left bower, ace, king, queen, 10, 9, 8 and 7. In no-trump hands there are no right or left bowers. The holder of the joker may then nominate it to represent any suit he wants. The joker becomes the highest card of that suit and can take any trick to which it is led or played.

Players cut to decide the dealer, with the lowest card dealing. For this, joker is lowest, ace next, then seven upwards to king high. Ten face-down cards are dealt to each player. The remaining three cards make up the 'widow' or 'kitty', and are placed face down on the table.

Do not ignore the importance of the kitty for increasing your holding of trumps if you have six or seven, but it is less likely if you are bidding eight to provide a ninth. But kitty is generally more important as a way of getting rid of the poor cards in your hand than actually increasing its strength.

•

Each player makes a bid in turn, starting with the player on the dealer's left. Each player nominates his choice of trumps, and the number of tricks he thinks he can take. The lowest number of tricks which can be bid is six, and the highest ten. The calls are ranked no-trumps (highest), hearts, diamonds, clubs and then spades. Any player who passes cannot make a further bid in that round. The player who wins the contract can try to improve his hand by choosing any or all of the three widow cards, but he must then discard the same number from his hand.

Before you bid, you should determine the maximum bid you can safely make, and make it immediately because there will be no chance to increase it if both opponents pass. If you are short of the joker, you should not think of making a no-trump bid unless you have aces or safe kings in all four suits.

•

If you are considering a suit bid, you should have at least five trumps, including a bower. It is possible to play four trumps with two bowers if you have good support from aces and safe kings.

•

If you have only three trumps, but a good number of another suit, you should still be careful about bidding, as you may be forced to use all the trumps before getting the opportunity to play the other good cards.

•

Rules of play are the same as in Whist. If a player leads the joker in a no-trump hand, he cannot claim it to be from a suit he has failed to follow. The winner of each trick leads to the next trick.

The players opposing the contract become partners for the game, but each scores ten points for each trick he makes. Provided he makes his contract, the bidder scores points according to the following table:

Tricks bid	Spades	Clubs	Diamonds	Hearts	No trumps
6	40	60	80	100	120
7	140	160	180	200	220
8	240	260	280	300	320
9	340	360	380	400	420
10	440	460	480	500	520

The opponents should play as partners and try to beat the contract rather than looking to score individual trick points. This means that you should, as an opponent, generally not trump or overtake tricks that your partner looks like winning. You should recall what he bid and play to that, even if it is only to make the successful bidder produces his trumps.

If the bidder fails to score the required number of tricks, he loses the value of the contract, and this could mean going into a minus score. There are no bonus points for tricks won above the number bid. However a player who has made a bid of less than 8 clubs, but has scored a 'grand slam' or all ten tricks, receives a total of 250 points.

A player can bid misere if he thinks he is able to lose every single trick, and open misere if he lays his hand on the table to play it. Both are played at no trumps, except for the best bower.

Misere is worth 250 and betters any bid of 240 or less. Open misere is worth 520 and betters any other bid.

Although there is a great temptation to go for misere, or even open misere, you should be very careful about doing so, by remembering what has been bid, and thinking through the likely hands to be played.

FIVE HUNDRED VARIATION
Two-hand Five Hundred: This is played in the same way as the three-handed game, with the third hand 'the dead hand' remaining face down throughout the game. This adds an element of uncertainty to bidding and play.

Four-hand Five Hundred: This pack is made up of 42 cards, the short pack used in other five hundred games, plus the 6s, 5s and two 4s – one of each colour. This variation is played like the three-handed game, but players facing each other act as partners.

NAP

This is a popular English game, sometimes called its full name, Napoleon, by its real enthusiasts. It is usually played for stakes.

COMPLEXITY RATING:	★ ★ ★
NUMBER OF PLAYERS:	**2 to 6 (best with 4 or 5)**
EQUIPMENT:	**Standard pack of 52 cards**
TIME REQUIRED:	**15 minutes**

Origins: The game probably has its origins from a combination of Triomphe and Ecarte. It was mentioned in Jerome K Jerome's 'Three Men in a Boat', which suggests it was particularly popular about that time.

Aim of the game: The player who bids to take the highest number of tricks then chooses the trump suit, and has to make that number to win.

Basic rules: Each player is dealt five cards. There then follows a round of bidding beginning with the player to the left of the dealer and ending with the dealer. There is only one opportunity to bid. A player may pass or make a higher bid.

The possible bids, in ascending order, and their stake value if won or lost are as follows:

One	(bid to win one trick)	1 unit
Two	(bid to win two tricks)	2 units
Three	(bid to win three tricks)	3 units
Misery	(bid to win no tricks, with no trumps)	3 units
Four	(bid to win four tricks)	4 units
Nap	(bid to win five tricks)	10 units if won, 5 if lost
Wellington	(bid to win five tricks)	20 units if won, 10 if lost

Wellington may be bid only to overcall a previous bid of nap and is a declaration to win all five tricks at double stakes.

Whether you should bid, or how much, is governed by the number of people playing, and also when you make your call. If you are playing a three-hand game, the odds that one of your opponents has an ace to better your king become progressively shorter the more players there are above three. If you have a queen, it is much more likely that it will be the highest card in its suit if three are playing than if there are five or six.

If you have just an average hand, you should be circumspect about making a bid of, say three, if you are first to call. However, if those before you have passed when you are in fourth or fifth position, such a bid would be much more realistic.

•

Unless three are playing, you should not bid nap without the ace of trumps, but it is acceptable to lose one in side suits because your opponents will not know which suit to hold back.

•

The player making the highest bid leads to the first trick and, except when the bid is misery, the card that is led determines the trump suit. Normal rules of trick-taking apply, as in Whist.

When playing it is best to get rid of your likely losers sooner rather than later except when nap is bid.

•

If you have not called the bid, you should win what tricks you can from the bidder rather than be conservative in your play and leave it to another player.

•

You should lead trumps when the bidder needs only one trick, and hold back when he needs two or more.

IT'S A FACT...
Napoleon was known to be a card-player and during his exile years on St Helena played Whist, Vingt-et-un and Piquet.

If the bidder wins his contract each of the other players pays him the appropriate stake. If he fails to win his contract, he pays each of the other players the appropriate stake. Stakes are paid only according to the number of tricks that were bid. No account is taken of any excess tricks or the number of tricks that were bid. No account is taken of any excess tricks or of the number of tricks by which a bidder fails to make his contract.

NAP VARIATIONS

Modern Nap: The skill has been increased in this game by stripping the pack from the lowest rank upwards until it consists of about one more hand than the number of players. Five players would use a 32-card pack with no card lower than seven. There is no wellington bid, but nap can actually be overcalled, and the bidder must lead his lowest trump. Played cards are left face-up in a pile.

Pool: A separate kitty or pool can be kept to be taken by the winner of a bid of five. It can be increased by requiring a bidder who fails his bid to pay to it as though it were an extra player.

Widow Nap: An extra hand of five cards is dealt face down. A player who bids nap or wellington may take up the cards and add them to his hand. He discards any five face down and then leads as normal.

Loo

Loo is a traditional gambling game, sometimes played as a party game with chips because when played for real stakes, it can be costly!

COMPLEXITY RATING:	★ ★ ★
NUMBER OF PLAYERS:	**3 to 8**
EQUIPMENT:	**Standard pack of 52 cards**
TIME REQUIRED:	**10 to 15 minutes per game**

Origins: Loo has a long history and was once one of the most popular and widely played gambling games in Europe. It was originally called Lanterloo from the French 'lanterlu', the refrain of a popular 17th-century song.

Aim of the game: Each player tries to win at least one of the three tricks. Any player who does not, must increase the pool.

Basic rules: At the start, the dealer contributes an agreed stake to the pool, usually three units. He then deals three cards to each player, and an extra hand of three called the 'miss' placed face down on the table. The next card is turned face up to establish trumps. Starting with the player to the left of the dealer, each player indicates whether he wishes to play or throw his hand in. The one who offers to play can then, if he wishes, exchange his hand for the miss, sight unseen. However he must remain with whatever cards he picks up. If all players pass, the dealer picks up the pool which includes his ante and any previous stakes.

If one player exchanges and the others pass, the exchanger wins the pool. If one player before the dealer plays, but does not take up the miss, the dealer cannot pass but can decide on how he meets the challenge of his opponent. He can play on his own behalf with or without exchanging, or he can defend the miss, but in that case he does not have any part in the transaction at the end of the play. This means that the other player settles only with the pool depending on the result.

The first player to choose to play leads with his highest trump if he has one. Each player who did not pass plays a card to each trick. He must a) follow suit if possible; or b) play a higher card of the leading suit than the one already played to that trick. If a player cannot follow suit, he should trump the trick with a higher trump than any already played to that trick. If he cannot do this, he may discard. The winner of a trick must lead to the next with a trump if possible.

The winner of each trick takes one-third of the pool. A player who has not won a trick is said to be 'looed'. In limited Loo, a looed player must play a set amount, say three units, into the pool. In unlimited Loo, he pays as many counters as there were at the beginning of the hand into the pool.

The strict rules of trick-taking mean that there is little opportunity for strategy, except in deciding whether to stay in or not to stay in. This makes it essentially a gambling game, based on the cards that are dealt.

•

LOO VARIATIONS

Five-card Loo: This is played in much the same way as three-card Loo except that:

i) five cards are dealt to each player

ii) contributions to the pool are usually five units instead of three

iii) miss is not dealt

iv) each player may exchange up to five cards for the same number drawn from the pack, but a player who exchanges must play the hand

v) the jack of clubs, called 'Pam', is the highest card in play beating everything including the ace of trumps. If the ace of trumps is lead, its leader can say 'Pam be civil', in which case the holder of Pam may not play it to that trick if he has any other trump.

vi) if anyone has a flush, either five cards of the same suit, or four of the same plus Pam, he 'loos' the board straight away having 'won' all five tricks. If there is more than one flush, the priority is a flush with Pam, a flush in trumps, the flush with the highest top card or cards. A player with a flush who loses in this way does not have to pay, and nor does any other player holding Pam.

vii) in some games, players use an optional winning hand called 'blaze' which is made up entirely of court cards. The same rules of precedence apply as with flushes, and a blaze outranks a flush.

Irish Loo: This is played like three-card Loo with the following differences:

    i) miss is not dealt

    ii) exchanging is carried out in the same way as in the five-card game

    ii) if clubs are trumps, every player must enter the game.

SPOIL FIVE

Spoil Five is similar to Loo, but with more opportunity for strategy. It was once regarded as the national game of Ireland.

COMPLEXITY RATING:	★ ★ ★
NUMBER OF PLAYERS:	**2 to 10 (best with 5 or 6)**
EQUIPMENT:	**Standard pack of 52 cards**
TIME REQUIRED:	**10 to 15 minutes for each hand**

Aim of the game: Each player tries to win at least three of the tricks played. If he is unable to do this, he will try to prevent anyone else from doing so. If he can achieve this, the five tricks are 'spoiled' and the pool is not claimed.

Origins: Spoil Five is derived from the old game of Maw, and became very popular in Ireland. It was taken to the United States and Canada, and its variant, Auction Forty-Five, became extremely popular in Newfoundland.

Basic rules: Spoil Five has an unusual ranking system for its cards. The highest card is always the five of trumps, followed by the ace of hearts, the ace of trumps (if not hearts), followed by the king, queen and other trumps in order. In the red suits this means from high to low, but in black it is from low to high.

Spades and clubs

Trump suit – 5, jack, ace of hearts, ace of spades or clubs, king, queen, 2, 3, 4, 6, 7, 8, 9, 10

Non-trump (or plain) suit – king, queen, jack, ace, 2, 3, 4, 5, 6, 7, 8, 9, 10

Diamonds

Trump suit – 5, jack, ace of hearts, ace of diamonds, king, queen, 10, 9, 8, 7, 6, 4, 3, 2

Non-trump suit – king, queen, jack, 10, 9, 8, 7, 6, 5, 4, 3, 2, ace

Hearts

Trump suit – 5, jack, ace, king, queen, 10, 9, 8, 7, 6, 4, 3, 2

Non-trump suit – king, queen, jack, 10, 9, 8, 7, 6, 5, 4, 3, 2

    Each player contributes an agreed stake to the pool, say one unit. Players are then dealt five cards, and the dealer places the remainder face down to form a stock, with the top card face-up to set trumps. If that card is an ace, it may be 'robbed' by the dealer before the first card is led, and exchanged for any card in his hand. His reject card is returned to the stock face down.

If the trump card is not an ace, any player who has the ace of trumps must declare the fact before he plays, but can wait until the player before him has played. He can then acquire the turned trump, exchanging it for another card which is placed face down at the bottom of the stock.

The player to the dealer's left leads to the first trick, and after that, the winner of each trick leads. If trumps are led, others must follow suit if they can. However if a player has any of the top three trumps, five, jack and ace of hearts, he does not need to play it in response if he has no other trump cards. In other words, he may renege. That means that when a trump is led, players must follow suit except with the five of trumps which can renege to any trump, jack of trumps which can renege to any trump but the five, and ace of hearts which need not follow any trump except jack and five.

When hearts are trumps and ace of hearts is led, five and jack may renege. When hearts are not trumps and ace of hearts is led, a trump must follow, although a player without a trump need not play a heart.

If a non-trump suit is led, players can choose whether they follow suit, or play a trump. A trick is taken by the highest card of the suit led, or by the highest trump.

The aim is to win three tricks in one hand. A player winning the first three tricks can either claim the pool without further play, or continue playing by leading to the fourth trick, or 'jinking'. If he continues to play he must win all five, or lose the pool. If he wins all five he wins the pool, and is paid an extra unit by each opponent. If no player wins three or more tricks, the game is spoiled, and the cards are dealt for a new hand. In this case, only the dealer contributes to the pool. Only when the pool is won do all the players contribute to a new one.

The important element of each deal is for you to decide whether to go for three tricks or to try to spread tricks among players and so to spoil. This depends to some extent on whether the ace of trumps is announced or not. As soon as one player has two tricks, the others should naturally combine to play against him to prevent him from taking a third.

•

If you have won the first three tricks, you should be certain of the strength of your cards before deciding to try to take five. Beware of one of the top three cards having been held back to try to baulk you in your attempt to take all the tricks.

•

SPOIL FIVE VARIATIONS

Forty Five: Only an even number of players can take part, divided into two equal partnerships. Because one side is certain to win at least three tricks there is no pool. A side scores

    i) 5 points for three or four tricks

    ii) 10 points for five tricks

or it scores

    i) 5 points for three tricks

    ii) 15 points for four tricks

    iii) 25 points for five tricks.

The target is 45 points, and the first side to reach it wins.

Auction Forty-Five: This is also a partnership game, but with bidding. The number 45 has no real relevance to the game.

Number of players: 4 or 6, in partnerships of 2 or 3. Each players sits between two players of the opposing side.

Basic rules: The basic rules are the same as for Spoil Five, but with a number of variations. Five cards are dealt to each player, but no trump card is turned up. Each player may then bid or pass, but having passed a player cannot re-enter. The bids, indicating the number of points each side needs to make, are 5, 10, 15, 20, 25 and 30. Each bid must be higher than the previous except for the dealer who may 'hold', outbidding the previous bid, but not actually increasing it. Trumps are nominated by the highest bidder.

Each player may then in turn discard any number of cards from the hand he has originally been dealt, and receive the same number of replacement cards.

The player to the left of the highest bidder leads first. The ranking of cards, the method of play and the play associated with the three top trumps are the same as for Spoil Five.

Each trick scores 5 points, and the highest trump in play scores an extra 5 for the side which has it. The non-bidding side scores all the points it makes in the game. If the bidding side achieves its bid, it scores the points bid plus the points scored with its tricks. If it fails to do so, it loses the number of points it bid.

The target is 120 points, and a side reaching 100 points may not bid less than 20 in the next hand.

HEARTS

Hearts is one of a number of games popular on both sides of the Atlantic in which the aim is to lose tricks rather than win them, a technique which involves a good deal of skilful play.

Origins: Games of the Hearts family probably originated with the highly complicated gambling game, Reversis, which dates from the 18th century.

Aim of the game: The object is to avoid winning tricks that contain certain penalty cards – hearts. The winner is the player with the lowest number of points after an agreed number of hands, or the player with the lowest number of points when any player's score reaches a set number such as 50.

COMPLEXITY RATING:	★ ★ ★
NUMBER OF PLAYERS:	3 to 7
EQUIPMENT:	Standard pack of 52 cards
TIME REQUIRED:	10 to 15 minutes

Basic rules: Before the game it is necessary for some cards to be removed from the pack, according to the number of players, so that the pack may be dealt out fully with each player receiving an equal number of cards. With three players, the 2 of clubs is removed; with five players the 2 of clubs and 2 of diamonds are removed; with six, all the 2s are removed; with seven, the 2 of clubs, 2 of diamonds and 2 of spades.

The cards are cut to select the dealer, who then deals the cards face down to each player in turn. The player to the left of the dealer leads to the first trick, and thereafter, the winner of each trick leads to the next. Players must follow suit if they can, otherwise they may play any card. There are no trumps, and a trick is always won by the highest card of the suit led.

At the end of the hand, each player counts the number of hearts in the tricks he has won, and scores that number of penalty points.

Most tricks including penalty cards are usually taken towards the end of the game by players who take over the lead, and then cannot lose it. It is therefore a good idea to lead aces and kings of safe suits as soon as you can in the game. This will make it less likely that you are left with the lead later in the game.

•

When you are able to discard in a trick without taking it, do not necessarily throw out a penalty card, but use the opportunity to get rid of cards which may force you to take the lead later. This is particularly important if you have no low cards of a suit.

•

An alternative method, when the game is played for stakes, is for each hand to be considered as a separate game. Each player pays into the pool one unit for each heart he has taken and the pool is shared by any players with no hearts. If all players have taken one or more hearts, the pool is carried forward to the next game.

BLACK MARIA

Black Maria is probably the most popular game of the Hearts group of card games. It is also known as Black Lady and Black Widow.

COMPLEXITY RATING:	★ ★ ★
NUMBER OF PLAYERS:	**3 to 7, although the fewer the better**
EQUIPMENT:	**Standard pack of 52 cards**
TIME REQUIRED:	**10 to 15 minutes a game**

Aim of the game: The aim is the same as for Hearts.

Basic rules: Black Maria is similar to Hearts except for the following differences:

i) the queen of spades (Black Maria) is an extra penalty card which counts a swingeing 13 penalty points.

ii) after the deal, but before the first lead, there is an exchange of cards. If there are three or four players, each one, after examining his cards, passes any three cards face down to the player on his right. A player may not look at the cards he has received until he has passed on the three discards from his own hand. If there are more than four players, only two cards are passed on.

It is not necessarily a good idea to pass hearts to the right. It is best to keep a good run of low hearts because they cannot be forced to take tricks. If you receive any high hearts from the player on your left, you should play the low ones if you have to follow suit with hearts, because you will be less likely to win the trick with them. Then, when you cannot follow suit in another trick, you can discard your high hearts.

•

In the same way, it is not necessary to pass on Black Maria if you have enough spades to avoid being forced to capture a trick with her. You should pass on the ace and king of spades in the initial exchange, but keep all spades lower than the queen so you can play them if the Black Maria is led.

•

With a bit of practice, you can usually learn a lot from the cards you receive from the left, and by watching the cards your opponents lead and discard. Good players can usually tell where all the remaining cards are by mid-game.

•

OTHER HEARTS VARIATIONS

Slobberhannes: This is a game for 3 to 6 players (although 4 is best). They use a short pack of 32 cards with all cards below 7 removed. If there are three, five or six players, the two black 7s are also removed. Cards rank from ace high to 7 low. The object of the game is to avoid winning the first and last tricks, and the trick containing the queen of clubs.

The cards are dealt one at a time and face down so that each player receives an equal number of cards and there are none left over. The player to the left of the dealer leads to the first trick. A player must follow suit if he can, or he may play any card of his choice. There are no trumps, and a trick is won by the highest card of the suit led. The winner of each trick leads to the next.

A player taking the first trick, the last trick or the one with the queen of clubs is penalised one point. A player unfortunate enough to win all three of these tricks scores an extra penalty point, making four in all. The first to reach the total of 10 is the loser.

Polignac: This game, of French origins, is similar to Slobberhannes and is sometimes known as Quatre Valets or Four Jacks.

It can be played by 3 to 6 people, but 4 is the best number. It is also played with a short pack of 32 cards. Polignac differs from Slobberhannes in that the penalties are for taking tricks containing jacks – two penalty points for the jack of spades, and one penalty point for each of the other jacks.

Auction Hearts: This is a game for four to six players, but the penalty suit is not necessarily hearts. Instead players bid for the right to nominate the penalty suit. The player who wins the bid, pays that amount into the pool. This is divided as usual, and the highest bidder leads the first trick.

Draw Hearts: This game is for two players who receive 13 cards each. The rest are placed face down as the stock. The winner of each trick takes the top card and adds it to his hand. When the stock has run out, the remaining 13 cards are played. Captured cards are counted in the usual way.

BEZIQUE

Bezique is an excellent game for two players, and is easy to learn and not too demanding to play.

COMPLEXITY RATING:	★ ★
NUMBER OF PLAYERS:	**2, although there are variants for 3 or more players**
EQUIPMENT:	**Two standard 52-card packs from which the 2, 3, 4, 5, and 6s have been removed, making 64 cards**
TIME REQUIRED:	**15 to 20 minutes per deal**

Origins: Bezique began in France and is derived from games such as Marriage, Brusquembille and Brisque which were played in the 17th century or earlier. It became particularly popular in Paris about 1860, and in London a few years later. It was helped to popularity in Britain by Alfred, Duke of Edinburgh, who discovered it in his travels.

Aim of the game: Players try to make winning melds or declarations, and to take tricks containing certain scoring cards known as brisques. The principal purpose of taking tricks is to enable a player to declare his combinations – and to prevent his opponent from doing so.

Basic rules: The cards rank ace high, 10, king, queen, jack, 9, 8, 7. Notice the position of the 10.

The two packs are thoroughly shuffled together and the players cut to deal. Each player receives eight cards and the rest are placed face down on the table to form a stock. The top card is turned face up beside the pile, its suit determining the trumps for the deal. If the card is a 7 the dealer scores 10 points.

The play is in two stages with the first consisting of 24 tricks. The non-dealer leads to the first trick, and thereafter the winner of each trick leads to the next. The winner of each trick is entitled to declare and score for any card combinations he may hold, according to the chart below. Both players replenish their hands by drawing from the stock. At this stage of the game, it is not necessary to follow suit – the second player to a trick may follow suit, trump or discard just as he pleases. A trick is won by the highest card of the suit led, unless it is trumped, and if two cards of the same value are played then the leader wins the trick.

The combinations are divided into a number of different classes: sequences, quartets and beziques.

Combinations and scores

Common marriage	king and queen of the same suit (not trumps)	20
Royal marriage	king and queen of the trump suit	40
Bezique	queen of spades with jack of diamonds	40
Double bezique	both queens of spades and both jacks of diamonds	500
Four jacks		40
Four queens		60
Four kings		80
Four aces		100
Sequence	ace, 10, king, queen, jack of trumps	250

A card used and which scores in one combination cannot be counted in a lower combination of the same class. However, a card such as a king could be used for a marriage and then later for four trumps, but not for another marriage. A king and queen of the trump suit may be used for a royal marriage, and may subsequently be used for a sequence with the addition of the ace, 10, and jack. It is also acceptable to use the two cards forming a bezique as part of a double bezique, though neither card could be used as part of another single bezique.

A player declares a combination by laying the appropriate cards face up on the table in front of him, and marking the score. Cards declared in combinations stay on the table until played – they still form part of the player's hand and may be played to tricks as and when required.

It is best not to make declarations too soon because this tells your opponent about what cards are available, and can help him plan his game. However, if you delay too long, you will have difficulty in winning enough tricks.

•

There is no point in winning tricks except for the purpose of declaring a combina-tion, winning a brisque, or to prevent your opponent from declaring one (particularly if you are near the end of the stock and there is the chance of preventing him from making any further declarations).

•

Keep an eye on the declarations your opponent makes to determine those cards which are not available to you. For example, it is pointless saving for a double bezique if he has declared four jacks. In the same way, it is best to play a card

from the table rather than one from the hand because this reduces the amount of information your opponent has about those cards he does not hold.

•

Your 10s should be kept for winning tricks when needed because there is no score from four 10s. If you do not want to break up a potential combination, you should usually discard a non-bezique jack to a 10 or another high card, as it is difficult to collect four jacks, and extremely difficult to produce a trump sequence unless you are dealt at least three of the cards needed for it at the beginning.

•

A player who holds the 7 of trumps may declare it and exchange it for the exposed trump card, scoring 10 points. The person who plays the second 7 of trumps also scores 10 points.

After the twenty-fourth trick has been taken there will be only one card left in the stock, plus the exposed trump card. The winner of that trick draws the stock card and the loser takes the exposed trump card. This is the last trick which allows the winner to make a declaration.

The second stage of the game now begins. The players gather any face-up cards in front of them into their hands, and play the last eight tricks. The rules for this stage are different. If he can, a player must play a higher card of the suit that was led; if he cannot do so, he must still follow suit if he can; if he cannot follow suit he must play a trump if he has one; otherwise he may discard. No declarations are made at this stage of the game, but the winner of the last trick scores 10 points.

When that trick has been won, each player examines the cards in the tricks he has taken to determine how many brisques he has. Brisques are each ace and 10 included in a trick, and they each score 10 points.

A game is usually played to 1,000 or 2,000 points.

BEZIQUE VARIATIONS

Rubicon Bezique: In this game, players use four short packs with a total of 128 cards. Each player receives nine cards, and each deal is a game. No card is turned for trumps and the trump suit is established by the first marriage declared. The 7 of trumps has no value.

Play is the same as for standard Bezique, except that the winner of the last trick scores 50 points. Declarations are also the same as in Bezique with a number of additions:

i) if either player receives a hand without a king, queen or jack, he may declare carte blanche and score 50 points. He proves the fact by turning the cards face up on the table, and afterwards if, in playing to a trick, he does not draw a court card he may show it and score a further 50 points. The privilege stops as soon as he draws a court card.

ii) a sequence in a non-trump suit (called a 'back door') counts 150

iii) triple bezique scores 1,500, and quadruple bezique scores 4,500.

A player can use the same cards more than once in the same declaration which is made and scored in the same way as in Bezique. If a card of that declaration is then played from the table, and a player who has won a trick adds a card which restores the declaration, he counts in full for the declaration again. Two marriages of the same suit may be rearranged to form two more marriages.

Brisques (ace and 10) are counted only if there is a tied score, or to prevent a player being 'rubiconned'. If the player with the lowest score for a hand has less than 1,000, including brisques, he has failed to 'cross the rubicon'.

The player with the highest score in the game takes 500 points plus the difference between his and the loser's score. If the loser is rubiconned, the winner gets 1,000 points, plus the sum of his and the loser's scores, plus 320 for brisques. This applies even if the winner has scored fewer than 1,000 points. If the loser fails to score 100 points, the winner scores an extra 100 points. Any fractions of 100 points are ignored in scoring, except if the scores are close.

Three-hand Bezique: This game involves the use of three short packs with a total of 96 cards. It is played in the same way as Bezique except that a triple bezique scores 1,500 points, but is valid only if all six cards are visible together. In the last eight tricks each player must win the trick if possible, and trump or overtrump if not able to follow. The game target is 2,000.

Four-hand Bezique: This game uses four short packs and 128 cards, and can be played in partnerships. A trick winner can declare, or invite his partner to do so. He may declare one or more cards to convert any of his partner's exposed cards into a combination of a different class or higher value. Double bezique scores 500 and triple bezique 1,500, but only when made from the hand of one partner. In the last eight tricks, each player must try to win the trick if he can, even if his partner is already doing so. The game is 2,000 points.

AUCTION PINOCHLE

Pinochle has many variations, and is one of North America's most popular games, but for some reason has never attracted a following in Britain. Auction Pinochle is the most popular version of the Pinochle family.

Origins: The original Pinochle was a game for two players, and very similar to Bezique. The modern game probably dates from about 1860. It is suggested that the word 'bezique' is very similar to the French word for eyeglasses 'besicles'. Another word for eyeglasses in both French and German is 'binocle' – hence Pinochle. The game is particularly popular with American Jews and the Irish.

Objects of the game: Players bid on a prediction of how many points they expect to score through melds and tricks.

COMPLEXITY RATING:	★ ★ ★
NUMBER OF PLAYERS:	**Best with 3, although usually played by 4, each taking a turn to deal and sit out**
EQUIPMENT:	**A 48-card pack, consisting of two 24-card packs shuffled together with no card under 9**
TIME REQUIRED:	**15 to 20 minutes**

Basic rules: Batches of three cards are dealt to each player, and after the first round, three cards are placed face down in the middle of the table as the 'widow'. Dealing continues until each player has 15 cards.

Each player in turn bids according to the number of points he expects to score. Bidding is expressed only in points and starts at an agreed minimum, usually 300, and rises 10 at a time. A player must bid or pass, but on passing may not bid again in that hand. Bidding ends when two players have passed, and the highest bid is the contract.

The bidder picks up the widow cards and shows them to the other players. He adds them to his hand, and lays down his melds. After doing so, he must lay down, or bury, any three cards which he has not melded to reduce the number of cards in his hand to 15. He must not show the cards he buries to his opponents. They will count to his credit after the cards are played. At the same time he announces his trump suit. He may change his mind on his melds, trumps and discards any time before the first trick. No other player can lay down melds during the game.

There are three types of meld, and they score on the following basis:

Sequences

Flush	A–10–K–Q–J of trumps	150
Royal marriage	K and Q of trumps	40
Marriage	K and Q of non-trump suit	20

Others

Pinochle	Q of spades and J of diamonds	40
Dix	9 of trumps	10

Quartets

Hundred Aces	One ace of each suit	100
Eighty Kings	One king of each suit	80
Sixty Queens	One queen of each suit	60
Forty Jacks	One jack of each suit	40

The bidder leads the first trick. Any trick containing a trick is won by the player who has played the highest trump; any other trick is won by the player who played the highest card of the suit led. Each player must follow suit if he can, and if trumps are led, must try to win the trick if he can. If a player cannot follow suit, he must trump rather than discard. This still applies after a trick has already been trumped, but he can play a lower trump if he wants to.

The winner of each trick leads to the next. The bidder collects all the tricks he has won into a pile, the cards he buried being at the bottom of the pile, and counting towards his total at the end. One opponent gathers all the tricks won by his side, and at the end the two sides agree on the number of points each has taken. If the bidder has scored, through melds and tricks, as many points as he nominated in the contract, the contract is made.

TIP

When bidding you should limit yourself to the cards you already hold in your hand, and not expect to find extra melds among the widow cards. If you hold a hand which is a sure score of 300, do not chance a 350 score if that looks doubtful. The same applies with a sure 350 hand and a doubtful 400.

•

TIP

You can get a good idea of the maximum bid you should make by assuming as trumps a holding of at least five and possibly six cards, counting the actual melding value of the hand but not more. You can also add 10 to 15 for each possible trick, and another 20 to 30 in the exchange.

•

TIP

If you have won the bid and picked up the widow, you should consider whether some other suit might be a better trump, especially if you have drawn cards for a sequence.

•

TIP

When you come to decide which cards to throw out, you should consider what your hand will look like. Do not discard a non-trump ace which will almost certainly win a trick. However tens from non-trump suits without an ace are good cards to throw out. A good hand will be made up of at least six trumps, a number of non-trump cards, and perhaps an ace or two from other suits.

It is also quite a sound move to try for a hand of two suits – trumps and a long non-trump suit. The advantage of a strong non-trump hand is that it may be led before you play your trumps, and if one opponent is short in that suit he must trump when he cannot follow suit. However, there may be cases when the non-trump suit is made up almost entirely of winning cards, and it might then be best to lead trumps to try to draw the opponent's trumps before leading the non-trump cards.

•

You will get a good idea of the strength of an opponent's hand by his bid. If he starts with a 300 bid, and allows himself to be pushed to 350, he could be allowed to play it because the fact that he did not start with 350 indicates he does not have a sure 350 hand.

•

Points for cards taken in tricks are allocated after each hand in this way:

A	10	K	Q	J
11	10	4	3	2

An alternative may be:

10 points for each ace or 10, and 5 points for each king or queen; or 10 points for each ace, 10 or king.

The bidder scores for any scoring cards among the three he discards, and if the bidder wins the last trick, he scores a bonus of 10. While scores may be kept, settlement is usually in chips. If the bidder succeeds, he receives the appropriate amount from each opponent. If however he concedes without playing, he pays the appropriate amount to each player. If he plays, but fails to score the required number of points, he pays double to each opponent.

A scale of payments might be:

i) a bid of 300–340, 3 chips
ii) a bid of 350–390, 5 chips
iii) a bid of 400–440, 10 chips
iv) a bid of 450–490, 15 chips
v) a bid of 500–540, 20 chips
vi) a bid of 550–590, 25 chips
vii) a bid of 600 or more, 30 chips

These amounts are doubled if spades are trumps.

PINOCHLE

Basic Pinochle is not as satisfying, and perhaps for that reason is less popular, than Auction Pinochle.

COMPLEXITY RATING:	★ ★ ★
NUMBER OF PLAYERS:	**2**
EQUIPMENT:	**A 48-card pack, as in Auction Pinochle**
TIME REQUIRED:	**15 to 20 minutes**

Object of the game: Each player tries to take tricks containing certain cards, and to make melds, so as to score points.

Basic rules: Draw for the first dealer, and after that the deal alternates. Twelve cards are dealt to each player, and the next is turned face up on the table to become trumps for that hand. If this card is a 9 (the 'dix') the dealer immediately scores 10 points. The rest of the pack, the stock, is placed face down on the table, half covering the trump card.

The non-dealer leads to the first trick, while the winner of each trick leads to the next. At this stage, a player can play any card to a trick, including a trump card when he actually holds a card of the non-trump suit which has been led. The highest trump wins a suit, or if none are led, the highest card of the suit led. If two cards of the same denomination and suit are played, the one played first wins.

TIP

In the early play, you should lead from the longest suit because your opponent is less likely to be able to cover your card without breaking up a possible meld. By the same token, you should not use a card from your longest suit to play to an unwanted suit because you should save that to make a lead.

After each trick, the winner can make one meld as described in Auction Pinochle, placing the cards face up on the table. Each card melded can also be used to form another meld of a different class when the player has another turn, but must involve the use of at least one card from the player's hand. A card used in a meld can be played to a later trick, but once a card has been played it cannot be used in other melds.

Whether or not a meld has been made, the winner draws the top card from the stock and the loser draws the next card. Players continue to draw after tricks until all the stock and the exposed trump card have been picked up.

If a player holds a dix at any time during the first stage of play, he can declare it and score 10 by placing it face up on the table after winning a trick.

In the first part of the game, it is important to meld, and to build up the strongest hand possible for the second phase of the game. However melding is the most important aim, both now and later. In the early stages of a game, you should hold cards which may be turned into melds as you draw from the stock. For example, if early on you take an opponent's 10 with an ace, it will count 21. However it would be much more valuable as part of a 100 aces group, and it is usually best to save it for that possibility. When it becomes obvious that it is no longer possible to meld such a group, then you should play it to an opponent's 10 lead.

•

If you have a high value sequence or quartet early in the play, you should delay melding them so that your opponent continues to hold onto cards he may be saving for an identical meld.

•

As the stock is used up, you should try to stop your opponents from winning tricks if he can still make melds. If it becomes obvious that there is nothing of particular value for him to meld, you can ignore the lower-scoring tricks and concentrate on building up a good playing hand for the last twelve tricks.

•

To start the second stage of this game, each player takes back any cards that he has melded. Players then continue for the remaining 12 tricks to use up the cards left in their hands. In this stage, they must follow suit if they can, and can trump only if they cannot follow suit. If a trump is led, the second player must play a higher trump if he can. Tricks are won just as they are in the first stage, but no melds are made.

If a player declares the first dix, it is exchanged for the trump card at the bottom of the stock pile, taking the trump card into his hand.

Points for cards taken in tricks are allocated after each hand in the same way as in Auction Pinochle:

The player who wins the last trick in the second stage receives a further 10 points. Scores for tricks of 7, 8 or 9 are rounded up to multiples of 10 before being added to the player's total score. The game is usually played to 1,000 points, but if both players reach 1,000 in the same hand, play continues to 1,250, or if the same thing happens again, to 1,500.

Sometimes you can draw such a poor hand that there is little likelihood of building up melds. In those circumstances, if you are playing a game of 1,000 points, you should try to win as many points in the play as you can. You should use tens to win tricks when kings or queens are led, and you should take aces when your opponent leads tens.

•

If you are playing separate games, and you have a poor hand, it is better to save cards which may turn into melds, hoping for good draws from the stock. It is very difficult to win a single hand on cards won in the play.

•

RUMMY

Rummy is one of the most popular card games in the United States. It is a good family game, easy to learn, but with many variations. This is the standard version.

COMPLEXITY RATING:	★ ★
NUMBER OF PLAYERS:	2 to 6
EQUIPMENT:	Standard pack of 52 cards
TIME REQUIRED:	15 to 20 minutes for each game

Origins: The earliest modern form of Rummy became popular in Mexico in the second half of the 19th century as Conquian. This spread to Texas and then the rest of the United States as Coon-Can in the early 20th century. The origin of the name, although associated with Rum, is unclear.

Aim of the game: Each player tries to be the first to get rid of all the cards in his hand (to go out) by 'melding', that is to form groups or sequences of cards. A group is three or four cards of the same rank (eg three or four kings). A sequence is three or more cards of the same suit in numerical order (eg 5, 6, 7 of clubs). Normally the ace ranks low, so that ace, 2, 3 is a sequence, but Q, K, A is not. Unlike most card games, the winning of tricks plays no part in the family of Rummy games.

A secondary objective is to reduce as far as possible the total face value of the

unmelded cards left in your hand because if your opponent goes out, he scores the points you have left.

•

Basic rules: The dealer is chosen by a cut of the cards with the lowest card the winner. Cards are then dealt face down, but the number varies according to the number of players: for two players, 10 cards each; three or four receive 7 cards each; five or six 6 cards each. After the deal, the remaining cards are turned face down to form the stock and the top card is then turned face up to start the discard pile.

The player on the dealer's left begins by drawing the top card from the stock or the discard pile and adding it to his hand.

It is important for each player to learn to identify any combinations or sequences he is holding at this stage ready for the play.

•

He may then meld a group or sequence, and as the game progresses, he may add or 'lay off' any individual cards that extend existing melds on the table – either his own, or his opponents'. Finally he discards one card, placing it face up on the discard pile.

A player goes out, and thereby wins the hand, when he plays the last card from his hand, whether as part of a meld, a lay off or a discard. His score for the round is the face value of all the cards left in the hands of his opponents. An ace counts as 1, and a court card counts as 10.

If a player goes out by melding his entire hand in just one turn without previously having melded or laid off any cards, this is 'going rummy' and his score is doubled.

If no player has gone out by the time the stock is exhausted, the discard pile is simply turned over to form a new stock and the game continues as normal.

The first player to reach a predetermined score wins the game.

GENERAL TIPS FOR RUMMY GAMES

Unlike most trick-taking games, in Rummy you play against the pack rather than other players. For this reason, when four or more players are involved, the only other hands you need to watch are those on either side of you. You need to watch the play of the opponent on your left to avoid discarding cards he might be able to use. By the same token, keep an eye on the play of the opponent on your right to see what he is discarding. This will help you to shape your own melds.

•

You must be flexible in your plans throughout the game, continually watching the cards which have been thrown out, and picked up in the discard pile. If you have the 7 and 9 of diamonds, and you see an opponent picking up an 8 of clubs or hearts from the discard pile, you have to accept that he might be collecting 8s, and may already hold the 8 of diamonds.

Because of the penalties for holding high-value cards when an opponent melds, it is wise to try to get rid of them as quickly as possible, even when you have cards which have the potential to become sequences. While it is fairly safe to hold on to cards like the 2 and 4 of diamonds in the hope of acquiring the 3, it is dangerous to keep hold of a 10 and queen in the hope of acquiring the jack.

However, because your opponent will probably be looking to use low-value cards, you might find it easier to make high-value melds. If you are dealt two high-value cards in sequence, or a pair, it may be worth holding on to them for several turns in the hope of a discard before getting rid of them.

Finally, because of the nature of Rummy games, the cards tend to end up in order, and should be thoroughly shuffled before the next deal.

GIN RUMMY

COMPLEXITY RATING:	★ ★ ★
NUMBER OF PLAYERS:	2
EQUIPMENT:	Standard pack of 52 cards

Aim of the game: As in Rummy, the object is to meld the cards in one's hand into groups or sequences. Unlike basic Rummy, however, it is possible for a player to win a hand without melding all his cards.

Basic rules: There are a number of important differences from basic Rummy in the way Gin Rummy is played. The players cut the pack to determine the lead, and the player who draws the highest card can deal first, or require his opponent to do so. After that, the deal alternates. Ten cards are dealt, one at a time, to each player. The remainder of the pack is placed down on the table to form the stock, the top card of the stock being turned over and placed face up as the first card of the discard pile.

The non-dealer may begin play by taking the face-up card. If he does not want it, the dealer may take it. If both players refuse it, the non-dealer draws the top card of the stock. As in Rummy, each player in turn takes the top card from either the stock or the discard pile and discards one card from his hand.

A player will pick up a discard to complete a meld in his hand, or to exchange an unmatched high-value card with one of a low value to reduce the 'deadwood' (the cards which do not form part of a group or sequence) in his hand.

TIP

You can develop a good picture of your opponent's hand by watching his discards and those cards he picks up, and can determine your play accordingly. It is

*possible to come to a reasonably accurate conclusion about an opponent's hand
by noting what cards do not appear in the stock or in discards.*

•

*It is sometimes worthwhile picking up a discard which you do not need in an
attempt to confuse a watchful opponent.*

•

Melds are not laid down on the table in the course of play. Instead, a player keeps
his melds in his hand and goes out by 'knocking' or 'going gin' when his deadwood
totals ten points or less. A player can knock only when it is his turn. After drawing
from the stock or discard pile, the usual practice is for the player to knock on the table
and then discard face down.

The player then lays his hand face up on the table, sorted clearly into melds and
deadwood. His opponent similarly lays down his hand without drawing from the
stock, but is then allowed to 'lay off' – to add odd cards from his own hand to melds
in the knocker's hand. If however the knocker has laid down a 'gin hand' – one with
no deadwood – his opponent may not lay off any cards.

If the knocker's deadwood count is lower than that of his opponent, he scores the
difference. If a player lays down a gin hand he scores the total value of his opponent's
deadwood plus a 25 point bonus. However, if a player knocks and his opponent has
an equal or lower deadwood count, then the opponent wins the hand, scoring the
difference plus a 25 point bonus for 'undercut'. A gin hand cannot be undercut.

The running score is kept with a player's score for a hand added to his previous
score, and then a line is drawn under it. A game ends when one player's score reaches
100. He then scores a bonus of 100 points for the game. If his opponent has failed
to win a single hand, the winner's total score is doubled for 'shut out'. Finally, to each
player's score is added 25 points (called a 'line bonus' or 'box bonus') for each hand
he has won.

The last two cards in the stock may not be drawn. If there are only two cards left
in the stock and neither player has knocked, then the hand is a tie and no points are
scored. The same dealer deals again for the next hand.

The general tips given for all Rummy games apply to Gin Rummy.

CANASTA

Canasta is another partnership game of the Rummy family.

Origins: Canasta originated in Uruguay and reached the United States after the Second
World War where it became enormously popular. It subsequently became fashionable in royal circles in Britain, and that ensured its popularity in this country. It has

COMPLEXITY RATING:	★ ★ ★
NUMBER OF PLAYERS:	4 playing in two partnerships
EQUIPMENT:	Two standard packs of 52 cards with four jokers, shuffled together
TIME REQUIRED:	60 to 90 minutes

also spread to Europe. Its name is derived from the Spanish word for 'basket', and probably comes from the tray placed in the centre of the table to hold undealt cards and discards.

Aim of the game: Partnerships play to be the first to score 5,000 over a number of hands, and points are mainly made by melds.

Basic rules: The double pack contains 12 wild cards: the four jokers and the eight 2s. A meld is a set of at least three cards of the same denomination. They can be natural cards, or a mix of natural and wild cards – but not fewer than two natural cards and not more than three wild cards. The scores for melds are awarded as follows:

Card	Points for each card in meld
Joker	50
Two	20
Ace	20
8, 9, 10, jack, queen, king	10 each
4, 5, 6, 7	5 each
Black 3	5
Red 3 (bonus cards)	100 (see page 61)

To begin, players cut the pack for partners, with the two picking the highest cards playing the other two. The player with the highest card becomes the dealer. The cards are dealt face down until each player has 11 cards. The remaining cards are then placed face down on the table as stock. The top card is turned face up to start the discard pile.

Play starts with the player on the dealer's left who takes the top card of the stock and then makes any meld he can. As play progresses he can add to any meld he or his partner have already laid out. Finally, he discards one card from his hand face up on the discard pile.

The first meld of a partnership must score a certain number of points, according to the table below – how many is governed by their score so far:

Total score of partnership	Card value needed for first meld
Minus	15
0–1,495	50
1,500–2,995	90
3,000 or more	120

Once either partner has achieved this first meld, both partners can make new melds of any value and can add to melds they have already laid out. Partners can add to their own or each other's melds.

A canasta is a meld of seven cards, and if the canasta is made up of cards of the same rank (a natural canasta), it scores a bonus of 500 points in addition to the card score. A mixed canasta is made up of natural cards and wild cards (no more than three though), and has a bonus value of 300 points.

When a canasta is completed, it is placed in a pile with a red card on top to indicate a natural canasta, and a black card for a mixed canasta. Further cards can still be added to a canasta, but a natural canasta is reduced in value if a wild card is added.

When you have made the initial meld, try to make as many more as possible, and add to those you have made. But try not to reduce your hand to too great an extent to do so.

•

Canastas are extremely valuable whether they are mixed or natural, and it is a good idea to use wild cards rather than hoarding them to achieving canastas.

•

A player can use the top card from the discard pile when it is his turn, but only if he has at least two natural cards of the same denomination. He must then lay them on the table, and meld the top discard with them. He also has to take all the remainder of the discard pile and can use as many of them as possible by adding to existing melds or laying our new ones. He continues to hold in his hand any cards he cannot use.

The player ends his turn by discarding one to start a new discard pile. A player can also take up the discard pile if he can meld the top discard with one card of the same denomination and one wild card, or if the top discard can be added to an existing meld made by him or his partner.

The best cards to discard initially are the low ones, and those ranks which the opponent immediately to your left also appears to be rejecting

•

It is essential for a player to remember what discards have been placed on the pile to determine how many of them can be useful for melding with cards in his hand. If there are a number of cards in the pile, particularly when the game is well

advanced, it is essential that the player should be able to make use of most of them.

•

It is extremely important to make the initial meld, but you should avoid reducing the cards in your hand too much in order to do so. The best way of achieving it is to do the very minimum, and preferably by taking the discard pack rather than making it entirely from the cards you already have in your hand. This will become more difficult as your initial requirement increases, but try to use no more than four cards from the hand to make 90, or six to make 120 if you can.

•

The discard pile is frozen:

i) for a partnership which has not made its initial meld

ii) if the top discard is a black 3. It becomes unfrozen when a player has drawn from the stock and discarded.

iii) for all players if the discard pile contains a red 3 or a wild card. When this happens further discards are placed across the top of the card which unfreezes the pile.

The pile remains frozen until a player melds the wild card or the top discard with two natural cards from his hand.

The best time to freeze the pack is when your opponents have melded and your team has not. The team which is best able to take the pack is the one with the greater number of cards in hand. Another good time to freeze the pack with a black 3 is when you have made an initial meld because this stops the player on your immediate left from taking it, and gives your partner opposite an opportunity to use it.

•

As indicated in the table on page 59, red 3s are bonus cards which count 100 points each. They cannot be melded. If the red 3 is drawn from the stock, it must be laid face up on the table and another card drawn from the stock. If a player receives a red 3 in his deal, he must lay it face up on the table and draw a card from the stock in addition to his normal draw. if a red 3 is picked up as part of the discard pile, it must be placed face up on the table without any extra card being drawn from the stock. If partners have all the red 3s, they score 800 points, but all red 3 points are subtracted from a partnership if it has not made its first meld when the game ends.

Black 3s cannot be melded until a player goes out, and they cannot be melded with wild cards. Their purpose is to freeze the discard pile so that the opponent immediately to the left cannot pick it up for that turn. A player cannot go out if he holds two black 3s, but if he holds one he can go out by melding all his other cards and discarding the black 3 last. If he holds three or four he can meld them together as part of going out. Wild cards cannot be included in a meld of black 3s.

Before going out, a player or his partner has to make at least one canasta. He then needs to meld all his cards. He can go out without having melded before, as long as his partner has already achieved a canasta, or he melds a canasta on going out. This is a concealed going out, and is done without consulting the partner. However, if a player is uncertain what his partner's hand is like, he can ask: 'Can I go out?' This is a signal to the partner to meld as many cards as possible so that the player making the request can go out on his next turn. The partner's answer of 'yes' or 'no' is binding for that turn. When a player goes out, each partnership receives bonus points according to the following table:

	Points
Natural canasta	500
Mixed canasta	300
Going out	100
Concealed going out	100 bonus

In addition players receive the total point value of all their melded cards, less the value of any cards still held by either player in the partnership at the end of play. If one partnership has not melded at all, the value of any red 3s it has laid down are subtracted from it. It is possible for partners to make a minus score on a hand.

It is more important for you to achieve high-scoring melds than to be first to go out because that tends to attract only low bonus points.

•

The partnership which first melds a canasta puts itself in a strong position to go out, but can increase the threat of doing so by increasing its score.

•

If you find yourself in the position where your opponents have melded a canasta, you should try to go out as quickly as possible to keep the score against you as low as possible.

•

CANASTA VARIATIONS

Two-hand Canasta: This follows the rules of the four-handed game except that players are dealt 15 cards each, and at each turn they draw two and discard one card. In addition, two canastas are needed to go out.

Three-hand Canasta: This is also based on the rules for the four-hand game except that players are dealt either 11 or 13 cards each, and for each turn they draw two and discard one. The first player to take the pack becomes a lone player, and the other two team up as partners against him. The score needed for the initial meld is fixed by the individual score the melder has so far achieved, and red 3s score separately rather than in partnership. Apart from that, each player scores the amount the partnership makes. The game target is 7,500, but if no one goes out, the hand ends when the stock runs out.

Six-hand Canasta: There are two versions of this. One has two partnerships of three players each, in which partners sit alternately around the table. They use three 52-card packs together with six jokers. Players are dealt 13 cards each, and two canastas are needed to go out. In scoring, red 3s count 100 each up to three, and 200 for four or more. The game target is 10,000 points and for a side with 7,000 or more, the requirement for the initial meld is 150. In the other version of six-handed canasta, there are three partnerships of two players each. Partners sit opposite one another.

Samba: Samba generally has the same rules as Canasta but with a few exceptions:

Three packs of 52 cards, plus 6 jokers, are used making 162 cards. Each player receives 15 cards, irrespective of the number playing. Instead of taking the discard pile, players draw two cards from the stock, but discard just one card to end the turn. Three or four cards of the same suit and in sequence are valid as a meld, and can be increased by cards in the sequence up to a total of seven when it becomes a samba. It is then turned down on the table. A samba cannot contain a wild card, and no card can be added to it. A samba ranks as a canasta for going out, and its bonus score is 1,500.

Wild cards can be used only in melds of cards of the same rank, and only two wild cards can be used for a meld. The top card from the discard pile cannot be added to a completed canasta – only natural cards from the hand can be added to a canasta.

The discard pile can be used only by melding its top card with a natural pair from a player's hand, or when it is not frozen, and then by adding its top card to a meld already on the table.

A partnership must have at least two canastas to go out. It then scores a bonus of 200, but there is no bonus for a concealed hand.

CRIBBAGE

There are a number of variations of Cribbage, the most popular being the six-card game for two players. Chance plays some part in this game, but a great deal of success can be achieved by players who develop skill in choosing how to play their cards.

Origins: Cribbage was invented by the 17th-century English poet Sir John Suckling. It was based on an earlier game called Noddy for which a special scoring board was

COMPLEXITY RATING:	★ ★
NUMBER OF PLAYERS:	**2, 3 or 4**
EQUIPMENT:	**Standard pack of 52 cards; Cribbage board for scoring (although the score can be kept with pencil and paper)**
TIME REQUIRED:	**20 minutes to an hour, depending on the game**

also used. Cribbage continues to be played in almost its original form, with the exception that in the modern two-hand game, each player is dealt six cards instead of five.

Aim of the game: Cribbage is all about scoring points both during the playing of a hand, and when they are shown at the end of play. Target scores vary from 61 to 181 points according to the game.

Cribbage board: The Cribbage board has four rows of 30 holes, two rows for each player, and extra game holes at one or both ends of the board. Each player has two pegs – red or black for one and white for the other.

A player marks his score by moving his pegs initially along the outer row of holes and then back along his inner row.

A player shows his first score by moving one peg that number of holes from the start. His next score is marked by placing his second peg that number of holes beyond the first peg. The third score is shown by moving his first peg that number beyond the second peg, and so on until a player's forward peg has passed all the scoring holes to end in one of the game holes.

SIX-CARD CRIBBAGE

NUMBER OF PLAYERS:	**2**

Aim of the game: The game is won by the first player to score 121 points, or to go round the Cribbage board twice.

Basic rules: The cards in each suit rank king high down to ace low, with the court cards worth 10, and the others their pip value with ace worth one. Players cut to deal, with the lowest going first. The deal then alternates. Six cards are dealt to each player, and the remaining cards are placed face down on the table.

Each player then discards two of his six cards face down. These form a crib of four cards, which belongs to the dealer, and will be used by him later to score points.

TIP

If you are the non-dealer you should discard cards which are least likely to score for your opponent.

•

The remainder of the pack is cut once more by the non-dealer and the dealer turns up the top card of the lower half. This is placed face up for the rest of the game, and is called the 'starter' or 'turn-up' card. If the starter is a jack, the dealer pegs 2 points – 'two for his heels'.

The non-dealer begins the play by placing one of his cards face up on the table and calling out its value. The dealer then lays a card from his hand in front of him, and calls out the sum of his opponent's card plus the card he has just played.

The non-dealer then plays another card, calling out the sum of the three cards which have been played. The dealer follows, and play continues in this way until the sum of the cards played is 31, or until neither player can play a card without exceeding 31.

If a player plays a card that brings the total to exactly 31, he says '31', and pegs 2 points. If one player is unable to play another card without exceeding 31, he says 'go', and his opponent must go on playing, if he can, until he reaches 31, or cannot play without exceeding the score. The player coming nearest to 31 scores a 'go' and is entitled to peg one hole.

TIP

At the beginning of play, your object should be to gain a 'go' or a 31. The 1 or 2 points involved will be very much to your advantage because they save you double that number of points by denying them to your opponent.

•

Other scores are achieved during the game according to certain combinations:

A player who plays a card to bring the total to exactly 15 scores 2 points. Points are also scored during the course of play for pairs and runs. A player laying down a card of the same rank as the card just played by his opponent scores 2 for a pair. Although court cards count as 10 they can only be scored as pairs if they are of the same rank, eg two kings, but not king and queen.

If the first player follows with a third card of the rank, three of a kind, he scores 6 for a 'pair-royal'. If the second player can then play a fourth card of the same rank, he scores 12 for a 'double pair-royal'.

A run is a sequence of three or more cards of consecutive rank, not necessarily of the same suit. Runs count 1 point for each card in the run. They do not have to be played in order – for example, if the first player puts down a three, the second player might then play a five, and the first player follows with a four, pegging 3 points for a run. The second player could then score 4 points for a run of four by playing a two or six.

SUMMARY OF SCORING

Single cards: The 12 court cards are worth 10 points each, while all other cards count their face value, the ace scoring one.

It is important to remember that there are 16 cards worth 10, the court cards and the 10s.

•

Combinations:

Pair – two cards of the same rank	2
Pair royal – three of the same rank	6
Double pair royal – four of the same rank	12
Run – three or more cards in sequence	1 for each card
Flush – three or more cards of same suit	1 for each card
Fifteen – any two or more cards totalling 15	2

Other scores:

For 'last' – to non-dealer (five-card game only)	3
His heels – to dealer if jack turned up	2
His nob – for holding jack of same suit as start	1
Go – for playing the last card towards 31	1 if under 31
	2 if 31

The safest card to lead is a four because the next player cannot make a 15. Any cards of lower rank are better held for later because of the chances they offer to make a 15, a go, or a 31.

•

You should try to avoid leading with sevens or eights, but it might pay to do so when you have cards of similar or close rank in your hand to back them up. For example, if you have eight, seven, seven, lead a seven. If the dealer plays an eight, obviously aiming for 15 and 2 points, you can follow with your eight for 23, and 2 points for the pair. If the dealer plays seven for 14 and 2 points for the pair, you can follow with your other seven for 21, and 6 points for the pair-royal.

•

Perhaps the worst card to lead is a five because of the large number of cards with a face value of 10 which will give your opponent many opportunities to make 15. If

you hold one of the 10-value cards and a five, lead with the 10. Then if your opponent plays a five for 15 and 2 points, you can then play your own five for 20, and 2 points for the pair you have made.

•

If you have a pair, you should play it because if your opponent pairs it, you can then play your own matching card for a pair-royal and 6 points.

•

If your opponent leads with a card which gives you the choice of pairing or making up to 15, it is better to make the 15 for 2 points. Your opponent could have been leading with one of a pair he holds, and for you to pair it will give him the opportunity to make a pair-royal. Even if you cannot make 15, it is often a good idea to play some other card widely separated in rank so that he cannot form a sequence or run. On the other hand, if you have cards which are close in rank, you can play a card close in rank to his in the hope that he will then form a sequence of three, and allow you to play a fourth card in the sequence for 4 points.

•

During play, you should try to avoid playing a card which will make the running total 21. Because as there are sixteen 10-value cards, it is likely your opponent will be able to play for 31.

•

As the count approaches 31, try to avoid playing cards which, if paired, will give your opponent the 31. For example, if you play a six to make 25, your opponent may pair it for 31 and 4 points.

•

Discarding for the crib is an important element of the game, and one which requires close observation of the opponent's moves, a feeling for the possibilities of the hand, the state of the game and the position of the board.

If you are the dealer, you benefit from the crib, and you should add cards to it

which you think will help to form scoring combinations. You also need to keep in your hand the cards which offer the best chance to score. However, it is best to favour the crib if you are in doubt, because the probable chances of gaining points in the crib are better than gaining them in the hand.

•

In discarding, keep the possibility of 15s in mind. There are more 10s in the pack than any other value, so you might throw out a pair of fives if you have them, though this will lessen to some extent your chances of scoring 15s in the play. Two fives in the crib will make one pair a certainty, and there is always the strong chance of using one or more 10s. You could throw out a five and a 10, making a 15 a certainty. Two cards of the same suit will give the possibility of a flush of three or four cards. Cards of identical value are also good as they form a pair to start with, and if you opponent happens to throw out a similar card, will make up a pair-royal or three cards of the same rank. Sequence cards, a series in face order, may also prove beneficial as throw-outs as they may be joined by a third that will continue the series. An eight and a seven (which already form a 15) have good prospects for a sequence. It is also better to throw out two alternate cards – a five and a seven for instance are better than widely separated cards because there is always the chance of the wanted sequences card joining them.

•

On the other hand if you are the non-dealer, try to discard the cards which you think will be least useful to the dealer, or will baulk him. You should therefore try to avoid putting out the type of cards and combinations which have been indicated as best for the dealer. A five is probably the worst card to put in the crib because it makes a 15 with any one of the sixteen 10-value cards. Perhaps the best single cards to discard are a king and an ace because they are of least value in making up a sequence. Avoid laying a jack in the crib if possible. Besides being one of the 10-value cards, a jack of the same suit as the turn-up card adds 1 point to the value of the hand you play with.

•

After the hands have been completed, both players gather up their own cards. The non-dealer shows and scores for his hand first. For this purpose, the starter or turn-up card is considered part of his hand, and he scores for all combinations in the four cards.

For each combination of cards which totals 15, 2 points are scored. The same card may be counted several times in different combinations. Therefore a hand of four,

four, five, six, six would score 8 points for 15s, 4 points for pairs, and 12 points for sequences to total 24 points. Finally, he scores '1 for his nob' if his hand contains the jack of the same suit as the starter.

The dealer then shows his hand and scores in the same way for any combinations in his three cards together with the start. He then turns over the four cards of his crib. The dealer scores for the crib, again together with the starter, in exactly the same way except that a flush, worth 5 points, is scored only if all five cards are of the same suit.

The number of possible combinations in Cribbage is enormous, and while it is not possible to go into them exhaustively, a list of some of the higher scores possible may benefit the beginner. N indicates 'nob' and 'S' the start:

5, 5, 5, 10 28	4, 5, 6, 6, 6 21	(It is not possible
	7, 7, 7, 8, 9	to score 19)
7, 7, 8, 8, 9 24	3, 3, 3, 4, 5	
7, 7, 7, 7, 1		5, 5, 10, N, Q 18
4, 5, 5, 6, 6	3, 4, 4, 4, 4 20	3, 3, 3, 6, 6
4, 4, 4, 4, 7	3, 3, 6, 6, 6	
3, 3, 3, 3, 9	3, 3, 4, 4, 5	5, 5, J, Q, K 17
3, 6, 6, 6, 6	6, 6, 7, 7, 8	2, 3, 4, 4, 4
	6, 6, 9, 9, 9	
5, 5, J, N, 5, S 23	7, 7, 7, 8, 8	A, A, 2, 2, 3 16
5, 5, 5, 4, 6	7, 8, 8, 9, 9	2, 2, 3, 3, 4
	7, 7, 7, A, A	2, 6, 7, 7, 8
5, 5, 5, 10, 10 22		6, 7, 8, 9, 9

If a player overlooks a score in his hand or in play, his opponent may call 'muggins' and claim the score for himself. Some players however do not follow this rule.

If a player reaches 121 before his opponent is half way round the board, he scores a 'lurch' and counts two games instead of one.

GENERAL TIP

Cribbage is an offensive as well as a defensive game. To play it well, you must change your tactics from time to time during the play. If you have a substantial lead, you should play carefully and defensively to maintain it. If you are behind, you will need to take risks to improve your position, and baulk your opponent's efforts to score.

After a little practice with someone who knows the game, the beginner will soon find that, in spite of the fact that the points seem small, high scores are possible from a few cards, and that cribbage can be as exciting as any other card game.

CRIBBAGE VARIATIONS

Five-card Cribbage: This is an earlier form of Cribbage than the six-card version. The rules are the same except that the deal is five cards to each player, and the target is 61 points. The crib consists of two cards from each player.

Before play begins, the non-dealer pegs 3 points to compensate for not having the crib. Hands are not played out after 31 is reached. Hands are then shown and scored, and a new deal follows.

Here are some of the scores for the five-card game:

5, 10, 10, 10 9

6, 6, 7, 8 10
5, 5, 10, J

5, 5, 10, 10 12
6, 6, 9, 9
3, 3, 3, 9
3, 6, 6, 6
6, 6, 6, 9
6, 9, 9, 9
7, 7, 7, A
7, 7, 7, 8
7, 8, 8, 8
4, 4, 5, 6
4, 5, 5, 6
4, 5, 6, 6

5, 5, 5, 10 14

5, 5, 5, 5 20

> **IT'S A FACT...**
> *Two Cribbage players have achieved the rare feat of having four maximum 29 point hands, Mary Matheson from Canada and William E. Johnson from the United States. One player, Paul Nault, also from the US, managed two maximum hands within eight games in a 1977 tournament.*

Seven-card Cribbage: This form is played in the same way as six-card Cribbage, except that the target is 181 points and each player receives seven cards, of which two go to the crib.

Three-hand Cribbage: The game is played to 61 points, and five cards are dealt to each player with one of those going to the crib. Play begins with the player to the left of the dealer and passes to the left. The player who leads also has the first show.

Four-hand Cribbage: This is a partnership form of the game with partners sitting opposite each other. Play begins with the person to the dealer's left. The game is played to 121 points, and the deal is five cards to each player of which one goes to the crib.

POKER

Poker is one of the most popular card games in the world. It is very much a gambling game, but that is not necessarily the same thing as a game of chance – poker requires a great deal of skill to play well. There are many hundreds of variations of the game, but these share certain basic principles and differ only in detail. A player familiar with these basic principles should have no difficulty in playing any of the variations.

COMPLEXITY RATING:	★ ★ ★
NUMBER OF PLAYERS:	**2 to 10. Certain forms of poker can be played by up to 14 people. The best games however involve 6 or 7 players. No alliances are allowed, and each player plays for himself.**
EQUIPMENT:	**Standard pack of 52 cards (sometimes with a joker added); betting chips or cash**
TIME REQUIRED:	**10 to 15 minutes for each play**

Origins: The earliest ancestor of Poker was probably a Persian game called As Nas, but Poker in its more modern form probably developed from a long line of European games, the first of which may have been Primero, believed to be the most ancient card game played in England. Modern Poker first began to emerge in the United States in the early 19th century; it has been called the national card game of America.

Aim of the game: The objective is to win the highest possible stakes by betting on which player holds the best hand. This involves calculation and bluff – the winner is not necessarily the player holding the best hand.

Basic rules: To choose the first dealer, one player takes the shuffled pack and deals one card face up to each player until a jack is dealt. The person receiving the jack deals, and thereafter, the deal passes to the next player on the left. In all variations of Poker, the cards are dealt one at a time in a clockwise direction, the first to the player on the dealer's left. Usually, each player receives five cards, but in some variations, each player may receive more than five cards, some face up – 'upcards' – and some face down – 'hole cards' – from which he selects five to be his playing hand. In other variations each player may receive fewer cards and some cards may be dealt in the middle to be shared by all the players. A playing hand, however, always consists of five cards.

All bets are made by players putting chips into a common pool – the pot – in the middle of the table. The pot may be won in either of two ways. In the first, the game may proceed to a showdown in which all players left in the game show their hands with the best hand winning. In the other, one player may make a bet which none of the others is prepared to match, and that player automatically wins without having to show his hand. This is where bluffing plays a part.

Much of the skill in bluffing is maintaining an impassive appearance – keeping a 'poker face' – so that your opponents do not get any hint of your hand from your demeanour. Another area of skill lies in the ability to surprise so that regular opponents will not be able to guess your actions from their knowledge of how you play.

In all variations of the game there will be at least one round of betting (known as the 'betting interval') and usually there will be two or more. The number of betting intervals and when they take place depend on the variation being played, as will the method for deciding which player starts the betting.

After one player has started or 'opened' the betting, each of the other players in turn has three options:

i) to drop out (or 'fold' or 'pass'). This means that he is not confident he can win, and discards his hand and takes no further part in the play. A player may drop out at any stage, and forfeits any stakes he may already have paid into the pot.

ii) to stay in (or 'call' or 'see'). This means that he pays into the pot just enough to make his total exactly equal to the greatest total stake put into the pot by any other player.

iii) to raise (or 'up' or 'go better'). This means he puts into the pot enough to stay in plus an extra amount – the 'raise'. The other players, to stay in, must then put into the pot enough to make their total stakes equal to his, or drop out, or raise again.

In some Poker games, players are allowed to 'check'. This means that, at the beginning of the betting, a player may stay in but bet nothing. But once any player makes a bet, the betting interval continues as normal and checking is not allowed.

Betting ends when all the players have checked, or when all but one of the players have dropped out – the player left in being, of course, the winner – or when all bets have been equalised, ie, all the players have bet the same amount and the turn has come round again to the last player to raise.

For example:

Player	Action	Bet	Total bet
A	checks	0	0
B	checks	0	0
C	checks	0	0

Player	Action	Bet	Total bet
D	opens for 5	5	5
E	stays in	5	5
F	drops out	0	0
A	stays in	5	5
B	raises 5	10	10
C	stays in	10	10
D	stays in	5	10
E	raises 10	15	20
A	drops out	0	5
B	stays in	10	20
C	stays in	10	20
D	drops out	0	10

B, C and E remain in and the betting has been equalised. There may be various limits placed on the size and number of raises allowed, and these are always agreed before the game begins.

Cards rank in the normal order, with ace ranking high, except in the 5–4–3–2–A sequence; while in a 'high–low' game it may rank either high or low. Sometimes low-ranking cards (2s, 3s, and even 4s and 5s) are removed from the deck to speed up the game. The suits are not ranked.

The card combination which determines which player has the best hand are common to all the variations of Poker. They are:

1. Straight flush Five cards in sequence of the same suit. An ace may be considered high as in A–K–Q–J–10 (which is known as a 'royal flush'), or low as in 5–4–3–2–A. If two or more players have a straight flush, the one with the highest-ranking top card wins – eg K–Q–J–10–9 beats J–10–9–8–7.

2. Four of a kind Four cards of the same rank (the fifth card being unmatched). If two or more players have four of a kind, the highest-ranking hand wins – eg four aces will beat four kings.

3. Full house Three cards of one denomination and two of another. As between two hands of this type, the one with the higher ranking three of a kind wins – eg K–K–K–2–2 beats Q–Q–Q–J–J.

4. Flush Five cards of the same suit, but not in sequence. As between two hands of this type, the one with the higher ranking top card wins, or if the top cards are equal, the one with the higher-ranking second card, and so on – eg K–J–10–9–4 beats K–J–10–8–6.

5. Straight Five cards in sequence though not all belonging to the same suit. An ace may be either high or low. As between two hands of this type the hand with the higher-ranking top card wins.

If you have any straight, flush or full house, and several players stay in ahead of you, you should raise. However, as you have such a strong hand, it may be worth just calling to try to encourage other players to stay in.

•

If you have a four-card straight you should fold. The odds against you making the hand are very long indeed.

•

6. Three of a kind Three cards of the same rank (the other two cards being unmatched). As between two hands of this type, the higher-ranking three of a kind wins – eg K–K–K–7–2 beats Q–Q–Q–J–9.

If you have any three of a kind, raise, no matter how many players stay ahead of you. If you have three tens or better you may wish just to call in order to entice other players to stay in.

•

7. Two pairs Two cards of one denomination, two cards of another denomination, and one unmatched card.

If you are due to start the second interval of betting, it is best not to open the betting unless you have at least two pairs with jacks high. Rather than fold though, check until you see what is happening.

•

8. One pair Two cards of the same denomination, and three unmatched cards.

It is not wise to open the betting with a hand of less than two kings.

If you have two aces or two kings and betting starts ahead of you, raise in an attempt to drive out other players and keep them from drawing against you.

•

9. High card Five unmatched cards. As between two such hands, the hand with the higher-ranking top card wins, or it they are equal the higher-ranking second card, and so on – eg A–Q–J–5–4 beats A–Q–10–6–5.

It could be worth staying in if you do not have a pair or better, but your higher card is a jack, queen, king or ace. If however your best card is a ten, you should fold.

•

The players may agree to designate certain cards to be 'wild'. A wild card is one that may represent any card that the player holding the wild card wants it to represent. Sometimes a joker (or two jokers) can be added to the pack as wild cards – usually 2s ('deuces wild'). With wild cards two additional poker hands are possible:

10. Five of a kind Four cards of the same rank plus a wild card. This hand beats all other hands.

11. Double ace flush An ace-high flush plus a wild card. This hand ranks higher than a flush, but lower than a full house.

After the first interval of betting, each active player may discard one or more of his original cards in turn and receive replacements for them (usually no more than three) from the unused cards. The discards are placed on the table without revealing what they are. Any player dropping out must place his cards face down on the table. There is then further betting, after which – if more than one player is left in – there is a showdown and the player with the best hand wins. Each active player in turn must place all five cards face up on the table to be seen by all players.

If you are due to start the second interval of betting, it is best not to open the betting unless you have at least two pairs with jacks high. Rather than fold though, check until you see what is happening.

•

As mentioned before, there are innumerable variations of poker, but the two main forms are Draw Poker and Stud Poker, each of which has its own variations.

Stud Poker is a faster game than Draw Poker, and allows for greater skill. There is no exchange of cards and the average rank of winning hands is lower than in draw poker. To play, one card is dealt face down (the 'hole card') to each player, then one card face up. Each player examines his hole card. The player with the highest ranking face-up card must open or drop out. A player dropping out turns all his cards face down and does not reveal his hole card. If two players hold equal-ranking cards, the player nearest the dealer's left opens.

TIP

You can generally decide after the first two cards are dealt whether it is worth continuing. Stay if you are dealt:

A–A, A–K, A–Q, A–J, A–10,
K–A, K–K, K–Q, K–J, K–10,
Q–A, Q–K, Q–Q, Q–J, Q–10,
J–A, J–K, J–Q, J–J, J–10,
10–A, 10–K, 10–Q, 10–J, 10–10

•

After the opener, each player drops out, stays in, bets, raises or reraises in the normal way. Further rounds of dealing one card face up to each player alternate with betting intervals until the end of the fourth interval. Each player then has one face-down and four face-up cards. The player who leads the betting is the one with the highest ranking completed hand of exposed cards. The showdown follows the fourth betting interval when all players still left exposing their hole cards. Because this form requires more skill than Draw Poker, and because the pot is usually larger (since there are more betting intervals) this is the form of the game preferred by the really expert gamblers.

GENERAL TIP

Knowledge of the probabilities is important in playing Poker. For example, the chances of receiving a hand of one pair or better is about 1 in 2; 1 in 5 for a pair of jacks or better, increasing to 1 in about 600 for a full house or better. The odds against improving the original hand range from about 2½ to 1 to improve a pair by drawing three, to more than 1,000 to 1 to make a pair and an ace into four of a kind by drawing two. Many books on poker have drawn up detailed tables of odds and statistics which apply to a whole variety of hands.

•

TIP

A player may use the draw to bluff in any way he wishes about the value of his hand. The dealer must indicate how many cards he has drawn, but there is no need for any player to give any other information – truthfully. The idea of the bluff is to try to frighten opponents out of the game, but there is no point in bluffing with nothing. In any case, do not bluff too often or too consistently.

•

A good card player learns that once his money is in the pot, it is not his any longer. He should say to himself: do the odds favour my playing regardless of the money I have already put in the middle?

•

You can get some idea from the draw what an opponent may be holding: someone who draws three cards may be holding a pair; drawing two suggests a hand of three of a kind; drawing one suggests a hand of two pairs, fours, four to a straight or four to a flush; a player refusing the draw could have a full house, a straight or a flush. The betting which follows may indicate whether the draw was a bluff or based on a real hand. Experience will teach you how to vary your draw.

•

To play well it is necessary to learn the winning chances of a hand before and after the draw. As a general rule, it is worth staying in the game only if you hold something better than average. The average pair or threes are eights; two pairs jacks and sixes; and in full hands a full house is nine times less likely than a flush and twelve times less likely than a straight.

•

Decisions on betting are based on the ratio of expected profit to the amount bet and on the chances of winning. If a bet of one chip can win 10 chips (odds of 10 to 1), and chances of winning appear to be 1 in 6, it is worth laying the bet. The fine points of psychological play, and adjusting your strategy to various types of games come through experience of playing.

•

You should study your own weaknesses as well as those of your opponents. It is essential to keep a straight, or 'poker' face, at all times to avoid giving any clues to your opponents about your hand. You should also remain silent as much as possible, as this aids concentration. It is a helpful rule not to grumble at losing hands, or to gloat about winning hands. As with any game of skill, it is advisable not to drink alcohol, even though others may do so and it may be part of a popular image. Drinking leads to carelessness.

POKER VARIATIONS

Brag

This is probably one of the forerunners of modern Poker.

COMPLEXITY RATING:	★ ★ ★
NUMBER OF PLAYERS:	3 or more

Basic rules: This is generally similar to Poker, but Brag hands, in descending order of value, are:

  i) **Prial** Three cards of the same rank (eg 9–9–9)

  ii) **Running flush** Three cards of the same suit in sequence (eg 10–J–Q of hearts)

  iii) **Run** Any three cards in sequence (eg 5–6–7)

  iv) **Flush** Any three cards in the same suit (eg 2–6–J of diamonds)

  v) **Pair** Two cards of the same rank, the third card being unmatched.

  vi) **High card** Three unmatched cards. As between two hands of this type, the hand containing the highest card wins.

Cards rank from ace high to 2 low, but an ace may also count low in the run A–2–3.

Before the game, limits for stakes and raises are agreed, as in Poker. To begin the game, the dealer puts an initial stake or ante in the pot. Three cards are then dealt, one at a time and face down, to each player. Thereafter, each player in turn has the option of calling, raising or folding. As in Poker, there can be an element of bluff. If all but one of the players fold, the remaining player wins automatically, otherwise there is a showdown and the player with the best hand wins.

Draw Poker

COMPLEXITY RATING:	★ ★ ★
NUMBER OF PLAYERS:	Best with 5 to 7

Basic rules: Before each deal, an agreed stake is put into the pot by each player. Five cards are then dealt, face down, to each player.

The deal is followed by the first betting interval, which starts with the player to the left of the dealer. He may either check or bet. If he checks, each player in turn after him has the same two options until one player opens by making the first bet. After that, players must call, raise or fold until the betting interval is completed. In one popular form of Draw Poker called Jackpots, a player may not open unless he has a pair of jacks or better.

When the first betting interval is over the draw takes place. The dealer takes the pack of cards left over from the original deal and asks each active player in turn (ie each player still in the game, not having folded) whether he wants to exchange any of his cards. A player may sit – keep all the cards he was originally dealt – or may discard from one to three cards from his hand. He puts them face down on the table, and is then dealt the same number from the top of the pack. In some variations of the game, a player can discard any number, even all five.

The second betting interval then takes place, starting with the player who opened the first round. If, after the second betting interval, all the players but one have folded, that player takes the pot without being required to show his hand. Otherwise there is a showdown and each player still in the game must place all five of his cards face up on the table. The player with the best hand wins.

Spit in the Ocean

COMPLEXITY RATING:	★ ★ ★
NUMBER OF PLAYERS:	Best with 5 to 7

Basic rules: This is normally played in the same way as Draw Poker except that each player is dealt four cards and an extra card (the spit) is dealt face up in the centre of the table. This card is considered to be the fifth card in every player's hand.

Five-Card Stud

This is the original Stud game from which Seven-card Stud and other Stud variations are derived. Five-card Stud has lost popularity in favour of other varieties because it is slower to play.

COMPLEXITY RATING:	★ ★ ★
NUMBER OF PLAYERS:	Best with 7 to 10

Basic rules: Each player receives a face-down card (the hole card) and than a face-up card. Each player examines his hole card without revealing it. Then follows the first betting interval which begins with the player who has the highest face-up card. Players may stay, raise or fold, but no checking is allowed.

Each active player then receives another face-up card. Then follows another betting interval beginning with the player whose face-up cards form the highest Poker combination. In this and the subsequent intervals, players may check until one of the players opens the betting. A fourth, and then a fifth card is dealt in the same way, each being followed by betting which is begun by the player whose face-up cards show the best Poker combination.

If at any stage there is only one player left in, all the others having folded, that player takes the pot. Otherwise the final betting interval is followed by a showdown, in which each active player turns up his hole card, and the player with the best hand wins the pot.

Six-card Stud

COMPLEXITY RATING:	★ ★ ★
NUMBER OF PLAYERS:	Best with 5 to 8

Basic rules: This is very similar to Five-card Stud except that each active player is dealt a sixth card, face down, and this is followed by one more betting interval. Each player selects any five of his six cards to be his final hand for the showdown.

Seven-card Stud

COMPLEXITY RATING:	★ ★ ★
NUMBER OF PLAYERS:	Best with 5 to 7

Basic rules: This, again, is very similar to Five-card Stud. Each player is dealt two face-down cards and one face-up. There is a betting interval. There are three more rounds of dealing in which each active player receives a face-up card, each round being followed by a betting interval. Then each player is dealt another face-down card and there is a final betting interval, followed by the showdown.

PONTOON

Pontoon is sometimes known as Vingt-et-Un or Twenty-One, and is similar to the American game of Blackjack. It is the best known game of a family of games in which the object is to acquire cards whose combined face value do not exceed a given total – in this game 21. It is one of the few banking games in which skill plays a part.

COMPLEXITY RATING:	★
NUMBER OF PLAYERS:	3 or more, although it is best with 4 to 6
EQUIPMENT:	Standard pack of 52 cards; betting chips
TIME REQUIRED:	Each hand takes from 5 to 10 minutes

Origins: Pontoon is one of a number of games, popular today in casinos around the world, which originated in Europe in the 15th and 16th centuries which are extremely simple to play. Pontoon was probably the most popular card game among the troops during the two world wars.

Aim of the game: The banker deals, and the players (punters) play against him and try to obtain hands which are better than his, without exceeding 21.

Basic rules: Players draw cards to decide who will be the banker. Suits of the cards are disregarded – all that matters is their numerical value. Court cards count 10; aces count 11 or 1 at the choice of the holder; all other cards count their pip value. A player who has a hand in which the cards add up to a total greater than 21 goes 'bust' and loses. A hand in which the total value of the cards is between 16 and 21 beats the banker if the value of his hand is lower or if it is bust.

A pontoon is a hand totalling 21 in two cards – an ace and a ten or court card – and this beats the banker unless he also has 21. A five-card-trick is a hand containing five cards totalling 21 or less, and beats the banker unless he also has a five-card-trick. A royal pontoon is a hand consisting of three 7s and beats the banker whatever cards he holds. The banker may not count a royal pontoon – if his hand consists of three 7s it counts only as a normal 21.

Stakes are won from and paid to the banker, and for this purpose, coins or counters are usually used. The cards are shuffled before the first deal, but not after that until the next dealer takes over.

The banker deals one card face down to each punter, and then one to himself. Each punter (but not the banker) looks at his card, and then stakes any amount up to an agreed maximum. The banker then deals a second card to each punter and one to himself. Each player looks at his second card, and at that point, the banker looks at his.

You should always remember that the banker has the advantage in this game because he always wins on equal hands, even when bust (qv).

•

When you receive your first card, the ones with the best potential are an ace or a card with the value of 10, and it is obviously best to stake high on either of these. A 7 or higher is not a bad opening card, but lower ranks do not show a lot of promise.

•

There is little point on speculating on the possibility of a five-card-trick until you have three low-rank cards.

•

If any player has a pontoon he declares it. If the banker has a pontoon, the deal ends and he collects from any punter who has a pontoon the stake he has wagered, and from any other punter double his stake. Otherwise the banker offers extra cards to each of the punters in turn, beginning with the player on his left.

A punter has three options:

i) to 'stand' (or 'stick'), which means that he takes no more cards from the banker. A player may stand only if the total value of his hand is 16 or more.

If you are banker, you should do best overall by sticking when you can, though the fewer punters you are playing against (ie, the more who have gone bust), the higher you can risk going.

•

If you are a punter, you should stick at 17 or more. To stick on 16 will leave you in a weak position.

•

ii) to 'buy' a card – that is, to lay an additional stake (not less than the amount for which he bought any previous card, and not greater than his existing stake), and to obtain an extra card face down from the banker.

iii) to 'twist' – that is, to be dealt an extra card face upwards without increasing the stake.

If the cards you have already received total 12 to 15 and you do not have an ace, you are in a weak position because about one in every three cards will cause you to bust. In this position, it is probably best to twist.

•

The banker finishes dealing with one player before proceeding to the next. Five cards is the maximum that a player can hold, and a player's fifth card, even if it is bought, is always dealt face upwards. A player who has bought a card may subsequently twist, but not vice versa. A player who goes bust or who gets a royal pontoon must declare the fact.

When all the punters have been given the cards they have asked for, it is the banker's turn to play. He turns his cards face up and deals himself as many extra cards as he wishes.

Settlement is then made, with the banker paying those players with better hands than he has, and collecting from the others. The following table summarises the normal scale of payments. Positive numbers represent payment from banker to punter; negative numbers represent payment from punter to banker; 1, 2 and 3 represent single, double and treble stakes. Punter's score in italics:

Banker's hand	Bust	16	17	18	19	20	21	Five card	Pontoon	Royal Pontoon
Bust	−1	+1	+1	+1	+1	+1	+1	+2	+2	+3
16	−1	−1	+1	+1	+1	+1	+1	+2	+2	+3
17	−1	−1	−1	+1	+1	+1	+1	+2	+2	+3
18	−1	−1	−1	−1	+1	+1	+1	+2	+2	+3
19	−1	−1	−1	−1	−1	+1	+1	+2	+2	+3
20	−1	−1	−1	−1	−1	−1	+1	+2	+2	+3
21	−1	−1	−1	−1	−1	−1	+1	+2	+2	+3
Five card	−2	−2	−2	−2	−2	−2	−2	−1	+2	+3
Pontoon	−2	−2	−2	−2	−2	−2	−2		−1	

A change of banker occurs when a punter wins with a pontoon, the winning punter becoming the next banker. If two or more punters win with a pontoon then the player nearest the left of the banker becomes the new banker. Alternatively, the bank can be bought at any time for a mutually acceptable sum.

An additional rule sometimes encountered is that when a punter is dealt a pair as his first two cards (eg two queens) he may 'split' the hand to form two separate hands, staking on each card the amount he originally staked on his first card. The banker then deals a second card face down to each of the two hands, which are thereafter dealt with independently.

When you have a pair, you should split aces, 4s, 6s, 7s and 8s, but keep any pair of 10-value cards. There is some debate about whether you should split 9s, but a pair of 5s gives you a total of ten, and is a good total to buy on. It is also best not to split a pair of 2s or 3s because they could provide the basis of a five-card trick if you are lucky.

•

PONTOON VARIATIONS

Baccarat: This is a game similar to Pontoon, but with the royal cards counting nought, and the ace one. The aim is to get as close as possible to nine in either two or three cards. After the dealer is chosen, several packs of cards are shuffled together, and stakes are laid before the cards are dealt.

After inspection, any punters of the dealer who holds eight or nine must turn up the hand and declare it. The other hands are then exposed, and the highest points under nine win. If neither dealer nor punters hold eight or nine, further cards must be offered by the dealer.

Only one total, five, gives a player the choice of standing or drawing. Varieties of Baccarat include Baccara Banque, Chemin de Fer and Punto Banco.

Blackjack This is the American equivalent of Pontoon. Players place their stakes before the deal. A player who receives two cards totalling 21 has a 'natural', and he collects from the banker who then collects from the other punters without further play. Otherwise punters may stick on any total and twist on as many more cards as they wish. If his first two cards total 11, a player can double his stake.

NEWMARKET

Newmarket is a very popular card game, played all over the world, and known by a variety of different names including Michigan, Boodle, Stops, Saratoga and Chicago. It is usually played for low stakes.

COMPLEXITY RATING:	★ ★
NUMBER OF PLAYERS:	**3 to 8 players (the more players, the better the game)**
EQUIPMENT:	**Standard pack of 52 cards and 4 from another pack, ace, king, queen and jack, each from a different suit; chips**
TIME REQUIRED:	**30 minutes, depending on the number playing**

Origins: Newmarket is one of the 'Stops' family of card games dating back two centuries. One of the earliest forms of the game was Comet which may have been inspired by the appearance in 1759 of Halley's Comet.

Aim of the game: Each player tries to play certain cards to collect chips, and then to be the first to get rid of all his cards.

Basic rules: The four extra cards (the 'Boodle' cards) are placed face up on the table where they remain throughout the game. Players draw for the deal, but before cards are dealt, stakes are placed on the Boodle cards – usually the dealer places two units on each, and each other player one on each.

All cards are then dealt even though some hands contain one more card than others. As part of the deal, an extra hand, or widow, is placed between the dealer and the player on his left. No one is allowed to see what cards are in the extra hand which belongs to the dealer. He may exchange it for his original hand, or if he does not he must sell it to the highest bidder. If everyone refuses it, no one may look at it. If a player does buy it, he discards his original hand, which must remain face down for the rest of the game.

By buying the widow, you are able to gain a complete knowledge of the stops in the dead hand. How much you should pay depends on how much has been placed on the Boodle cards, the worth of your original hand, and the possible number of Boodle cards in the original hand. You should hold onto a hand with a higher than average number of high cards, even if it does not have any Boodle cards.

•

The player to the left of the dealer then leads with the lowest card he has in any suit. The player (the one who has just led or any other) with the next highest card in the same suit then plays it regardless of where he sits on the table. The game proceeds in this way until the ace is reached or because a card of the sequence is in the widowed hand.

It is a good idea to lead cards in the suits where you hold Boodle cards.

•

When one of these stops is reached the player who last played must start a new suit and has to put out the lowest card he holds in that suit. If he does not have any other suit, the lead passes to the next player on his left.

You should get rid of low cards in a stopped suit as quickly as you can.

•

If a player puts out one of the Boodle cards he takes all the chips off that Boodle card. The first player to get rid of all his cards is given one chip by each of the players for each card they have been left with. Any chips on the Boodle cards that have not been claimed are left for the next round.

It is quite often useful to help another player get rid of all his cards quickly to stop someone else winning a lot of chips on a Boodle card.

•

RAT-FINK

This is a light-hearted card game ideally suited for all the family but especially children, and is played at high speed to add to the excitement. It's guaranteed to liven up the quietest children's party.

COMPLEXITY RATING:	★ ★
NUMBER OF PLAYERS:	**5 to 8, though as few as 3 and as many as 10 can play**
EQUIPMENT:	**A pack of playing cards and teaspoons**
TIME REQUIRED:	**45 minutes**

Aim of the game: It is a game of quick wits in which players have to grab a teaspoon as quickly as possible to avoid becoming a Rat-Fink – a North American expression for a bad person.

Basic rules: Not all the cards are needed, just four of the same numerical value per player. If there are five players, then five lots of four identical cards are taken from the pack. It doesn't matter which ones, it could be four kings, four queens, four jacks, four tens and four nines. The remaining cards are not needed for the game. There should be one less teaspoon than there are players (it doesn't HAVE to be a teaspoon), ie in this example you would need four. The players sit in a circle with the teaspoons in the centre, an equal distance away from each of the competitors. This is important to ensure fairness. The cards being used are thoroughly shuffled and then dealt, face down, to the players who will get five each. (The dealer can be chosen in the normal way.) The cards must be left on the table and only when the dealer says so can all five players, including himself, pick them up. Each player is trying to get four of a kind in his hand so he or she arranges their cards accordingly. Then on the command of the dealer each player passes their least-wanted card to the player on their right. (To add a little chaos the dealer can sometimes vary this command by telling players to pass to their left.) The dealer keeps this sequence going at quite a fast pace, which keeps players on their toes, until one of them gets four of a kind in their hand. This is where the teaspoons come in. When a player has four of a kind he picks up one of the teaspoons. This is a signal for all the other players to pick up a spoon as well. But as there are not enough spoons to go around, one player will be left spoonless. This player is then 'awarded' a letter, in the first case the letter 'R', the first letter in Rat-Fink. If and when that player loses again they will be given an A, then a T, then an F and so on. Eventually one of the players becomes a 'Rat-Fink' and loses the game. However, that person continues in the game until just one person is left who is not a Rat-Fink – and he or she is declared the winner.

TIP

When a player gets four of a kind, he or she can pick up the teaspoon so that the others can see. But sometimes it is more fun to pick it up quietly, hoping someone will not notice – and get left behind in the rush for the teaspoons.

•

TIP

Players are allowed to bluff in Rat-Fink. When a player picks up a spoon he or she is not obliged to show their hand. This means that a player may pick up a spoon even if they do not have four of a kind. The player will get away with this unless they are challenged by another player. If a challenge is successful then the person who wrongly picked up the spoon is penalised with two extra letters in Rat-Fink. However if the challenge is incorrect, and the player did have four of a kind, then the unsuccessful challenger him or herself is penalised by two letters.

•

IT'S A FACT...

Perhaps the greatest name in the history of cards in Britain is Edmond Hoyle who died in 1769 in his 90s. Hoyle wrote a 'short Treatise' on whist, or 'whisk' as it had been called, in which he described whist and other card games. His name is now synonymous with the rules of card games and his surname has been used on books in Britain and the United States explaining the rules of countless card games, the majority of which he would not have known. Curiously, Hoyle, who was a whist tutor, never actually described the rules of any card game in his best-selling treatise, not even whist.

IT'S A FACT...

The invention of the sandwich, ascribed to the 4th Earl of Sandwich in the 18th century, occurred while His Lordship was indulging in a marathon session of gambling, including the playing of whist.

DOMINO GAMES

Dominoes probably originated in China, as many as 2,000 years ago, and were introduced into Europe by Venetian traders in the 14th or 15th century. From Italy, they were subsequently introduced into France, and it is thought that the English may first have learned about dominoes from French prisoners-of-war during the Napoleonic wars.

For nearly all their history, dominoes have been especially popular among working men. In the days when paper was expensive, dominoes were made of bone. They were easier to produce, and more durable than the playing cards which were popular among wealthier people.

Most of the games are easy to learn, and a novice can reach an acceptable level of play, although real expertise comes only with practice.

•

Dominoes are rectangular tiles, made these days from bone, wood or plastic. The use of ivory to produce them has, thankfully, been outlawed. A standard set, or pack, used in Europe and the USA consists of 28 tiles. The face of each is divided by a central line into two equal squares, each of which is either blank or marked with pips from one to six in number. A tile that has identical halves such as 3:3 or 0:0 is known as a double. All other tiles are called singles. This set of dominoes is known as the double-6 set, as the double-6 is the top domino in the set. All games described in this section are played with this set. Double-9 packs using 55 tiles and double-12 packs with 91 tiles are sometimes used. These allow more players to take part in more sophisticated games, but their use is not widespread.

Almost all games for a double-6 set can be played with the larger sets, although in some cases a slight modification of the rules is needed.

For some games, tiles are classed in suits. There are eight suits, each consisting of seven tiles making up all combinations of the suit numbers.

The suits are:

Blank suit: Double-blank, 6-blank, 5-blank, 4-blank, 3-blank, 2-blank, 1-blank
1 suit: Double-1, 6-1, 5-1, 4-1, 3-1, 2-1, 1-blank
2 suit: Double-2, 6-2, 5-2, 4-2, 3-2, 2-1, 2-blank

3 suit:	Double-3, 6-3, 5-3, 4-3, 3-2, 3-1, 3-blank
4 suit:	Double-4, 6-4, 5-4, 4-3, 4-2, 4-1, 4-blank
5 suit:	Double-5, 6-5, 5-4, 5-3, 5-2, 5-1, 5-blank
6 suit:	Double-6, 6-5, 6-4, 6-3, 6-2, 6-1, 6-blank
Double suit:	Double-6, double-5, double-4, double-3, double-2, double-1, double-blank

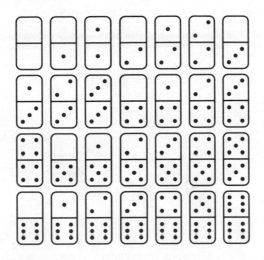

All single dominoes belong to two suits, corresponding to their pip values, so a 3-2 tile belongs to both the 3 and 2 suits, and the double-3 belongs to the 3 suit and to the double suit.

Although there is a range of domino games, certain general principles apply. These are described here to avoid repetition in the descriptions of the games that follow.

The players:

Some games are for two players, some for four and some for any number from two to five. Where there are four players, they may play individually or in partnerships of two. Partners should sit on opposite sides of the table.

Shuffling:

Before each game or hand, the dominoes are all placed down on the table and are moved about until they are thoroughly mixed. All players take part in the shuffle.

Drawing a hand:

After shuffling, each player selects the number of dominoes required for the game. In all but a few games, the player looks at his tiles, but keeps them concealed from other players. The dominoes left after all players have drawn their hands are known as the 'boneyard'. They are moved to one side, face down, whether they are needed later in the game or not.

Leading:

In some games the lead or first turn goes to the player who has drawn the double-6. If no player has this, the lead goes to the player holding the next highest double. In other games, the lead is decided by lots before the hands are drawn.

Direction of play:

Play always proceeds to the left, or clockwise, around the table.

The play:

In a few games, the dominoes are played so that tricks may be taken, but in most games they are played so that matching ends are adjacent. In most games the players may build on either end of such a row, known as the line of play. The row may bend at right angles (particularly when nearing the edge of the table). Doubles are usually played across the line of play, whereas the other dominoes are played with the line of play.

Usually one can play only against the sides of the doubles, as in the illustration above, but in a few games the tiles can be placed like this:

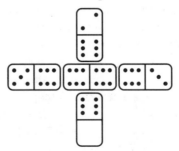

Passing:

In some games, if a player cannot match a domino from his hand with either end of the line, he is said to pass or to be knocking, and usually knocks on the table. Play immediately passes to the next player. In some games, the player who is unable to play a matching domino must draw a tile from the boneyard.

End of play:

A hand ends when one player has played all his tiles, or 'goes out', or when all players are unable to play from their hands, and have passed in turn (this is known as a 'blocked game').

Types of games:

There are two main types of games, scoring and blocking games. The scoring game is one in which scores are made during the play, and at the end of the hand, and the blocking game is one in which the object is to go out first and scoring takes place at the end of each hand.

Scoring:

There are various scoring systems, depending on the game being played. Most consist of a number of hands or rounds, and are played until one player attains an agreed number of points such as 100. The scoring is usually based on the number of pips on the dominoes remaining in the players' hands. A cribbage board may be used to record the score, in which case the game is usually played to 61 or 121 points.

GENERAL TIPS

You need to develop your memory and logic to play both drawing and blocking domino games well. You always need to concentrate on the game, and watch closely what the other players are doing, including your partner when you are playing with one. Remember the count all the time, and think through your move before you make any play.

•

Perhaps the most important skill in dominoes is the knowledge of suit control, and one you need to develop. Each tile belongs to suits, or number sets, from 6 down through blank. Each of the six singles dominoes of a particular suit, such as the number 1, can be played on any domino that puts up that suit number.

It is very important to play your double early enough to avoid it being left as an orphan. If the other six tiles of the suit are played, you will not be able to get rid of the double, preventing you from going out, and possibly giving your opponents a gift of that score.

GENERAL TIPS

The skill in playing dominoes is in choosing which play to follow by making the best use of the dominoes in your hand.

•

For blocking games, the aim for you and your team is to go out by playing your last domino and to receive the score in your opponents' hands. If you are unable to go out, you should try to reduce the count in your hand so that you will give your opponents the least number of points possible.

For scoring games, such as Five-Up, your main aim is to score on your plays and preventing your opponents from scoring. You should also try to keep your hand moving, while at the same time trying to force your opponents to draw from the boneyard if it is to your advantage. There will be occasions when your opponent will benefit from drawing a number of dominoes.

VARIATIONS

It would be impossible to describe all the variations of each game. We have included a number of variations here, and although players may find others, the basic principles remain the same. The accepted practice is to play house rules.

BLOCK

Block is probably the most popular of all domino games. It is best played as a game for four players in partnership.

COMPLEXITY RATING:	★ ★
NUMBER OF PLAYERS:	**2, 3 or 4. Four may play individually, or in partnerships.**
EQUIPMENT:	**Set of double-6 pack of dominoes**
TIME REQUIRED:	**15 minutes for each game**

Aim of the game: The object is to be the first player to dispose of all tiles in hand. The player who goes out scores the total of the pips on his opponents' remaining tiles. In a partnership game, the sum of the remaining pips on one side is subtracted from the remaining pips on the other to give the game score. It is therefore possible for a player to go out, but for his side to lose because his partner has a higher pip count than the opponents combined. In the case where all players knock, then the player with the lowest pip count scores the total of his partners' pips less his own. Where there are partnerships, the lowest combined total scores the difference between that total and their opponents' combined total. Play continues for an agreed number of games, or time, with running scores being kept.

Basic rules: If there are two players, each draws seven tiles. If there are three or four players, each draws five. The lead player is chosen by lot, and plays any domino from his hand. The next player must play a tile which matches either end of the starter, or pass if he cannot do so. Play continues around the table in this way with each player adding a tile to either end of the line or passing.

To allow yourself to be the first player to play all your tiles, you should try to play dominoes which will block your opponents and force them to pass. Therefore a good hand is one which has a number of tiles of one suit. If you are leading, you should play a tile of your strongest suit, preferably the double. If the line stands at:

and you hold the double-6, 6-3 and 6-4, then your opponents are fully blocked because all the sixes have either been played or are in your hand. You may play the double-6, and your opponents will still be passing. You can then play either the 6-3 or the 6-4 and your opponents will be restricted to playing on that one end – you still hold a block on the other.

•

If you are playing a partnership game, it is not always a good thing to go out as quickly as possible, because it may leave your partner with a high pip count. It is therefore important to check the number of tiles your partner holds compared with those of your opponents. Look too, to see how many high-value tiles have already been played in the line.

•

To minimise the possible penalty if someone else goes out before you, try to play out your high-suit tiles early.

•

Try also to play out your doubles since the opportunities for playing these are half those of the singles.

•

Watch carefully all tiles that are played to give you a better feel for what tiles are left, either held by other players or as sleepers. Experienced players can deduce which suits are sleepers by remembering the suits on which their opponents pass.

•

BLOCK VARIATIONS

Draw: The Draw game is a derivative of Block played in a line except that each player is allowed to draw from the boneyard. This gives him the chance to overcome the luck of the draw in his original hand. A score is made only at the end of each hand. *Number of players:* 2, 3 or 4. Four can play individually or as partners.

Aim of the game: Players try to go out or close the hand and score the total left in their opponents' hands. The game is played to 61 points, or to 100 if a longer game is preferred.

Basic rules: With two or three players, each takes seven dominoes while four take six each.

The play is the same as in Block, but after the first tile is led, each player may play from the dominoes in his hand, or draw from the boneyard, even if he has a playable tile in his hand. However, the last two dominoes in the boneyard may not be drawn. If a player has no playable domino in his hand he must draw from the boneyard until he has one.

In the two-handed game, the advantage of the first player in being able to lead is neutralised by the other player having the right to draw more dominoes. This offers more possible plays, and the chance to control the game. However, in the four-handed game, there are only two dominoes in the boneyard which can be drawn, and it is generally a bad thing to draw, and should be avoided. Rather, you should attempt to force your opponent to do so.

•

Passing: In the Passing game, like Draw, drawing is allowed. As an extra element, players also have the opportunity to pass. Therefore he has the choice of playing from his hand, of drawing from the boneyard, or passing.

Number of players: 2, 3 or 4. Four play in partnerships.

Aim of the game: Players try to go out, or close the hand and score the total in their opponents' hands. The game is played to 61 points, or 100 if a longer game is preferred.

Basic rules: The method of play is the same as in block and draw, but after the first player has led a tile, each player may play from the dominoes in his hand, draw from the boneyard, or pass, even if he has a playable tile in his hand. As in draw, the last two tiles cannot be drawn. Players need not draw from the boneyard, even though they cannot play. If each player then passes, the hand is closed, and a count is made.

To play a good passing game, you will need to develop skill in deciding when to play and when not to, either to force your opponent to play or to confuse him about your intentions. You will also need to develop a skill in working out the count in your opponents' hands, by applying averages based on what you have in your hand and what has already been played.

•

Sebastopol: This is a four-handed blocking game, but different from the others. The players play as individuals and each draws seven tiles, so there are none left for the boneyard.

The player who holds 6-6 leads, and the next four dominoes are played against the sides and ends of the first tile to form a star as in the following example:

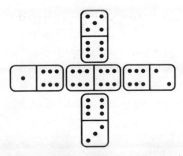

If a player does not have a 6 in his hand he must pass until the star has been completed. Play then proceeds as for block except that there are four ends to play instead of two. Scoring is the same as for block.

Cyprus: Cyprus is similar to Sebastopol except that after the double-6 has been led, the next six dominoes must be played against it to form a star with ends like this:

If a player does not have a 6 in his hand, he must pass until the star has been completed. Thereafter, play proceeds as for block except that there are now six ends to play on.

Cyprus is sometimes played with a double-9 set of dominoes, and in that version the double-9 is led and the star is formed with eight ends.

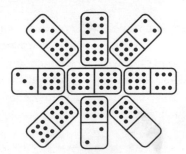

FOURS

Fours is a simple game which is particularly suitable for young players, and is often the first domino game they learn.

COMPLEXITY RATING:	★
NUMBER OF PLAYERS:	**3, 4 or 5**
EQUIPMENT:	**Set of double-6 pack of dominoes**
TIME REQUIRED:	**10 minutes for each hand**

Aim of the game: The object is to be the first player to get rid of all his dominoes.
Basic rules: The first player to lead is chosen by lot, and each player then draws his dominoes. If three are playing, each draws nine dominoes, four draw seven each, and five draw five. Left-over tiles are not used at all in the hand.

The first player leads with any domino from his hand. He can continue playing from his hand as long as he is able to match either end of the line of dominoes already played. When he is unable to do that, the turn passes to the next player on the left.

If you lead, choose the domino that will allow you to get rid of as many dominoes as possible. Do this by mentally matching your tiles as far as you can, and then try any other combination which may run further. Be careful though that you do not choose to hold onto high-value tiles if you can get rid of them because you may be caught with them and they could count against you.

•

Occasionally, it is possible to play all dominoes in one turn, but usually it will take at least two turns. In some cases the game will become blocked when all players are left with dominoes that cannot be played. When this occurs, each player adds up the number of pips on the dominoes left in his hand, and the winner is the player with the lowest total.

FIVE-UP

Five-Up is a game of chance and skill which has gained recent popularity in the United States. Because of the possible variations, Five-Up gives much opportunity for strategy and skilful play.

COMPLEXITY RATING:	★ ★
NUMBER OF PLAYERS:	**2, 3 or 4 with the 4 usually playing as pairs**
EQUIPMENT:	**Set of double-6 dominoes**
TIME REQUIRED:	**About 15 minutes per hand**

Origins: Five-Up was developed in San Francisco at the beginning of the 20th century, and was played a great deal in northern California. Its popularity has now spread elsewhere.

Aim of the game: The object of the single game or hand is to score points by making the ends of the line of play add up to multiples of five, and to get rid of all the dominoes. A number of hands are played until a score of 61 is reached.

Basic rules: The game's outstanding characteristic is that every double is a possible spinner, that is, a double which has been played on both sides and which may then be played on both ends.

There are two objectives: the first is to build up the highest score by playing tiles so that the pips on the exposed tiles at the two ends of the leg add up to 5 or a multiple of 5. One point is earned for every five pips, so that if the two ends add up to 10, 2 points are scored. With doubles, all pips are counted, so a display of 20 (double-6 and double-4) would be worth 4 points.

Keep track of the count on the table at all times. In this way, you will know what is going on, and it will help you to keep check on the scores claimed by your opponents.

•

Remember who led, and what was led, particularly if you are playing in partnership, because it will help to influence your play.

•

The lay-out on the table tells you what has been played, what you can play and where.

•

The second object is to go out. The remaining pips are totalled by the other players as in Block, but in Five-Up the winner scores 1 point for every five pips that the scores differ. Numbers are rounded up to the next multiple of 5.

For example, in a partnership game, one player goes out and his partner has six pips left. The total pip for the opposition is 12. The pips of the winner's partner are deducted, leaving 6. This is rounded up to the next highest multiple of 5 for a score of 10. Points scored during play are then added on. Games continue until an agreed score, usually 61, is reached.

Your running score should determine how you play the later hands. If you are way behind, you should build up the count on the table for higher scores. If you are way ahead, cut down the count to protect your lead.

•

Lots are drawn to determine who starts. If that player happens to lead with a double-5, he immediately scores 2 points. The game is then similar to Block, with each player in turn trying to match one of the ends of the leg. If he is not able to play, a player must draw a tile from the boneyard until he can get one that can be played. If the boneyard is empty, he must pass.

Singles are matched end to end, while doubles are played across singles. The second play on the double must be made off the side of the double.

A double may be played on the same singles number only, and it must cross the number. Both of its ends are included in the count until both sides have been played on. When plays have been made on both sides, the double is dropped from the count.

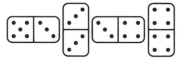

As plays can be made on the ends of all doubles as well as the sides, four plays can be made off all doubles. Every double on which plays have been made on both sides becomes a spinner.

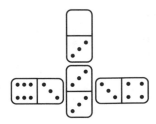

A domino played on a spinner is an open end, and the number turned out forms a new line. It may be played on in the same way as any other open end.

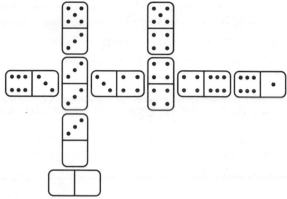

A singles domino may be played any place where it can be played – off the end of another matching singles, off the side of a matching double, or off the end of a spinner. However, the two sides of a double must be played on before playing on the ends.

Players score 1 point for each 5 and multiple of 5. Points are scored throughout the play on the tiles which are laid, and on completion of the hand. When a player or team makes a play so that the total count of all open ends on the table total 5 or a multiple of 5, they score 1 point for each multiple of 5. For a double, all spots are counted when it is an end. If, however, the count does not add up to 5 or a multiple, the player does not score.

The first player or team to have laid down all the dominoes held receives the total in the opponents' hands as a bonus. He scores 1 point for each multiple of 5. Where there are remainders of 1 or 2 they do not count, but remainders of 3 or 4 score 1 point. For example, if one player goes out and his two opponents have a total count of 16, the player scores 3.

MUGGINS

Muggins is one of the family of domino games in which points are earned during play as well as at the end. It is a good starting game, especially for young children.

COMPLEXITY RATING:	★ ★
NUMBER OF PLAYERS:	2, 3 or 4
EQUIPMENT:	A set of double-6 dominoes
TIME REQUIRED:	15 minutes or so for each game

Aim of the game: Muggins is another game, like Sniff, in which the aim is to play so that the ends of the line of play add up to multiples of 5.

Basic rules: Preparation is the same as for Block. Two, three or four players (who are best in partnership) take part, and draw respectively seven, six or five tiles at the start.

There are two objects: The first is to build up the highest score by playing tiles so that the pips on the exposed tiles at the two ends of the leg add up to 5 or a multiple of 5. One point is earned for every five pips, so that if the two ends add up to 10, 2 points are scored. With doubles, all pips are counted, so it is possible to display 20 (double-6 and double-4) for a total of 4 points.

The second object is to go out. The remaining pips are totalled by the other players as in Block, but in Muggins the winner scores 1 point for every five pips that the scores differ. Numbers are rounded up to the next multiple of 5.

For example, in a partnership game, one player goes out and his partner has 6 pips left. The pips total for the opposition is 12. The pips of the winner's partner are deducted, leaving 6. This is rounded up to the next highest multiple of 5 for a score of 10. Points scored during play are then added on. Games continue until an agreed score, usually 61, is reached.

To start, the player who has the highest double leads with that domino. If it happens to be double-5, he immediately scores 2 points. The game is then similar to Block, with each player in turn trying to match one of the ends of the leg. If he is not able to play, a player must draw a tile from the boneyard until he can get one that can be played. If the boneyard is empty, he must pass.

TIP

If you can, you should play a domino that puts up a number to make both ends the same as a number you have in your hand. This is particularly valuable if you have two or more. In a game with two players, you are certain of another play if you can get up two open-end numbers like those you have in your hand. This may force your opponent to the boneyard.

•

TIP

If you are playing a partnership game, and your partner leads, your strategy is to help him to go out. To do this, play a double on his number, put up his number at the first opportunity, or play a number that leads back to his number.

•

If a player fails to claim points that he is entitled to, any other player can score the points by calling 'Muggins'.

MUGGINS VARIATION

All Fives: All Fives is similar to Muggins, but with these differences:

i) regardless of the number of players, each player draws only five tiles.

ii) the player who leads for the first hand is chosen by lot, and he may play any domino he chooses from his hand. The lead passes to the next player on the left for each subsequent hand.

iii) When a player plays a double, or a domino from which he scores points, he has an extra turn. If he does not have a playable tile for this extra turn, he must draw from the boneyard until he draws a domino that he can play or until the boneyard is empty. If the boneyard is already empty when it is his turn to play his last domino he may not play it and must pass.

iv) A player may not go out by playing a double or a domino that scores points. When such a domino is the last one in his hand he must play it, and then draw from the boneyard until he draws a domino that he can play or until the boneyard is empty.

SNIFF

Sniff is another game of the Muggins family of domino games.

COMPLEXITY RATING:	★ ★
NUMBER OF PLAYERS:	2, 3 or 4
EQUIPMENT:	set of double-6 dominoes
TIME REQUIRED:	15 minutes for individual games

Aim of the game: Like Muggins, the aim of Sniff is to play so that the ends of the line of play add up to multiples of 5. In Sniff, however, the line of play may have up to four ends, so higher scores may be achieved. Players score 5 points for the count of 5 and each multiple of 5.

Origins: The game originally comes from Europe, but is particularly popular today in parts of industrialised America.

Basic rules: The first player is chosen by lot, and the players then draw their dominoes. If there are two players, each draws seven dominoes; if three players, each draws six; and if four, each draws five dominoes. The first player leads with any domino he chooses from his hand, and the turn passes round the table in the usual way.

Until the first double is played, the line of play has to ends, as in Fives. The first double to be played (and it can be the first tile placed on the table) is called 'the sniff', and may be played across the line of play, or with the line of play, as the player chooses.

If the sniff is played with the line of play, dominoes can be played on the sides of the sniff, but only after the open end has been played on. If the sniff is played across the line of play, dominoes can be played on the ends of the sniff, but only after the open side has been played on, and only their sides can be played on.

The sniff is included in the count until both sides and both ends are played on. When plays have been made on both sides, it becomes a spinner, but both ends are still included in the count until they are played on. However, as the ends of the sniff are played on, they are no longer included in the count.

Where doubles are played across the line, all spots on the doubles are counted while they remain ends. The sniff is the only double on which plays can be made on the ends. Plays on other doubles can be made off the sides only.

The following illustration shows how a game might develop:

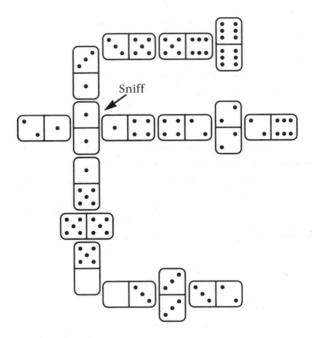

A player who does not have a domino he can play in his hand must continue to draw tiles from the boneyard in an attempt to find one he can play. If the boneyard is empty, he passes. In games of three or four players, all tiles may be drawn from the boneyard, but in the game for two, the last two remain unused.

Your aim is to score and prevent your opponents from doing so, forcing them to the boneyard if possible, and if it is to your advantage. However, this ploy has to be treated with caution because if a player has a lot of tiles in his hand, he can take control with a number of scoring plays. This applies particularly in Two-hand Sniff.

◄ TIP ►

Some dominoes give greater opportunity to score than others, and they should be held for scoring if at all possible. However, the 5 and 0 tiles do not necessarily ensure a scoring total because the end of sniff is lost when played on. However, if the spinner is 0-0 or 5-5, the 0-5 would go on to score if there was a score on the previous move.

Count -11
5 of sniff is
closed off

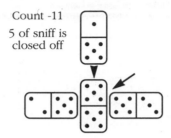

Again, if the spinner is either 1-1 or 6-6, the 6-1 tile will score if there was a score on the previous move.

The first player or team to play his last tile goes out, and is credited with the total count remaining in his opponents' hands, to the nearest multiple of 5. A remainder of 3 or 4 is rounded up to 5, but a remainder of 1 or 2 is rounded down to 0. If no player can play, or draw from the boneyard, the hand is 'blocked', and the player or team with the lowest count receives the score in the opponents' hands. The game is played to an agreed number of points.

SEVEN ROCKS

Seven Rocks, sometimes known as Single Spinner, is a game of skill. It was the favourite domino game of the former American president, Lyndon Johnson.

COMPLEXITY RATING:	★ ★
NUMBER OF PLAYERS:	2, 3 or 4 with the 4 playing either singly or in partnerships
EQUIPMENT:	Set of double-6 dominoes
TIME REQUIRED:	20 minutes for a single game

Origins: Seven Rocks has grown and developed in the southern states of America, and is also popular in Latin America.

Aim of the game: Like other scoring games such as Five-Up and Muggins, the object of Seven Rocks is to score points by making ends of the line of play add up to multiples of 5, and to get rid of all the dominoes. A number of hands are played until an agreed score, 100, 200 or 250 or more, is reached.

Basic rules: The dominoes are shuffled, and the player who draws the highest leads. Each player draws seven tiles, so that in a four-hand game, the players hold all the tiles. In two- or three-hand games, the remaining tiles become the boneyard.

The first player leads with any domino in his hand, and each player then follows in turn if they have playable tiles. If he cannot play, and there is no boneyard, he passes. If there is a boneyard, the player draws until he can play. All dominoes can be drawn.

When the total count of the open ends makes 5 or a multiple of 5, the player making that score receives 5 points for each multiple of 5. All spots on a double are counted when it is an end.

Your aim in this game should be to score where possible, and to prevent your opponents from doing so – to ensure that you keep in play, while your opponents have to pass or draw from the boneyard.

•

Because the main aim of the game is to score, it is not sensible to keep turning an end to the same number, say a 3, in an attempt to block the game. A good player will prepare a defence against this by playing off the spinner, particularly if he has the double of the suit being played.

•

If you are playing partnerships, make sure you watch your partner's play, and try to act as a team.

•

The player (or team) first to put down his last domino receives the count in the opponents' hands to the nearest multiple of 5. A remainder of 3 or 4 is rounded up to count 5, but a remainder of 1 or 2 is rounded down for no score.

If all players have dominoes left in their hands but cannot play any of them, and cannot draw from the boneyard, the hand is blocked. The player (or team) with the lowest count in his hand receives the score in the opponents' hands in the same way as he would if he had gone out.

In this game, unlike Five-Up, the first double is the only spinner. Tiles may be played on the ends of the first double as well as on the sides, but the two sides must be covered before the ends can be used. As a result, four lines of tiles run from the spinner, but other doubles cannot be used in this way. These doubles must be played across the last tile, and both ends are included in the count until other dominoes are played on it. However, a player can build only on the side of all doubles after the spinner.

Scoring is on the basis of 5 points for a count of 5 or multiple of 5 during the game, and at the end of the hand.

A player who does not have a domino he can play in his hand must continue to draw tiles from the boneyard in an attempt to find one he can play. If the boneyard is empty, he passes. In games of three or four players, all tiles may be drawn from the boneyard, but in the game for two, the last two remain unused.

Your aim is to score and prevent your opponents from doing so, forcing them to the boneyard if possible, and if it is to your advantage. However, this ploy has to be treated with caution because if a player has a lot of tiles in his hand, he can take control with a number of scoring plays. This applies particularly in Two-hand Sniff.

BERGEN

Bergen is based on scoring, which makes it unlike any other domino game.

COMPLEXITY RATING:	★ ★
NUMBER OF PLAYERS:	2, 3 or 4
EQUIPMENT:	Set of double-6 dominoes
TIME REQUIRED:	20 minutes

Aim of the game: The objectives are to be the first player to get rid of all his dominoes, to block his opponents and to score special points by ensuring that the same number appears at both ends of the line of play.

Basic rules: If there are two or three players, each draws six dominoes. If there are four, each draws five.

The player holding the highest double leads, and immediately scores two points for a double-header. If no one has a double, the player holding the highest domino leads, but does not score with that tile.

Play proceeds clockwise, with players matching tiles in a straight line. Singles are placed end to end, and doubles cross singles. If a player cannot match one of the open ends, he must draw from the boneyard until he can play. The last two tiles must be left. If a player is unable to play or draw, he passes.

In Bergen it is important to try to make as many double-headers or triple-headers as possible. A double-header is made by matching the tile at one end of the line so that the number actually at the end is the same as the one at the other end.

For example:

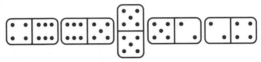

When the same number appears three times at the ends, i.e. when one end is a double, this is known as a triple-header.

Because the object of the game is to score points, you should try to hold on to doubles as long as possible to make triple-headers.

•

A double-header counts 2 points, a triple-header 3 points. When a player is within 2 points of winning the game, either header counts only 1 point. A player within 3 points of winning the game who makes a triple-header receives only 2 points.

The first player to play his last tile wins the hand and scores 2 points. If the game is blocked and no player can match the ends or draw from the boneyard, the player with no doubles left in his hand is the winner. If no one has a double, the player with the lowest count wins. If more than one player has a double, the lowest double wins. The winner of a blocked game scores 2 points. The winner in a game with three or four players is the first to reach 10, and with two players the winning score is 15.

MATADOR

Matador is a popular pastime which differs from all other domino games because it is not played by matching like-numbers.

Origins: As the name suggests, Matador is a game of Spanish origins.
Aim of the game: The object is to be the first player to dispose of all tiles in hand. The player who goes out scores the total of the pips on his opponents' remaining tiles. In the case of a block, the player holding the least number of spots scores all the spots held in the opponents' hands. The game is usually 200 points, or whatever is agreed.

COMPLEXITY RATING:	★ ★
NUMBER OF PLAYERS:	2, 3 or 4 for the double-6 set, playing individually, or in partnerships with 4 players.
	3 to 8 players for the double-9 and double-12 sets. The players play individually.
EQUIPMENT:	set of double-6, double-9 or double-12 dominoes
TIME REQUIRED:	10 to 15 minutes for a single game

Basic rules: Instead of seeking to match numbers, the aim in Matador is to form combinations of numbers which add up to a required total. With a double-6 set, a tile is added to the open end so that two adjoining numbers total 7. For example, if a 5-5 is led, it is not matched with a 5, but with a 2 to make 7.

For a double-9 set the total is 10, and for a double-12 the adjoining numbers need to total 13.

In the double-6 set, four dominoes are trumps and are called matadors, in the double-9 set there are six trumps, and in the double-12 there are seven trumps. They are wild, and can be played at any time, and are the only tiles which can be played on the blanks. When they are played the join does not have to add up to seven. Matadors are placed across the line of play.

In the double-6 set, the matadors are 6-1, 5-2, 4-3 and the double-blank.

In the double-9 set, the matadors are 9-1, 8-2, 7-3, 6-4, 5-5 and the double-blank.

In the double-12 set, the matadors are 12-1, 11-2, 10-3, 9-4, 8-5, 7-6 and the double-blank.

The double-6 game

The player who leads must play a double if he has one. If not, he plays his highest tile. Play then proceeds in turn, with the next player needing to make the required 7. For example, if a 5-5 is led, a domino with a 2 must be played on either end of the 5-5 by the next player. If he does not have a 2 or a matador, he must continue to draw from the boneyard until he gets a 2. Players can continue to draw from the boneyard until there are two tiles left when a player must play a domino if he can, and pass if he has no playable tile.

The key to strong play is to hold two strong suits such as 6s and 1s, 5s and 2s or 4s

and 3s because their total makes 7. You should aim to set up numbers to ensure your play, to force your opponents to provide helpful numbers, and make him play his matadors.

•

The blanks are very strong tiles to play because it is not possible to make a 7 against them. If you play them, you can easily block the game. so that your opponent cannot make the ends blank, you should play only those tiles which match the dominoes with blanks already down. The 0-0 is the strongest of all the matadors, so it is important to hold it back until your opponent makes the ends blanks. You can then force him to play a matador.

•

The double-9 game

The principle is the same as with the double-6 set, but 10 is the number needed for each play.

The double-12 game

The principle is the same again as with the double-6 and double-9 games, but 13 is the required number to make on each play.

In play, double tiles are played end to end like single tiles, and count as singles. However, when scoring at the end of the game, all the spots are counted.

Play continues until one player has played all his dominoes – in which case he is the winner, scoring one point for each pip in his opponents' hands – or until none of the players can play any more dominoes. Then the player with the lowest number of pips in his hand is the winner, and his score is the total number of pips in his opponents' hands minus the number of pips in his own.

A game is played to an agreed number of points, usually 200.

BINGO

Although this may appear at first to be complicated, it is probably one of the best domino games for two players, and is well worth the trouble of learning. It requires skill and a good memory.

COMPLEXITY RATING:	★ ★ ★
NUMBER OF PLAYERS:	2
EQUIPMENT:	Set of dominoes
TIME REQUIRED:	30 to 45 minutes

Origins: Bingo is based on the card game, Bezique, and towards the end of the 19th century was rated as 'king of the domino games'.

Aim of the game: Players attempt to be the first to win seven sets, each set being worth 70 points.

Basic rules: Most of the scoring comes from dominoes which are won by taking tricks, but some scoring comes from the dominoes held in the hand.

The dominoes which score points in a trick are:

i) the double of a trump suit which scores 28 points

ii) the double-blank (called bingo) which scores 14 points, unless blanks are trumps, when it scores 28

iii) the other doubles, which score their pip value

iv) the dominoes of the trumps suit (other than the double) which score their pip value, with a blank counting as 7

v) the 6–4 and the 3–blank which each score 10 points

The total possible score from any round is different for each of the different trumps as shown:

Trumps	Total possible score
Blanks	143
Ones	135
Twos	138
Threes	131
Fours	134
Fives	147
Sixes	140

Each player draws seven bones, and the remaining fourteen form the boneyard. The first to play is then decided by lot. After the deal, the player who is not leading turns up one tile from the boneyard, and the higher number on it fixes the trump suit.

The leader may play any tile, and the opponent may play any tile, until the boneyard is empty. A trump wins any non-trump tile, and the player who leads wins if his opponent does not follow suit or trumps. The higher number tile wins if two played to a trick are of the same suit. The winner of a suit leads to the next one. When each trick is completed, each player draws one tile from the boneyard.

A player who holds two or more doubles in his hand at any stage of the game can try to increase his score by leading one of the them, and saying how many he holds. To claim these points a player must lead one of the doubles and show the others to his opponents. The calls and points he claims are:

i) for two doubles, the player calls 'double' and claims 20 points

ii) for three doubles, he calls 'triplets' and claims 40 points

iii) for four doubles, the player calls 'double doubles' and claims 50 points

iv) for five doubles, the player calls 'king' and claims 60 points

v) for six doubles, the player calls 'emperor', claiming 70 points

vi) for all seven doubles, the player calls 'invincible', claiming 210 points

The player must win the trick in order to gain the points he has claimed. Each player should record the points he has gained from tricks and doubles at the time the tricks are taken.

◆ TIP ▶

You should always watch the number of doubles you have in your hand because you can get points whenever you have more than one.

•

◆ TIP ▶

You do not have to claim for two doubles because you may think it better to try to get three or more doubles before making your claim. But if you do want to wait you must not put out a double as the first domino of a new trick

•

◆ TIP ▶

If you do not claim 'double' or one of the other possible claims when you put out your double, you lose the score.

•

The first phase continues until all tiles have been drawn. The last to be drawn must always be the domino that was turned up to establish trumps. In the second phase the remaining tricks are played with a change in the rule about the dominoes the second player may play.

From this point the second player must always follow suit if he can. If he cannot, he must play a trump or bingo if he can. Only if he does not have a domino of the suit being led, a trump or a bingo, may he play any other domino.

It is possible to go from the first phase into the second phase before all the dominoes have been drawn from the boneyard. If a player, after he has won a trick, thinks his hand is good enough to score at least 70 points from tricks and doubles without drawing any more from the boneyard, then instead of drawing a tile he turns the trump domino face down. This is known as 'closing' and from that point on the rules of the second phase apply – there is no further drawing from the boneyard, and the second player must follow suit if he can.

The object of the game is to score seven sets which are scored as follows:
i) one set is scored for every 70 points gained from tricks and doubles
ii) one set is scored by the first player to score 70 points – if his opponent has scored 30 points or more
iii) two sets are scored by the first player to score 70 points – if his player has won a trick but has scored less than 30 points

iv) three sets are scored by the first player to score 70 points – if his opponent has not yet won a trick

v) two sets are scored by the opponents of a player who closes and then fails to score 70 points

vi) one set is scored for taking the double of the trump suit with Bingo.

GENERAL TIP

It is important to remember the varied ways of scoring, but it could be worth while making a note of them to remind yourself as you play. There is nothing in the rules to prevent this.

•

BLIND HUGHIE

As players in Blind Hughie cannot see what dominoes they are playing this version is purely a game of chance, but it is a good way of introducing children, in particular, to a domino set.

COMPLEXITY RATING:	★
NUMBER OF PLAYERS:	**2 to 5**
EQUIPMENT:	**Set of double-6 pack of dominoes**
TIME REQUIRED:	**15 minutes**

Aim of game: To get rid of all your dominoes as quickly as possible. Sometimes, though, the game will end in stalemate because no one is able to get rid of all their dominoes. This is more likely to happen when there are fewer players.

Basic rules: The players choose who goes first by lot. When there are four or five players each player will take out five dominoes, but when there are only two or three the players will have seven dominoes each. A key part of this game is that players must not look at their own dominoes and must keep them face down on the table in front of them and in an orderly row. The first player now picks the domino furthest to his or her left and places it, face up, in the middle of the table. The next player now turns up the domino on his left. If there is a match with the domino in the centre, then the player is allowed to match it up. If not then the player has to replace it, face down, at the other end, ie right hand side, of his dominoes, and the next player goes. The game is won by the player who gets rid of all his or her dominoes first, unless of course as mentioned above there is stalemate because no one is able to go.

MALTESE CROSS

This simple version depends on one rule to make it distinctive from other games.

COMPLEXITY RATING:	★ ★
NUMBER OF PLAYERS:	4
EQUIPMENT:	**Set of double-6 pack of dominoes**
TIME REQUIRED:	**10 to 15 minutes for each game**

Aim of game: A player tries to get rid of all the tiles in his or her hand as quickly as possible. If no one can manage this then the lowest number of pips left in a hand wins.

Basic rules: The four players draw seven dominoes each and as usual the player with the double-6 plays first. The next player can move from any of four directions from the double-6, that is from either end or from either side. Normal tactics apply in Maltese Cross, but what makes it different is that players can only match a number if that number's double tile has been played. In other words there are fewer openings to match a tile than normal. In the illustration below, the game has been opened up at (i) because a double 5 has been played, but at (ii) no one can move until a double 3 has been used and similarly a double is needed at (iii) before anyone can play a 2. This makes it even more advantageous to have double numbers in your hand.

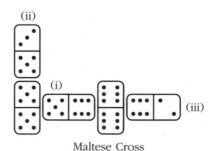

Maltese Cross

If you are fortunate in having a number of doubles in your hand try to play them as late as possible to hold your opponents up, unless doing so will hold you up later.

•

DICE GAMES

Dice are the oldest gambling implements of all. They are also the most widespread, having been in use in virtually every part of the world since earliest times. Today they are used in some games of skill such as Backgammon, but they are mainly used in games of chance, and for the playing of a variety of social games.

Each side of a standard die is marked with small dots or spots from one to six in number. They are arranged so that the spots on opposite sides always add up to seven: one and six, two and five and three and four.

Archaeological finds have shown that dice were in use in Egypt in at least 2000 BC, and in China as early as 600 BC. Over the centuries they have been made of many materials ranging from peach stones and animal horns to shells and teeth, and in a variety of shapes and markings.

Modern dice are almost all made of cellulose or some other type of plastic material. There are two types, perfect dice which are true to a tolerance of one-twentieth of a millimetre and used in casinos, and imperfect dice used for social games.

The skill in most dice games is in knowing the mathematical probability of the likely totals when dice are thrown at random. In most dice games they can be determined by simple arithmetic. The assumption is that any side of the die is as likely as any other side to land face up. This means that any number is likely to come up once every six times, its odds against appearing therefore being 5 to 1.

With two dice, each of the six sides of one die is combined with each of the six sides of the other to form 36 combinations. The chance of a combination of two like numbers such as two 1s appearing is 1 in 36, or odds of 35 to 1.

IT'S A FACT...

The Romans were great players of dice games, including a version of the modern-day backgammon. The Emperor Claudius, who reputedly wrote a book on dice playing, was so enamoured with the pastime that he is said to have had a special board mounted in his chariot to play while on the move.

CRAPS

Craps is the most popular dice game in the United States, but its popularity has spread to many other countries as well.

COMPLEXITY RATING:	★
NUMBER OF PLAYERS:	2 or more
EQUIPMENT:	2 dice; counters for stakes.
TIME REQUIRED:	No time limit

Origins: The modern game of Craps is derived from the old English game of Hazard, and its name comes from a losing throw of 1–1 or 1–2 which was called crabs as long ago as the 16th century.

Aim of the game: Players bet against themselves on the chance of throwing certain combinations of numbers.

Basic rules: Players enclose the playing area called the centre, which in an informal game may be the floor or ground. In a gambling house it is a table which is marked out to accommodate betting.

Each player rolls the dice once and the one who throws the highest number shoots first. The shooter places a bet to say that he will win, and others are asked to 'fade' it, ie, put up an equal amount to bet that he will lose. When the shooter's bet has been covered by other players, he rolls two dice.

The bets are settled on this throw if any one of five numbers comes up:

If the shooter rolls 7 or 11 (a 'natural') the shooter wins immediately.

If the shooter rolls 2, 3 or 12 ('craps') the shooter loses immediately.

If the shooter rolls any other number, ie 4, 5, 6, 8, 9 or 10, the number rolled becomes the shooter's 'point'. He continues to roll the dice and for him to win, he must 'make the point' or throw the same number again before he throws a 7. If he does, he wins, but if he throws a 7, he loses. Any other totals are disregarded. When the shooter wins he is said to 'pass', and when he loses he is said to 'miss'. When he misses, those who faded him take their winnings (always double the amount they bet), and when he passes, all the money in the centre belongs to him.

IT'S A FACT...
*Dice are sometimes still known as
'African Dominoes' because of
their traditional popularity among
black Americans.*

While the shooter wins he remains the shooter (unless he decides to pass the dice on), but when he loses he must give the dice to the man on his left who becomes the shooter.

There is scope for a wide range of betting between shooters and faders, and the other players betting among themselves.

There is little skill in playing craps other than knowing the odds of various bets, and not placing bets when the odds are not favourable. The odds are slightly against the shooter by about 251 to 245, but most players willingly accept this disadvantage. Other odds on bets most frequently placed are: 2 to 1 against making the point 10 or 4; 3 to 2 against making the point 9 or 5; 6 to 5 against making the point 8 or 6; 8 to 1 against making 4 or 10 'the hard way' ie with doubles 2–2 or 5–5 (a popular side bet); 10 to 1 against making 6 or 8 the hard way. A hard-way bet loses if the shooter throws a 7 or makes his point with another number before his double shows up.

•

Odds for bets on or between single numbers:

No.	No. of ways	Single Before throw a 7		Comparative odds								
	(a)	(b)	(c)	(d)								
12	1	35–1	6–1	12								
11	2	17–1	3–1	2–1	11							
10	3	11–1	2–1	3–1	3–2	10						
9	4	8–1	3–2	4–1	2–1	4–3	9					
8	5	6–1	6–5	5–1	5–2	5–3	5–4	8				
7	6	5–1	–	6–1	3–1	2–1	3–2	6–5	7			
6	5	6–1	6–5	5–1	5–2	5–3	5–4	1–1	5–6	6		
5	4	8–1	3–2	4–1	2–1	4–3	1–1	4–5	2–3	4–5	5	
4	3	11–1	2–1	3–1	3–2	1–1	3–4	3–5	1–2	3–5	3–4	4
3	2	17–1	3–1	2–1	1–1	2–3	1–2	2–5	1–3	2–5	1–2	2–3	3
2	1	35–1	6–1	1–1	1–2	1–3	1–4	1–5	1–6	1–5	1–4	1–3	1–2	2

Notes:
(a) This represents the number of different combinations of two die number which will give the total in the first column.
(b) The figures in this column represent the odds against making the number in a single throw.
(c) The figures in this column represent the odds against throwing the number before throwing a 7

(d) This column represents the odds against making the higher number before the lower number, eg 12 before 6: 5–1

In the casino, all bets are made against the bank, although players still roll the dice. As in the private game, a shooter wins, or passes, if he rolls 7 or 11 (natural) on his first roll, or if he establishes a point and rolls it again before he rolls a 7. He misses if he rolls 2, 3 or 12 on his first roll, or if he establishes a point and rolls a 7 before he rolls his point.

TWENTY-ONE

Twenty-one is the dice equivalent of the card game, Twenty-one or Blackjack.

COMPLEXITY RATING:	★
NUMBER OF PLAYERS:	**2 or more**
EQUIPMENT:	**Two dice**
TIME REQUIRED:	**From 5 to 10 minutes depending on the number playing**

Aim of the game: Each player throws the dice to decide who has first turn. The player with the highest score goes first.

There is an advantage in going last because you can see how high you have to score to win, and you can take risks accordingly.

•

Each player places an equal stake into the pot.

A player has just one turn in each game. He may cast the dice as many times as he wishes on that turn, and can sit on any total of 21 or less. Each time he throws the dice he adds the total number to his score for that turn. When he reaches 14 or more, he then uses just one die.

If a player scores over 21 he has gone bust, and is out of the round. After players have had a turn, the player who has the total closest to 21, but not over 21, wins the pot. If two or more players tie, they roll again to decide the winner.

If you have reached a total of 17 or less, it is worth risking another throw.

•

*If you have reached 19 or more you should stick with that total, unless another
player has already scored 20 or 21.*

•

*If you have reached 18, you have a 50–50 chance of adding to your
score, or going bust.*

•

*If you are one of the later players and one or your opponents has already reached
20, you should roll again even if you have scored 19. The odds are against you
staying under 22, but there is no point in sticking with a losing total.*

•

LIAR DICE

Liar Dice is a fascinating game of deceit, deception, bluff and counter-bluff, and is
considered by many to be by far the best of all dice games.

COMPLEXITY RATING:	★ ★ ★
NUMBER OF PLAYERS:	**3 (but 4 to 6 is best)**
EQUIPMENT:	**Set of 5 poker dice, or standard dice; 3 counters for each player.**
TIME REQUIRED:	**10 to 20 minutes**

Aim of the game: Players aim to make the highest poker hand, but in Liar Dice, as in
Poker, it is possible for inferior hands to win.
Basic rules: To play it is best to have a set of poker dice which have pictures of playing
cards on their faces, and not spots. The ones usually chosen are the 9, 10, jack, queen,
king and ace.

*You need to get to know the different patterns you try to throw on the dice, and
their different values. These are given below with the lowest first. They are not in
the same order as the hands in Poker played with cards because the chances of
getting them with dice are different.*

1. Ace high (ranking according to the value of the highest 'backers' – for example ace, king, jack, 10, 9 beats ace, queen, jack, 10, 9.

2. One pair (a pair of aces ranking highest and a pair of 9s lowest)

3. Two pairs (the higher pair determines the value – for instance: ace, ace, 10, 10, 10 beats king, king, queen, queen, 10)

4. Three of a kind (three aces ranking highest and three 9s lowest)

5. Straight (five consecutive values – ace, king, queen, jack, 10, 9)

6. Full house (three of a kind and a pair – ranking according to the three of a kind – for example, king, king, king, 9, 9 ranks higher than queen, queen, queen, jack, jack)

7. Four of a kind (four aces ranking highest and four 9s lowest)

8. five of a kind (five aces ranking highest and five 9s lowest).

To begin a game, each player throws a single die, and the highest becomes the first dealer. The winner of each deal is the dealer in the next. Each player puts three counters in front of him. These are his lives, and when he loses all three he is out of the game.

To begin, the first players rolls all five dice, concealing them with the dice cup or with his hands so that he, but none of the other players, may see what he has thrown. He then declares his hand (eg 'pair of queens', 'full house', 'nines and jacks'). This hand may be the hand he has thrown, or it may not. If it is not, the player may declare a hand higher or lower than the one he has thrown.

TIP

A straight on the first throw should be announced correctly because this is the worst hand to try to improve. The best thing is to try to force an opponent to throw for a full house.

•

IT'S A FACT...
Both King John and his more illustrious brother Richard the Lion Heart enjoyed playing dice games for money. However, the popularity of gambling became such a problem that, during the Third Crusade in the 12th Century, Richard banned anyone beneath the rank of a Knight from gambling at all – and even noblemen were limited in the stakes they could use.

If you bluff, you should avoid making a call which is so high that your opponent is bound to challenge you.

•

If you throw a good hand such as full house or better, you should call it truthfully. If you call it at a lower value, your opponent may call your exact hand, and you have lost out.

•

Calls of three of a kind are good openers because they raise the chance of your convincing your opponent that you have a full house or four of a kind in your throw.

•

The next player on the left may accept or challenge the call. If he accepts, the first player passes the dice to him, taking care that they remain concealed from the other players. The second player examines the dice. He may then decide to throw none, some or all of them again. He must say how many dice he is throwing, but the dice must stay concealed from other players.

The second player then has to declare a hand better than the one declared by the previous player. It may be a higher type of hand, or a higher-ranking hand of the same type. If the first player has declared 'pair of queens', then he could for example declare 'three tens'. Again this may be true or bluff – equal to, higher than or lower than the actual hand.

The next player has the choice of accepting the hand or challenging it. If he accepts it, he may throw any number of the dice again, and must then declare a higher hand.

The play continues around the table in this way until a challenge is issued. The player being challenged exposes the dice. If the declarer can refute the challenger by showing that his declaration was equal to or less than the actual hand, then the challenger must pay one counter into the pool. If, on the other hand, the declarer has called a hand that was better than the actual hand, then it is the declarer who must pay a counter into the pool.

After a challenge a new round is started by the challenger if he is still in the game. The game continues until all but one of the players have lost their three lives and have been eliminated. The last player in is the winner.

YACHT

Although Yacht can appear difficult to play at first, it is quite easy to pick up, and can be very exciting.

COMPLEXITY RATING:	★ ★
NUMBER OF PLAYERS:	**2 or more, although it becomes very slow with more than 6**
EQUIPMENT:	**5 dice; score sheet**
TIME REQUIRED:	**30 to 45 minutes, depending on the number of players**

Aim of the game: Players try to score the highest number of points.
Basic rules: Each player throws the five dice with the one throwing the highest total starting the game. That player throw the five dice again to try to score points by making the numbers on the dice form the patterns shown below.
Ones (only the 1s score – maximum 5 points)
Twos (only the 2s score – maximum 10 points)
Threes (only the 3s score – maximum 15 points)
Fours (only the 4s score – maximum 20 points
Fives (only the 5s score – maximum 25 points)
Sixes (only the 6s score – maximum 30 points)
Little straight (1–2–3–4–5 – scores pip value, 15 points)
Big straight (2, 3, 4, 5, 6 – scores 20 points)

IT'S A FACT...
*The Aztecs of what is now called
Mexico played a dice and board
game called 'patolli' which had
some similarities to an old version
of backgammon.*

Full house (three of any number and two of another score pip value – for example, 1, 1, 1, 2, 2 would score 7 and 6, 6, 6, 5, 5 would score 28 points)
Four of a kind (four of any number score the pip value for four dice – for example, 1, 1, 1, 1, 6 would score 4 while 6, 6, 6, 6, 1 would score 24 points)
Choice (no pattern is needed and the score if the total pip value of the five dice – the aim is to obtain as high a total as possible – for example, 3, 3, 5, 6, 6, would score 23 points)
Yacht (all five dice showing the same number – scores 50 points)

To achieve any of these patterns, he is allowed to have two more throws, but can use as many or as few dice for these throws as he likes. When he has had his three throws his score is written down on a score-sheet like this showing each player:

Category	Maximum score	Players 1	2	3	4	etc
Yacht	50					
Big straight	30					
Little straight	30					
Four of a kind	29					
Full house	28					
Choice	30					
Sixes	30					
Fives	25					
Fours	20					
Threes	15					
Twos	10					
Ones	5					

Each player is allowed to choose the same pattern only once. Only after a player has said which pattern he is trying for is he allowed to take his other two turns at throwing the dice.

Choosing which pattern to go for introduces the element of skill, and a player's strategy in choosing the right patterns is as important as good luck in throwing the dice. Since each group scores differently, and with five 1s scoring 5 points, but five 6s scoring 30 points, you should aim to choose the pattern which will give you the greatest score. Since you can only used each pattern once, you should also choose between making small, certain scores, and trying for the larger ones with the risk of not scoring at all.

•

Once a player has thrown the five dice and named the pattern he is aiming for, he has to make another choice – which dice to leave and which to throw again. He puts the dice he wants to keep to one side and throw the rest. He can then choose to put any of the dice he has thrown with the dice from the first throw, and have his third and final throw. A player can decide not to throw any more dice after his first or second throw and this ends his turn. His score is calculated and the dice are then passed to the next player.

If a player throws 2, 2, 2, 3, 3 on his first throw, he might call 'Full house', throw no more dice and score 12 points. He might however call 'Twos' and put the three

2s to one side and throw the remaining dice to try to get more 2s. If the second throw gives him another 2, he would put it with the other three dice, and throw the remaining die for his third and final turn. If he scores no more 2s, he at least will have 6 from his first throw. He may, however, try for Four of a Kind. Again he will put the 2s to one side and try for a fourth 2. If he does not achieve it, he scores nothing.

When a player selects the Choice pattern, he throws the dice three times as before but scores the total value of all the pips when he has finished his turn – the dice do not have to make any particular pattern.

Play goes round the table with each player choosing one of the twelve patterns on each turn until they have all chosen all of them. The scores are then added up and the player who has the largest total is the winner.

It is a good idea to aim for Yacht, the two Straights, Four of Kind and Full House early on in the game because they are the hardest to throw.

YACHT VARIATION
Double Cameroon: This variation of Yacht is played with ten dice, and demands greater strategy.

COMPLEXITY RATING:	★ ★
NUMBER OF PLAYERS:	**2 or more**
EQUIPMENT:	**Ten dice and score sheet**
TIME REQUIRED:	**10 to 20 minutes, depending on the number of players.**

Aim of the game: Players try to score the highest total of points.
Basic rules: Each player rolls five dice to decide who starts, with the lowest score leading. If Double Cameroon is being played as a gambling game, each player puts an equal stake in the pot.

A score-sheet similar to this showing each player, is prepared:

Category	Maximum score	Player 1	2	3	4	etc
Five of a kind	50					
Large Cameroon (2, 3, 4, 5, 6)	30					
Little Cameroon (1, 2, 3, 4, 5)	21					

Category	Maximum score	Player 1	2	3	4	etc
Full House	28					
(three of a kind and pair)*						
Sixes	30					
Fives	25					
Fours	20					
Threes	15					
Twos	10					
Ones	5					
Totals	234					

*A Full House scores the total number of pips on the five dice.

A player's turn is made up of three throws of the dice. On his first throw, the player throws all ten dice. He then selects and sets aside the dice he wishes to keep from the opening throw. He then uses the remaining dice for his second throw, again choosing the dice he wishes to keep, setting them aside, and using the rest for his first and final throw.

After that throw, he selects two categories, and groups the dice into two hands of five each. Each hand scores in one category. Once he has scored in a category, he may not score in that category in a subsequent turn. A player must therefore enter scores in two open categories on the score-sheet after each turn.

The number categories are the same as in Yacht so that the number of dice a player throws showing his selected number are multiplied by the number itself. In that way, five 6s score 30 in the Sixes category while four 4s score 16 points in the Fours category.

Scoring applies to each five-dice hand individually with the dice in one hand having no effect on the scoring of the second hand. After five rounds of play, each player will have scored in each of the ten categories. The totals are added up, and the player with the highest total is the winner.

If you throw a hand which does not score, or scores poorly in a more valuable scoring category, you should choose a less valuable category such as 1s, 2s or 3s, and enter a score for the turn in that category.

•

You should score zero in the lower categories rather than lose your opportunities to score in the higher-ranking categories in subsequent turns.

•

SHUT THE BOX

Shut the Box is a dice game which can be played by both young and older players.

COMPLEXITY RATING:	★ ★
NUMBER OF PLAYERS:	**2 or more, with 2, 3 or 4 best**
EQUIPMENT:	**Special box with two dice**
TIME REQUIRED:	**15 minutes**

Origins: This is a traditional dice game of northern France, particularly popular with the sailors of Normandy over the past 200 years.

Aim of the game: Players aim to cover as many of the numbers as possible in accordance with the throws of the dice.

Basic rules: The proper equipment consists of a wooden box with a tray for throwing the dice, and a row of nine numbered boxes with sliding lids which can cover or disclose the numbers. If such a box is not available, players can use a sheet of paper on which they draw a row of nine squares, numbered from 1 to 9, and nine counters to cover the numbers.

To begin, each player throws the two dice. The player throwing the largest total starts. At the beginning of his turn all nine numbers are uncovered. The player throws the two dice and adds up their scores. He can then shut any boxes which add up to the same total number. for example, if he throws a 6 and a 5, he could close the 9 and 2 boxes, or the 8 and 3 and so on. He must choose one set of boxes and close them before he throws the dice for his second throw.

When a number is hidden it cannot be used again, so that if a player has closed the 9 and 2, and then throws a 9, he cannot close the 9 again, but must close 8 and 1 or 6 and 3 and so on. It is usual to allow a player who has closed the three top boxes (the 7, 8 and 9) to throw only one die if he likes at any time after the third box has been closed. A player's turn ends when he is unable to make the open boxes add up to his throw. The numbers which can still be seen are added up, and this gives the player's score. The next player then has his turn, and this goes on until all players have tried to shut the box. The winner is the player who has the lowest score.

High-numbered boxes should be closed first because it is the player with the lowest score who wins.

•

PIG

Pig is one of the simplest dice games, but can also be very exciting.

COMPLEXITY RATING:	★
NUMBER OF PLAYERS:	**2 or more**
EQUIPMENT:	**One die**
TIME REQUIRED:	**10 to 15 minutes**

Aim of the game: Each player tries to be the first to reach a total score of 101.

Basic rules: Before the game begins, a preliminary round is played in which each player throws the die once. The player throwing the lowest number begins the game.

The order of play is important because the first and last players have a natural advantage.

•

The first shooter rolls the die as many times as he wishes, adding up the score as he goes. His turn ends if he throws a 1, in which case he loses the entire score he has made that round. Alternatively he can decide to end his turn before that, making a note of his total. The next player then throws until he decides to end his turn (keeping his total) or throws a 1 in which case he forfeits the total for that turn. the game continues until one player reaches the target score.

Given a bit of luck, the first player is the one most likely to win. The last shooter also has the advantage of knowing the scores made by all his opponents. He can continue to throw until he has beaten all those scores. There is the danger that the success of an earlier player might force you to press your luck too far, and wipe out a fairly promising turn with an ace.

•

The fairest way of playing is to have a series of games with each player taking it in turns to throw first. Over the course of a number of games, this eliminates any advantage, and the game becomes one of pure chance.

MATTERHORN

Matterhorn is a simple game which could be a valuable aid to children learning addition. However, it is also suitable as a gambling game for a large number of adults.

COMPLEXITY RATING:	★
NUMBER OF PLAYERS:	**2 or more, but best for 5 or more**
EQUIPMENT:	**Three dice; score-sheet for each player**
TIME REQUIRED:	**5 to 15 minutes**

Aim of the game: Players throw for scores from 1 to 12 and then from 12 to 1. The first to achieve this is the winner.

Basic rules: Each player draws two rows of numbers on his score-sheet, the top one from 1 to 12, and the bottom one from 12 to 1 like this:

1	2	3	4	5	6	7	8	9	10	11	12
12	11	10	9	8	7	6	5	4	3	2	1

Each player rolls the dice to decide who plays first. That player then throws the dice, and crosses off numbers on the score sheet according to the result. He may choose to use the numbers of his throw individually, or in combination, but may use them only once. For example, a player who throws 1–3–5 can cross off either numbers 1, 3, and 5; numbers 4 and 5; numbers 3 and 6; numbers 1 and 8; or number 9.

When each player has crossed off his numbers after each throw, the player to his left has his turn. After a player has crossed off all the numbers in the top row, he then proceeds to do the same in the bottom row.

You should cross off the higher numbers in each row first. The lower numbers from 1 to 6 can be made easily on any throw, but the higher numbers need combinations which are less frequently produced, and should be crossed off as quickly as possible.

•

MATTERHORN VARIATION

Centennial: Centennial is played in the same way as Matterhorn, but players must cross the numbers off in sequence, from 1 to 12 in the top row, and from 12 to 1 in the bottom. There is not the same room for strategy in Centennial as there is in Matterhorn.

CRAG

Crag is the same type of game as Yacht, and is considered by many to be one of the best dice games. It needs a little preparation before the game.

COMPLEXITY RATING:	★ ★
NUMBER OF PLAYERS:	**2 or more, although it becomes slow with more than 6**
EQUIPMENT:	**3 dice; score-sheet and pencil**
TIME REQUIRED:	**30 to 45 minutes**

Aim of the game: Players aim to make the highest total score in thirteen rounds.
Basic rules: Before the game begins, a score-sheet like this is drawn up:

	Player 1	Player 2	Player 3
Ones			
Twos			
Threes			
Fours			
Fives			
Sixes			
Odd straight			
Even straight			
Low straight			
High straight			
Three of a kind			
Thirteen			
Crag			
Totals			

Each player throws the dice once to determine who starts; the highest score wins.
The first player then throws the three dice to start the game. He is trying to score points by making the numbers on the dice form one of the patterns described below:
1 Ones (only the 1s score – one point each for a maximum of 3)
2 Twos (only 2s score – two points each for a maximum of 6)
3 Threes (only 3s score – maximum of 9 points)
4 Fours (only 4s score – maximum of 12 points)
5 Fives (only 5s score – maximum of 15 points)

6 Sixes (only 6s score – maximum of 18 points)

7 Odd straight (1, 3, 5 – scores 20 points

8 Even straight (2, 4, 6 – scores 20 points)

9 Low straight (1, 2, 3 – scores 20 points)

10 High straight (4, 5, 6 – scores 20 points)

11 Three of a kind (all three dice the same – scores 25)

12 Thirteen (a total of 13 without a double – 2, 5, 6 or 3, 4, 6 – scores 26 points)

13 Crag (a total of 13 including a double – 1, 6, 6 or 3, 5, 5, or 5, 4, 4, – scores 50 points.

When each player has thrown all three dice on his turn, he can use the dice as shown, or he can throw one, two or all three dice again for a second turn. He then chooses which pattern he wants to score under, and once he has chosen and recorded the score, it cannot be altered. If a player can score in only one pattern, he must record the score for that pattern, but if he can score in more than one pattern, he can choose which one he likes. If he cannot score in any pattern he must choose which pattern he will leave blank on the score sheet.

The last seven patterns are the most difficult to throw, and it is a good idea to aim for them at the beginning. Great skill is needed in choosing which die or dice to set aside so that your score will be as high as possible. for example, a throw of 1, 4, 6 could become an Even Straight or a High Straight if the 1 is thrown. You could also try for a 4 and a Crag. Near the beginning, it would be best to try for the Crag, even though it is a more difficult pattern to achieve. Towards the end, if is probably better to try for the easier scores.

•

Once a player has scored for a particular pattern, he must try for another if he throws it again. When all players have filled in all thirteen spaces on the score sheet, with blanks if necessary, the scores are added up and the player with the largest total is the winner.

IT'S A FACT...

The witch doctors among the Zambesi were called 'dice doctors' by missionaries, because of their use of dice to tell the future. The dice were also used, more mundanely, to divine which people in the village were stealing.

BATTLESHIP

This is a simple game which can be played by the family, but is also suitable for gambling. It is also known by a number of other names including Ship, Captain, Mariner, Mate and Crew and Destroyer.

COMPLEXITY RATING:	★
NUMBER OF PLAYERS:	**2 or more (3 to 6 best**
EQUIPMENT:	**Five dice; and score-sheet**
TIME REQUIRED:	**Up to 10 minutes a round, depending on the number of players**

Aim of the game: Players try to reach 100 points, or score the highest number of points in ten rounds.

Players throw the dice to determine the order of play with the lowest score leading. In a gambling game, each player places an equal stake in the pot.

The first player begins by rolling all five dice. If he does not throw at least one 6, he throws all five dice again for his second throw. If his first throw does produce a 6, the player has his ship, and throws the other four dice again. If he has thrown more than one six in his first throw, only one counts, and he still uses four dice for his second throw.

If the first throw produces a 6 and 5, the player has his ship and his captain. He sets them aside and uses the three other dice for his second throw. If a player's first throw produces a 6, 5 and 4, he has the ship, his captain and his mate.

He is then ready to take on his crew. He sets aside the 6, 5 and 4 and can either throw the remaining two again, or use their total.

A player who rolls a 5 or a 4 on his first turn, but does not roll a 6, cannot count the 5 and 4 as captain and mate. He must recast all five dice until he has a ship. In the same way he cannot collect his mate until he has a captain.

A player who collects his ship, captain and mate on his first throw may take up to two more throws to pick up his crew, keeping whichever die or dice he wants to from these two throws. Any dice thrown in the third roll must be kept. If a player chooses to throw again to try to get a higher number of crew members, he must accept the total of his later throw, even if it is lower.

An average score for a round would be 7, so if you are able to get your ship, captain and mate in fewer than three throws, and your crew totals more than

seven members, you would be wise to settle for such a total and not take your remaining throws. If the crew numbers less than 7, you should generally make an attempt to improve your score. However, your strategy should be determined by your position compared with that of your opponent. If you are trailing, you should try to catch up to the leader by attempting a high score for the round, even if it is against the odds.

•

If a player does not establish his ship, captain and mate in three throws, he cannot take on a crew and does not score in that round.

When the player has finished his turn, he scores one point for each crew member (excluding captain and mate) and enters this total in the score-sheet as his score for the round. The dice then go to the player on his left.

Play continues till one player reaches 100 points, or for 10 rounds. If two players are level after ten rounds, a further round is played. If stakes are laid, the winner takes the pot.

HOOLIGAN

Perhaps appropriately in view of its name, this is a popular dice game in bars and also for gambling.

COMPLEXITY RATING:	★ ★
NUMBER OF PLAYERS:	**2 or more**
EQUIPMENT:	**Five dice, pencil and paper**
TIME REQUIRED:	**No real time limit**

Aim of the game: Gaining the highest number of points from a determined sequence of throws.

Basic rules: First of all, each player keeps his score on a sheet of paper, which should be divided into seven columns, six marked 1 to 6 and the final one marked H for hooligan. A 'hooligan' in this game is getting either 1, 2, 3, 4, 5 on the five dice or 2, 3, 4, 5, 6. The players then throw to see who starts.

The first player then takes his first of seven 'frames', that is three throws. Once he has thrown his first dice, he may select any of the numbers which come up as his 'point' number. His or her aim then is to get all the dice showing the 'point' number in the next two throws. If for example he selects 2 as his point, he puts all the dice with 2 to one side, and throws the remainder. Let us assume that two dice had 2. If in the second throw all the remaining dice – here that would be three – came up with 2, then the player can use all five dice for his final throw of the frame. This would also happen if all five dice came up with the same number on the first throw. To find out how many points he or she has scored at the end of the frame, the player counts up the number of times the 'point' numbers came up and multiplies this by its numerical value. So if in this case 2 had come up seven times in total, the score for that frame would be 7 times 2, that is 14. Each player takes it in turn to throw a frame. The next time a player throws, they go for a different number as the 'point', that is in this example it would be 1, 3, 4, 5 or 6. The points scored on each of these frames is recorded on the player's score-sheet.

It may happen that by chance a hooligan sequence, as described above, comes up on a player's first throw. He or she is then given 20 points in the H column. However, when the player has thrown for every number (1 to 6) except a hooligan, then they must try for a hooligan sequence. In the same way as the other frames, they have three throws to achieve this, and the reward is still 20 points.

Note that a player is not obliged to put aside any dice on his or her first two throws in a frame. But if no dice are put aside, then any similar dice from the earlier throws cannot be added to the 'point' number chosen on the third throw. At the end all the seven frame totals are added up, and the winner is the one with the highest number of points.

If say two 3s and three 2s came up on your first throw, although 3s are worth more it is best to go with the 2s, as there's more chance of you getting all five by the second throw – allowing you an extra throw.

•

ACES

This interesting game is especially popular in Asia and is very enjoyable when played just for fun.

COMPLEXITY RATING:	★ ★
NUMBER OF PLAYERS:	**2 or more**
EQUIPMENT:	**Five dice for each person**
TIME REQUIRED:	**30 minutes**

Aim of the game: To throw the final ace in the game
Basic rules: To start, each player throws his or her five dice and the one with the highest poker hand starts – 1 represents the ace, and 6 the king, 5 the queen and so on. The second player starts on the first player's left and throws second, the third on

his left and throws third, and so on. The first player throws the die. Any die which comes up with a 1 (or ace) is placed in the centre. All dice which come up with a 2 are given to the player on their left; all dice with a 5 go to the player on their right. The player keeps throwing until he or she fails to throw a 1, 2 or a 5, or until all his dice are gone. Note that a player who has lost all his dice keeps in the game, because he or she can receive dice from the player on their right. After the first player has thrown, the player on the left throws and so on right around the table. Eventually the point comes when there is just one die left as all the others are aces in the centre. The players who throw the last 1 or ace is the loser; though in some versions of the game the winner is the person who throws the final ace.

INDIAN DICE

This is a very simple game, based on the rules of poker, but which can be played using ordinary numerical dice. It is mainly played in North America.

COMPLEXITY RATING:	★
NUMBER OF PLAYERS:	**2 or more**
EQUIPMENT:	**Five dice**
TIME REQUIRED:	**No time limit**

Origin: The game appears to have developed in the United States as a simple alternative to poker, though it lacks the options of bluff as all the other players know your hand.

Aim of the game: To score as good a poker hand as possible over three throws of the dice.

Basic rules: The players throw a die first to see who starts. The highest goes first. In Indian Dice the 1 or ace is a joker, that is it can represent any number you like. The 6 is high, with 2 low. Each player has three throws in his or her round. If a player scores well on the first throw they may 'stick' on that. The interesting thing here is that the other players cannot take more throws than the first player, and in this case that would be just one. A player may stick after two throws or use all three. The object is to get a good poker hand. The best 'hand' is five of a kind (possibly using an ace), then four of a kind, full house (three of a kind plus a pair), three of a kind, two pairs and finally one pair. So for example on a first throw a player may have two 4s and a 3, 5 and 6. They may decide to keep the 4s and throw the other three in the hope of perhaps a full house or even four or five 4s. If on the second throw there is an ace, a 2 and a 5, the player might keep the ace as another 4, giving him three of a kind, and shoot the other two dice hoping for another 4 or a pair of different numbers. At the end of the round the best hand naturally wins.

Always be prepared to stick after your first throw if you have a reasonable fall of the dice, as the other players will only have one throw themselves to beat you.

•

Always put an ace to one side, even if you have no other decent combinations of numbers as its flexibility can always be adapted to a hand in your second or third throws.

•

THREE DICE GAME

Also known as Four-Five-Six this North American version is primarily a gambling game.

COMPLEXITY RATING:	★ ★
NUMBER OF PLAYERS:	1 or more plus a banker
EQUIPMENT:	Three dice
TIME REQUIRED:	No time limit

Aim of the game: To throw a better combination of dice than the banker.

Basic rules: Normally each player will put down his bet against the banker, who will match the bet and play each player in turn. The banker will go first, throwing the three dice once. The combination the banker is looking for is three of a kind, any pair with 6 as the third number, eg 4, 4, 6, or 4, 5, 6 – hence the alternative name of the game. All these combinations win the bets for the banker against that player. The losing combination, for the banker, and the winning one for the player, is if the banker throws 1, 2, 3 or any pair with 1 as the third dice, eg 3, 3, 1. These are the winning and losing combinations. However, if the banker throws a pair with another number as the third dice, eg a pair plus 2, 3, 4 or 5, then this third number represents his or her 'point number', and the game is thrown open and becomes more exciting.

If this happens it is the players' turn to throw the dice. Moving left from the banker, each player in turn throws the three dice once. The rules are the same as before; three of a kind, 4,5, 6 or any pair plus a 6 wins the banker the bet. A throw of 1, 2, 3 or any pair with a 1 wins the player the bet. If the player throws a pair with a 2, 3, 4 or

5 then the contest is decided by who has the highest 'point number'. So if a banker has thrown 3, 3, 2 and the player throws 2, 2, 3, then the player wins even though his pair is smaller than the banker's. If the point number is the same then the contest is a tie, a non-decision. Note that each player keeps throwing until he has won, lost, or tied, in which case the next player to his or her left throws against the banker. All combinations of dice other than those outlined are void and the thrower simply throws again – this applies both to the banker and the players.

This is essentially a game of luck with the odds stacked in favour of the banker, who has more winning combinations than the players and who has the chance to throw first in any case. So the best tip is to make sure you are the banker! However, the rules make it an interesting variation of a simple gambling game and it can be played for fun with, say, matchsticks if you are not feeling lucky.

•

ENGLISH HAZARD

This old-fashioned gambling game has quite a few complex scoring rules and is not much played these days, though it can be an exciting contest.

COMPLEXITY RATING:	★ ★ ★
NUMBER OF PLAYERS:	**2 or more**
EQUIPMENT:	**2 dice and a cup**
TIME REQUIRED:	**No time limit**

Origins: The game became very popular in English gambling dens in the 17th and 18th centuries. English Hazard has a ritual flavour to it and it's very easy to imagine the flourish with which bets were laid down and accepted in past times. It is the ancestor of the popular modern North American game of Craps.

Aim of the game: To score chance combinations which beat your opponents.

Basic rules: One player is nominated as the thrower or 'caster', who then places his or her bet in the centre of the table. In past times there would have been a circle drawn for this purpose in the middle of the table. Other players then decide whether to take up the bet, which they do by putting their in the centre also. The caster then indicates he is accepting the bet by tapping the cup on the table next to the other player's money.

Now the caster throws the two dice from the cup. The object here is to establish what will be the 'main point' number. This number can only be 5, 6, 7, 8 or 9. If the dice do not add to any of these numbers, the caster keeps throwing until they do. Once the main point has been determined, the caster then throws again to find what is called the 'chance point'. This can only be 4, 5, 6, 7, 8, 9 or 10. Again, he will throw until he reaches one of these. Now the two point numbers have been established the contest really begins. The caster's aim now is to throw the dice to replicate the chance point score, which wins him or her the bet. If, however, the caster replicates the main point, he loses the bet.

However, the result can be decided even before this contest. When the caster is throwing to determine the chance point, if he or she throws a 12, and the main point is 5, 6, 8 or 9, then he automatically loses the bet; this is known as an 'out' throw. Similarly, if in determining the chance point the caster throws a 2 or 3, he loses the bet no matter what the main point score is. These throws were called 'crabs' – from where the name of the modern game Craps comes. However, the caster can also win immediately when he throwing to determine the chance point. Such a throw – called a 'nick' – occurs when he throws a chance point which is the same as the main point. Also, if the main point is 12 and the caster throws a chance point of 6 or 8 he automatically wins, and when the main point is 7 and a chance point of 11 is thrown the caster wins as well.

HEARTS

This is a game more suited to the family than many gambling dice games.

COMPLEXITY RATING:	★
NUMBER OF PLAYERS:	**2 or more**
EQUIPMENT:	**6 dice. In theory they should be dice with the letters HEARTS on them, which are available, but it is in fact perfectly possible to play the game with ordinary numbered dice**
TIME REQUIRED:	**30 minutes**

Aim of the game: To reach a fixed score by throwing the correct combinations of letters or numbers.

Basic rules: As with many dice games, there is a small advantage in going first, so each player throws the six dice once to see who gets the highest score and starts. Each player then has one throw of the dice in turn. The aim is to get as near to spelling the word HEARTS with the dice as possible. The scoring is done like this:

HE	=	5 points
HEA	=	10 points
HEAR	=	15 points
HEART	=	20 points
HEARTS	=	25 points

Should the same letter come up more than once, only one counts for scoring purposes. If you are using ordinary dice with numbers then simply adapt the scoring accordingly, so that for example the combination 1, 2 equals five points, 1, 2, 3 equals ten points, 1, 2, 3, 4 equals fifteen points and so on. The winner is the first person to reach 100 points; or the loser can be the last person to reach 100 points, whichever way you want to play. It is also possible to play for a set number of throws or rounds and see who has the most points then, but this is more likely to result in a number of frustrating draws.

BEETLE

This really is a good dice game for children and all the family, as it involves not just the throwing of dice but also the drawing of a beetle as the game progresses.

COMPLEXITY RATING:	★
NUMBER OF PLAYERS:	2 to 6, though it lends itself well to team groups
EQUIPMENT:	One die and pencil and paper
TIME REQUIRED:	20 minutes

Aim of the game: To throw the right numbers to enable you to draw a complete beetle.
Basic rules: The beetle in question is made up, for the purposes of this game, of 13 parts: a head, body, tail, two eyes, six legs and two feelers. There are special dice available with letters corresponding to these parts of the body, with a H for head and F for feeler and so on. But it's just as possible to play with numbered dice and make the numbers correspond to the parts. This might be done in this way:

1 – body
2 – head
3 – each leg
4 – each eye
5 – each feeler
6 – tail

No player can draw a part of the beetle without first scoring the appropriate number. Each player throws once in turn, but has to start with the body first, so he or she must throw a 1 before beginning. With the body drawn, a player can add legs or the tail by scoring 3 or 6, but must score a head (2) before moving on to the eyes or feelers. The winner is the first player to complete a beetle. Another way of playing is to award players points, which would give a player with the complete beetle 13 points, and the other players would get a point for each part of the body they drew. The winner would be the first person to reach 51 points.

ROUND THE CLOCK

This is a very simple and undemanding game which might perhaps be suitable for people on a long and boring journey.

COMPLEXITY RATING:	★
NUMBER OF PLAYERS:	2 or more
EQUIPMENT:	2 dice
TIME REQUIRED:	20 minutes

Aim of the game: To score the correct numbers in the correct order.

Basic rules: This very simple game involves each player throwing the two dice in turn. The aim is to score the numbers 1 to 12 in the right sequence. The players are allowed to use either the score of one single die or the combined value of the two dice. Naturally, to start with the players will be looking to throw a 1. To get 2 they might throw two 1 dice or a single die may come up 2, and so on. The winner of the game is the first player to reach 23 having arrived there in the correct order. To add variety to what can become a slightly tedious game, Round the Clock can be played backwards, ie starting from 12. Even better, you can add a rule that scoring a pair penalises a player, and he or she has to go one number back.

HELP YOUR NEIGHBOUR

This is one of the oldest dice games around but still remains very enjoyable because it is so unpredictable and, as its name suggests, you can end up unwittingly helping your opponents in the game. It's ideal for parties and family occasions.

Aim of the game: A game of luck where a player tries to get rid of his counters as quickly as possible.

Basic rules: As with most dice games, the players each throw the dice once to see who

COMPLEXITY RATING:	★ ★
NUMBER OF PLAYERS:	2 to 6
EQUIPMENT:	Three dice and ten counters per player
TIME REQUIRED:	25 minutes

gets the highest score and starts first. Now each player is given a number 1 to 6, with the first player being number 1 and so on. If there are only two players, the first will be 1, 2 and 3, and the second 4, 5 and 6, while if there are three players the first will be 1, 2, the second 3, 4 and the last 5, 6. If there are four players the 5 and 6 are forgotten, and if five then 6 is left out. Each player will have his or her ten counters in front of them (it can be more or less depending on how long you want the game to last and for six players you may have fewer counters). The first player throws the dice. The players whose number comes up on the dice have to put one counter in the centre for each time it occurs. So if for example you are number 3 and there are two 3's in someone's (or your) throw, you put in two counters. If you are representing two numbers then the same principle applies. Say you are number 3 and number 4, and someone throws a 1, 3 and 4, then you would put two counters in the centre. The person who gets rid of all his or her counters the first is deemed the winner. To make the game last longer, players can be given more than ten counters.

IT'S A FACT...

Dice which have been loaded or shaped for cheating are not a new phenomenon; examples have been found at ancient sites in the Middle East and South America

BOARD GAMES

The earliest games appear to have been invented by primitive people to try to learn more about themselves, and the future. Through them, they thought, the gods provided signs which would describe their destinies – if they could read them. Dice, cards and wheels have all been used in fortune telling. It is unclear when the mystical equipment began to be used for pleasure and relaxation.

Around the world, games developed in a variety of forms ranging from those simulating battles between opposing forces to positional contests. Some cultures such as the people of South America and the Australian Aborigines had no board games. Those which they have played were variations on games brought from Europe and Africa.

The oldest gaming boards were found by British archaeologists in the royal tombs of Ur, and date from about 3000 BC. Players had a series of marked pieces and moves were made by using pyramidal dice. There is no indication of how the game was played. Centuries later the Egyptians devised their own board games based on the Ur game. Some were built into a box which contained the dice and pieces. Throwing sticks were used as a form of dice. Also discovered was another Egyptian game which became known as the Game of Thirty Squares.

The Romans adapted the game and introduced cubic dice. A series of modifications transformed the game into the Tables game of the Middle Ages. From this was developed Backgammon, today one of the world's most popular games but one which bears little resemblance to its ancient predecessors.

ALQUERQUE

Alquerque is one of the most enjoyable games played on a small board.

COMPLEXITY RATING:	★ ★
NUMBER OF PLAYERS:	2
EQUIPMENT:	Board and 24 pieces
TIME REQUIRED:	10 to 20 minutes

Origins: Alquerque dates back at least 3,500 years, a version of it being found in the Temple of Kurna in Egypt. It is one of the forerunners of Draughts but is still played today.

Aim of the game: As in Draughts the game is won by capturing all the opponent's pieces.

Basic rules: Each player starts with twelve pieces which are set out on the board like this:

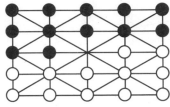

The players draw lots to start, and then have alternate moves. A piece may be moved along a line in any direction to any adjacent point that is empty, or if an adjacent point is occupied by an opponent's piece and the point beyond it is empty, then that piece may be captured by being jumped, and removed from the board. Two or more captures may be made in this way in one move, changes of direction being allowed. A player who may make a capture must do so, and he must capture all the pieces possible in that move, otherwise he is 'huffed' and the offending piece is removed from the board.

Initially the game is very cramped, and moves are confined. Once the board opens up however, there is much scope for strategic play. It helps to look two or three moves ahead so that you can plan sacrifices of pieces in order to capture a greater number of pieces.

•

Alquerque perhaps requires greater concentration than Draughts because moves are made vertically, horizontally and diagonally. It is therefore likely that your opponent will miss a jump he should make, particularly at the side of the board. The offending piece can then be huffed with no loss to you. If you have the greater number of pieces towards the end you should be able to force a win.

•

If you have fewer pieces than your opponent, it is a good idea to play defensively, ie by keeping to the side lines and making him bring the game to you. Try to keep just ahead of him as you move around the side. This way, it is possible that you can take advantage of any errors he commits, and even restore the balance.

•

ALQUERQUE VARIATIONS

High Jump: High Jump may well be older than Alquerque, and comes from north Africa. The starting position is the same as for Alquerque, but players cannot move diagonally, and the huffing rule does not apply when a piece which could be captured is not taken.

Five Field Kono: Five Field Kono comes from Korea, and is played on a similar board to Alquerque, but with only 7 pieces for each player. At the start they are positioned like this:

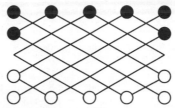

Each piece can move diagonally in any direction onto an empty square. The object for each player is to be first to move his pieces into the opposite starting position.

BACKGAMMON

Backgammon is one of the great games of the world, and although it does not have the depth and complexity of Chess or Go, it makes up for this in being exciting and fast-moving. It has lots of opportunities for strategic play, but also includes an element of chance which means that even a beginner can sometimes beat the expert.

COMPLEXITY RATING:	★ ★ ★
NUMBER OF PLAYERS:	2
EQUIPMENT:	**Board and 30 men; four dice; and a doubling die (optional)**
TIME REQUIRED:	**20 to 30 minutes**

Origins: It has been claimed that Backgammon is one of the oldest games in the world, and its history can be traced back thousands of years. However this is not strictly true. Backgammon, as we know it, first appeared in England in the 17th century, and the rules were codified by Edmund Hoyle in about 1750. Except for the introduction of the doubling die in the 1920s in the USA, they have changed little since.

Backgammon has some features in common with a variety of earlier games, all of which shared the same name of Tables, and which had reached Europe from the

Middle East in the 11th century. Earlier games played by the Romans or the ancient Egyptians – which are claimed to be forerunners of Backgammon – had little in common with the game as we know it apart from the fact that they were race games using counters and dice.

Aim of the game: Backgammon is a race game, and the object is to be the first player to move all his pieces round the board into his home or inner table and from there to remove them from the board, or to 'bear them off'. The first to bear off all his pieces wins the game.

Although the moves in Backgammon depend on the throw of the dice, it is a game of skill. Although the outcome of a single game may to some extent be determined by luck, over a number of games the element of luck will cancel out, and the more skilful player will win.

Basic rules: Each player has fifteen men, one playing with the black set and the other white. Each player also has two dice. The board is divided into four sections known as 'tables', and each table has six long tapering triangles, or points, which are coloured alternately red and white. The two inner tables are separated from the two outer tables by a strip known as the 'bar'. The board is placed so that black has his inner table to his right.

The diagram shows how the men are set out on the board at the beginning. The points and descriptions are show for reference – they are not normally printed on the board.

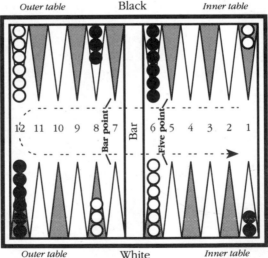

Players may decide to use a doubling die whose faces show the numbers 2, 4, 8, 16, 32 and 64. Its significance will be explained shortly.

Each player throws one of his dice, and the one with the highest number moves first. If both throws are the same, the players roll again. The player with the higher number moves his men according to the numbers on the two dice, his own and his opponent's. For example, if white throws a 6 and black throws a 5, then white has the first move and his throw is considered to be a 6–5. After that the players move alternately, each rolling his own two dice to determine his move.

Each player advances his men a number of points – towards his inner table – according to the numbers thrown with the dice. The numbers are not added together, but are taken separately. For example, if a player throws a 6–1, he may advance one man six points and another one, or vice versa. He may also more one piece six and then a further one, or vice versa. This is not the same as moving the one piece a combined total of 7, as he has to have regard for the position on both points reached by the two numbers.

When a double is thrown, a player moves twice the values shown. For example, a double 6 gives a player four moves of six points each. He may move:

i) one man four times 6 points

ii) one man twice 6 points and another man twice 6 points

iii) one man twice six points, and two other men six points each

iv) four men 6 points each.

The position of the men on the board may affect a player's choice of moves, or may even prevent him from moving at all. Provided that none of his men is off the board, a player may move to any point that is:

i) clear of any other men

ii) occupied by any one or more of his own men

iii) occupied by only one of his opponent's men.

When there is only one man on a point, it is called a 'blot'. A player who moves a man to a point where he already has a man is said to 'make' that point, as his opponent cannot then land on it. If a player can use the number shown on only one of his dice because of closed points, the other number is disregarded. A player may play one of his men on to a point occupied by an enemy blot. It is said to be 'hit', and the opponent's piece is removed from the point and placed on the bar.

A player who has any hit men on the bar must re-enter them before he can move any of his men on the board. To re-enter a man, the player must throw the number of an open point or blot on his opponent's inner or home table. If, for example, white has a man on the bar and throws a 2–3 and the points B2 and B3 have been made by black, then white's throw is void. But if black had a blot on B2, white could enter that point, hitting the black blot and sending it to the bar. He could then use the 3 to move the same man or another man. Both players may have any number of men on the bar at the same time.

Having the opening move in backgammon is an advantage, and it is important to know how to play it. The game's experts have determined which are the best opening moves for any throw of the dice. Some are quite clearly advantageous, and for others there are possible alternative best moves.

Best opening moves if you throw:

6–5 move one back man from black 1 point to black 12 point.

6–1 move one man from black 12 point and one from your own 8 point to your bar point.

5–4 move two men from black 12 point to your 8 and 9 points.

5–2 move two men from black 12 point to your 8 and 11 points.

4–3 move two men from black 12 point to your 9 and 10 points.

4–2 move one man from your 8 point, and one from your 6 point to your 4 point.

3–1 move one man from your 8 point and one man from your 6 point to your 5 point.

Good players never ignore the odds, which are not difficult to gauge, but they do demand a certain mental ability. It is necessary to know the odds against a number coming up, the chances of having a blot hit, of being able to enter a man from the bar, and the number of throws needed to bear off.

•

In the early game, each point you make constitutes a block against any opposing men who may want to pass it. So it is important to try to make points to block your opponent's progress so that he has as few places as possible on which to land. Another important object must be to get your back men (those on black one point in the diagram up and moving.

•

Secure the five-point in your opponent's table, both bar-points and your own four-point if you can.

•

When a player has moved all his men into his own inner table – but not before – he may begin 'bearing off' (removing his men from the board). A man may be borne off each point indicated by the number on either side of the dice. For example, if white throws a 4–2 he may bear off a man from W4 and another from W2. He may alternatively use all or part of the throw to move men inside his inner table.

On a throw of 4–4, white might move a man from W6 to W2, move another from W5 to W1 and bear off two men from W4.

If a number thrown is higher than any point on which the player has men left, then he may bear off from the highest occupied point. For example, if black is left with men only on the points B4, B2 and B1, and he throws a 6–2 he may bear off from B4 and B2. If a player has a blot that is hit while he is bearing off, that man must be re-entered from the bar into his opponent's inner table, and be moved around the board into his own inner table before he can continue bearing off.

It is not a good idea to occupy the 1, 2 and 3 points until getting ready to bear off because the blocks do not provide an effective barrier and can be easily jumped. The men would be better further back.

The winner is the first to bear off all his men. If the loser has borne off one or more of his men, he loses a single game, but if he has not borne off any men he loses a 'gammon' or double game. If he has not borne off any men, and in addition he has one or more men left on the bar or in the winner's inner table, then he loses a 'backgammon' or triple game.

If you were able to complete a round from the starting position without any hindrance, the minimum number of points from throws of the dice to bear off all your men would be 167. This would involve more than 20 throws of the dice without taking any account of the effect of blocks or your men being sent to the bar. It is important therefore to make full use of your turns when your opponent is blocked. You should then bear off first because you will need fewer turns to do so.

Blots do not always work to your advantage. If you hit a runner your opponent has brought round into his inner board, then he has been set back two or three turns. If however, you send a man to the bar from your home board, it is moved back just a couple of points. In addition, the hit may be returned when the man re-enters, and this could be more serious for you with your man close to bearing off.

Avoid leaving blots towards the close of a game – certainly never leave two blots on your own inner table.

The doubling die is a modern introduction to increase further the value of a game and is used when the game is played for stakes. Either player, at any stage in the game when he thinks he has an advantage and when it is his turn to play, may propose the first double by saying 'I double'. His opponent then has the option of declining –

thereby conceding the game and paying the original stake – or accepting the double, in which case the game proceeds for double stakes. If he accepts the double, the doubling die is placed, with the 2 uppermost, at his side of the board and he is said to control the die.

As long as he has control, his opponent cannot double again. However, if the balance of advantage shifts, as it often does, he may redouble. If the redouble is accepted, the die is then turned to show the 4 and passed back to the first player, otherwise the game is conceded by the first player who pays double stakes. The doubling die may be passed back and forth in this way several times in the course of a game, each player having the right to double.

The result of the game – whether it is a single win, gammon or backgammon – acts as a multiplier of the value of the doubling die. So if your basic stake is £1, the double die shows 32, and you win a backgammon, your opponent has to hand over £96.

If you are using the doubling cube, accept a double only if the odds against you are better than 3–1. Apart from the odds for the game, you will then hold the valuable doubling option.

•

GENERAL TIPS
In the beginning the best way to gain skill and confidence in backgammon is to practise by yourself. Set up the men and locate the inner tables first on one side and then on the other. Study the board, and become familiar with its features to help you speed up your moves. Remember that when you throw an even number, your man will land on a point of the same colour, while a man moved on an odd number will land on a different colour point.

•

For practice, play alternately the black and the white men, throwing the dice and making the moves as in a real game. Follow all the moves, but do not attempt to use any strategy. From the beginning always think of your moves in terms of the individual numbers thrown: for example, five and four or four and five, not nine.

It helps to learn the technique of moving two men with the single motion of one hand, rather than individually. Once you become familiar with the board and the moves, the value of quick play will become apparent to you in actual play.

IT'S A FACT...
*A 17th century writer described
Backgammon as an antidote to
'the gout, the rheumatism, the
azure devils, or the yellow spleen'.*

IT'S A FACT...
Homer refers to a Greek form of backgammon in his epic work The Odyssey. *The Greeks called a 6 throw of a die 'Aphrodite' after their goddess of love; while a 1 was dismissed as a 'dog'.*

IT'S A FACT...
In 1437 James I of Scotland is said to have spent the last evening of his life playing chess and 'tables' – an early version of backgammon. The next day he was murdered.

BACKGAMMON VARIATIONS

Dutch Backgammon: This is the same as the standard game except for the following differences:

i) at the start of the game, all the men are placed on the bar. A player must enter all 15 of his men before making any other move.

ii) a player is not allowed to hit a blot until he has moved at least one man around the board into his own inner table.

Plakato: This form of Backgammon is very popular in Greece. It is played in the same way as Backgammon except for these basic differences:

i) at the start of the game each player has all his men positioned on the number 1 point in his opponent's inner table.

ii) there is no bearing off. Instead, each player has to move all his men right around the board to his own number 1 point.

iii) blots are not hit and sent to the bar. Instead, they are blocked, and may not be moved while an opponent's man is on the same point.

You should try to establish as many points as possible as quickly as you can, unless you have a chance to pin one man or more.

•

Gioul: Gioul is popular in the Middle East but is slower than Backgammon. It also differs in these respects:

i) at the start of the game, each player has all his men positioned on the number 1 point in his opponent's inner table.

ii) blots are not hit and sent to the bar. Instead, they are blocked, and may not be moved while one of the opponent's men is on the same point.

iii) when a double is thrown, a player is allowed to move according to that double – and then for each subsequent double up to double 6. For example, if he throws a double 3, he has moves for double 3, double 4, double 5 and double 6.

iv) if a player is unable to use any of the moves resulting from the throw of a double, these moves may be claimed by his opponent.

You should try for a position in which you will be able to move doubles (mainly 5s and 6s), while at the same time preventing your opponent from doing the same.

•

Acey Deucey: Acey Deucey is a type of Backgammon popular in the US Navy. It differs from the standard game in the following respects:

i) the game starts with no men on the board.

ii) players throw a single die, as usual, to decide who will play first, but the first player then throws both his dice for his first turn.

iii) throws may be used to enter additional men on to the board or to move those already entered. Blots are hit and sent to the bar in the normal manner. Men may be moved before all 15 men have been placed on the board but – as in the normal game – may not be moved while a man that has been hit remains on the bar.

A tactic used by Navy men who are behind in the game is to bring only 14 men into play, while holding the fifteenth (the 'clammy') back. In due course, your opponent will have to expose one man or more while bearing off. The clammy can then be used to hit a blot, and switch the advantage.

•

IT'S A FACT...
Boards from an Egyptian game which bore some resemblance to backgammon and dating from 1500 BC were discovered in the tomb of King Tutankhamen.

iv) a throw of 1–2 (Acey Deucey) has special status. Having moved a 1 and a 2, the player throwing 1–2 may then name any double he chooses and move his men accordingly. He then has an extra turn and is allowed to throw both dice again.

However, if he cannot use any part of the throw, he forfeits the rest. If for example, he can use the 1 but not the 2, he foregoes the double and the extra throw.

v) There are a number of other variations concerning doubles and scoring. Some allow automatic doubles every time a 1–2 is thrown. Some replace the standard doubling and tripling for gammon and backgammon by a system whereby the loser pays one unit of the stake for each man left on the board or for the number of points needed to bear it off.

In the early part of the game you should try to establish advanced points as quickly as possible, and if possible to establish advanced points as a base for a prime – six successive points you make anywhere on the board. Your opponent cannot move his men past a prime. If both players develop primes against one another, the prime that is further advanced has the advantage.

•

CHESS

Chess is perhaps the most popular board game in the world, and one of the few games where international matches are regularly covered as news events by the media. Although highly complex and sophisticated, Chess can still be enjoyed at a simple level by beginners.

COMPLEXITY RATING:	★ ★ ★
NUMBER OF PLAYERS:	2
EQUIPMENT:	**Board and 32 pieces**
TIME REQUIRED:	**In rare cases, games can be completed in just a few moves, but most will take 30 minutes to 1 hour. Games can last much longer, and many experienced players use a clock to ensure than at agreed number of moves are made in a given time.**

Origins: The first recorded game of Chess comes from 8th-century India. From there, it appears to have spread to Persia and was probably introduced into Europe during the Moorish occupation of Spain after the eighth century. The game has gradually evolved over the centuries, and features of Chess as we know it today were probably determined in the 16th century.

Aim of the game: The pieces are lined up on each side of the board, rather like opposing armies, and the objective of each player is to 'checkmate' his opponent's king, ie to force it into a position where it could be taken at the next move, and the danger cannot be overcome. Unlike all the other pieces, the king cannot be removed from the board.

The player forcing the checkmate wins the game, even if his opponent has more pieces on the board. A player who recognises that his king is in a losing position can resign before checkmate, and the player forcing the resignation wins the game.

A game can also end in a draw: when there are not enough pieces left on the board for either player to win; when one player continues to threaten his opponent's king ('check'), but cannot checkmate it; when the player whose turn it is can make no legal move but is not in check ('stalemate'); when exactly the same position occurs three times with the same player having the next move, either player can claim a draw; when no capture or pawn move has been made by either player during his past fifty moves; or by agreement.

Basic rules: Chess, like Draughts, is played on a square board made up of 64 squares coloured alternately black and white. The board is always positioned so that both players have a white square on their right hand side – white on the right.

Each player has sixteen pieces: 1 king, 1 queen, 2 bishops, 2 knights, 2 rooks and 8 pawns. Not all have the same value. If you assume the pawn is worth one point, the approximate worth of the other pieces are:

bishop – 3 points

knight – 3 points

rook – 5 points

queen – 9 points

These values provide only a rough guideline, and can vary throughout the game. The king is priceless. If you lose the king, you lose the game.

At the beginning of each game, the 32 pieces are set out on the board with the queen always placed on the square of her own colour – black queen on black square. white queen on white. The rows across the board are usually called 'ranks' and along the board called 'files'.

Each different piece follows different moves.

The king is the most important piece on the board, It can move only one square at a time, but in any direction, provided this square is not one where he can be taken. Opposing kings can never stand on adjoining squares. The king can capture an opposing piece by taking its place on the square, and removing the other piece from the board, provided the square it moves to is not threatened by an opposing piece.

When a king is attacked, or in check, it must immediately be moved out of check, the threatening piece captured, or another piece interposed between the king and the attacking piece (this is not possible if the attacking piece is a knight).

If none of these is possible, the king is said to be checkmated, and the game is over. Although this is usually a part of the end game, it can happen at any time.

Castling: Just once in a game, the king is allowed a special move of more than one square. This move, regarded as a single move, also involves the rook. Called castling, it is made to improve the king's defensive position, and to bring the rook more into play. To castle, the king can move two squares either to the left or right towards one of the rooks. The rook then moves to the square over which the king has just passed. Castling is allowed: if neither the king nor the rook has moved before in the game; there are no pieces of either colour standing between the king and the rook; and none of the squares involving the king's move is threatened.

Castling provides valuable protection for the king, and it is generally a good idea to carry it out earlier in the game as you are building up your defensive position, rather than later on. If the three pawns to the front, immediate left and right of the king's new position have not yet been moved, you should move the one closer to the side of the board forward one square as soon as possible. This may help to avoid the king being trapped behind the rank of pawns later in the game.

•

The queen is the most powerful attacking piece, and therefore the most valuable. It can move any number of clear squares along a rank, file or diagonal, provided the squares it crosses are not occupied by other pieces. If its ultimate square is occupied by an opposing piece, the queen can capture it by removing it from the board, and taking its place on the square.

A common mistake by beginners is to use the queen early in the game, moving it aimlessly around the board, attempting attacks which are easily countered, and meanwhile leaving their other pieces on their original squares. This can result in a player being left in a poor attacking and defensive position later in the game.

•

The rook, occasionally called a castle, moves forwards, backwards and sideways along ranks and files through any number of clear squares. It can capture an opposing piece by removing it from the board and taking its place.

The rook is a particularly valuable mid- to end-game piece when the board is not so congested. Castling is a good method of ensuring that one of your rooks is brought towards the middle files ready for the later stages. Try to do the same with the other rook once the knight and the bishop have been moved out of the way.

•

The bishop moves diagonally backwards or forwards, crossing only clear squares, but like other pieces, can capture by landing on a square occupied by an opponent's piece, and removing that piece from the game. Each bishop remains on the same square colour throughout the entire game.

Because each bishop keeps to the same square colour, it can cover only half the squares on the board. Therefore bishops are often at their most effective when they work in tandem.

•

The knight's move is a combination of the rook's and bishop's moves. It travels one square in any direction along a rank or file and, still moving away from its original position, a second square in a diagonal move. This means that whenever a knight moves from a black square, it must land on a white square – and vice versa. In its move, a knight may cross a square occupied by any other piece rather like a horse jumping an obstacle – the only piece allowed to do so. It also captures an opposition piece by taking its place on the square.

Like the bishops, the knights are often at their most effective when used together, particularly when the board is crowded in the first part of the game.

•

The pawn can move only forwards, usually one square. However, in its opening move, a pawn can, as a matter of choice, be moved forward either one or two squares. This helps to speed up the game's first stages. Unlike other pieces, the pawn does not capture in the same way it moves, ie in a forward direction. It does so diagonally, and then only by moving one square. It can also capture an opposing pawn *en passant* (in passing). If the opposing pawn moves forward two squares in its first move, the square it crosses over is open to attack as though the pawn had been moved just one square. Therefore the capturing pawn may make the usual taking move (ie one square diagonally forward) onto the square just crossed by the opposing pawn. The opposing pawn is then removed from the board. The capture can only be made immediately the opposing pawn has moved forward two squares.

Pawn promotion: Whenever a pawn reaches the end of the file along which it is moving, it must then be exchanged immediately for a queen, rook, bishop or knight, irrespective of how many of those pieces are still on the board. In this way a player can have more than one queen.

IT'S A FACT...
*The youngest-ever world Chess
champion was Gary Kasparov who
won the title in 1985 at the age of 22.*

IT'S A FACT...

Kasparov won the title from
Anatoly Karpov who had held it
for 11 years.

TIP

Do not disregard the importance of the pawn, which, by itself, is the least valuable piece on the board. It is very helpful in protecting and shielding more important pieces from capture. In the later part of the game, if you still have a number of pawns moving forward towards the end rank, your opponent may have to delay his own attack to prevent you from promoting your pawns.

•

CHESS NOTATION

For recording games, there are two different systems of notation in general use – descriptive notation which is in common use in the UK and the USA, and algebraic notation which is common on the Continent and in Russia.

Pieces are identified by the side of the board they stand on. From left to right, you start with queen's rook, queen's knight, and so on. Pawns and files are named in turn after those pieces: eg queen's knight pawn.

The symbols generally used are:

P=	pawn	check or +	=	check
R=	rook	0–0	=	castles on king's side
Kt or N =	knight	0–0–0	=	castles on queen's side
B=	bishop	X	=	captures
Q=	queen	e.p.	=	en passant
K=	king	!	=	good move
		?	=	bad move

In the descriptive system, each square has two names, depending on whether it is from white's point of view, or from black's. For example, white's king's rook starts the game on his square, KR1, which is black's KR8. They remain the same throughout the game, irrespective of where the pieces are on the board.

A move is described by writing the piece which is moved and the square it is moved to. If, for example, white's first move is the pawn in front of his queen two squares forward, this would be written P–Q4 (read as 'pawn to queen four').

In the algebraic system, each square is represented according to the rank and file it is on – the eight files being represented by the letters a to h, and the eight ranks by the numbers 1 to 8. The squares are always described from white's point of view.

For our purposes, we shall use the descriptive system.

In the opening phase, both players try to move their pieces into the most advantageous positions. It is during the middle part of the game that players attempt to capture opposing pieces, to reduce the opponent's attacking potential, and to weaken the defence of the king. In the end game, players attempt to checkmate the opposing king.

To start the game, players draw for colour, with the player securing white making the first move. The game's etiquette requires a player to move one of his pieces if he touches it, assuming a legitimate move can be made. A player must also go ahead with the capture of an opposing piece if he touches it, and it is possible to take it.

It is a good idea to begin by moving at least one of the centre pawns forward two squares. As many pieces as possible should be brought into play as quickly as possible. There is an old saying that you should never move a piece twice until you have moved each piece once. While it should not be taken too literally, it suggests that you should not start an attack until all your soldiers are in the field.

•

Successful play often hinges on control of the centre squares. The four in the middle of the board are especially important and you should try to gain and keep control of those four squares. This does not of course mean that you should try to plant all your pieces there. They would merely get in each other's way. It does mean you should keep those squares under control, particularly with bishops, knights and pawns. Try never to make a move in the opening which does not either increase your control of the centre squares or lessen your opponent's. There is a need for balance, to keep your position free and open, but not letting any of your pieces stray far away from covering the centre.

•

Ten sound opening moves would be (in this order): P–K4; P–Q4; Kt–KB3; Kt–QB3; KB–B4; QB–B4; Q–K2 or Q–Q2; 0–0; P–KR3; QR–Q1.
It is unlikely you will be able to achieve all these, because you also need to respond to your opponent's moves. However, if you can achieve most of them, you will have a very solid attacking and defensive base.

•

IT'S A FACT...
The first British chess player to be
officially designated as an
International Grand Master was
Anthony John Miles in 1976, who
was just 20 years old at the time.

TIP

Examine each move made by your opponent to see what it threatens. Do this every time, and at once. If its threat is dangerous it must be attended to before anything else. Even if it is not immediately dangerous, try to work out the idea behind it. When you have examined your opponent's move, and its options, come back to your own plan.

•

TIP

If there are no immediate threats and you are not sure which move to make, decide which of your pieces is least usefully placed and move that piece to a square where it will be more useful.

•

IT'S A FACT...
In 1990, Kasparov and Karpov met for their latest world title series, over 24 games. Kasparov retained his title 12½ points to 11½

IT'S A FACT
The 1990 series brought the total number of games between the two players to 155, the most sustained series between champion and challenger in the history of the game. Their record then stood at Kasparov 23 wins, Karpov 20 and 112 drawn games.

IT'S A FACT
The longest-reigning undisputed World Chess Champion was a German called Dr Emanual Lasker whose supremacy lasted 26 years and 337 days between 1894 and 1921. Vera Francevna Menchik-Stevenson, a Soviet citizen who took British nationality, was World Women's Champion from 1927 until her death in 1944.

IT'S A FACT

*The Cuban chess player Jose Raul
Capablanca lost just 34 games
during his adult playing career,
the least ever by a world
champion. He was unbeaten from
1916 to 1924 and was world
champion from 1921 to 1927*

GENERAL TIPS

*Many books have been written about Chess, and Chess strategy, and a great deal
can be learned by studying the moves, particularly the openings. It is quite helpful
to learn two or three of the strongest openings which have been developed by Chess
masters. These generally produce sound attacking and defensive positions and a
sound basis on which to move into the middle game.*

Examples of various openings include:

1. P–K4, P–K3 (the French Defence)

1. P–K4, P–QB4 (the Sicilian Defence)

1. P–K4, P–K4; 2. Kt–KB3, Kt–QB3; 3. B–Kt5 (the Ruy Lopez)

1. P–Q4, P–KB4 (the Dutch Defence)

1. P–Q4, Kt–KB3 (the Indian Defence)

1. P–QB4 (the English Opening)

*Players develop skills with practice and knowledge (much can be gained from
following the recorded games of good players), and the best games are between
players of about the same level of ability. However, the best and quickest way of
improving your Chess is to play as often as possible against an opponent slightly
better than you. If you always play inferior players, or those who are very much
better, then you will learn little from them. It helps to play as many different
opponents as possible.*

•

IT'S A FACT...

*What is thought to have been the
slowest game of chess in an official
event occurred in October 1857.
The contest was between Germany's
Louis Paulsen and Paul Charles
Morphy of the USA who drew after
56 moves and 15 hours of play.*

CHESS VARIATIONS

Randomised Chess This is played in the same way as conventional Chess, except that at the beginning of the game the pieces on the first rank are arranged in a random manner, provided it is the same for both players.

Refusal Chess This is played in the same way as normal Chess except that at each move, a player has the right to refuse his opponent's choice of move, and to insist that he play some other move instead. The right of refusal may be exercised as often as one likes during the game, but only one refusal is allowed per move.

Pocket knight Chess This is played the same way as normal Chess except that each player starts the game with an extra knight in his pocket. At any stage of the game, when it is his turn to move, a player may place his extra knight on any vacant square on the board. This counts as his move, and thereafter the extra knight functions as a normal piece.

Two-move Chess The normal rules apply, except that each player has two moves at a time instead of one. A player giving check on his first move forfeits the second, and a player in check must get out of it on his first move.

Progressive Chess This is a very challenging variation, requiring the ability to think ahead. White has one move, black then has two, white then has three, and black has four, and so on. When a player gives check this ends his turn, and he forfeits the rest of his move. A player who is in check, must get out on his first move.

DRAUGHTS

Draughts, or checkers as it is called in the United States, is widely played throughout the world, and has many variations. It is comparatively simple to learn, but can be a game of great skill and complexity.

COMPLEXITY RATING:	★ ★ ★
NUMBER OF PLAYERS:	2
EQUIPMENT:	Board and 24 pieces
TIME REQUIRED:	20 to 40 minutes

Origins: Draughts was played in southern Europe in medieval times and appears to have been based on much older games. Games similar to Draughts were played in the days of the early Egyptian pharaohs in about 1600 BC. It was played in 16th century France as 'jeu des dames' (because in early times it was dismissed as 'women's chess'), and spread to Scotland. The first English description of draughts appeared in 1566. William Payne, an English mathematician, published the first book on Draughts in England, 'Introduction to the Game of Draughts' with a dedication by Samuel Johnson who enjoyed the game. In the 19th century the game was extensively analysed and made popular by a number of English and Scottish experts.

Aim of the game: A player attempts to capture all his opponent's pieces and remove them from the board, or to position his own pieces so that his opponent is unable to make any move.

Basic rules: Draughts is played on a square board which is divided into 64 smaller squares which are alternately black and white. Play is confined to the squares of one colour. At the start of the game the board is positioned so that each player has a black square at his left hand corner.

One player has twelve black pieces or men, the other has twelve white pieces. Each player's men are set out on the black squares of the three rows nearest him. The board when ready for play looks like this. The notation will allow the description of moves:

	1		2		3		4
5		6		7		8	
	9		10		11		12
13		14		15		16	
	17		18		19		20
21		22		23		24	
	25		26		27		28
29		30		31		32	

To start the game, players draw for colour with the player securing black making the first move. After that, the players move alternately. Moves must be made diagonally, and pieces can be moved only to an empty square.

TIP

The first moves open to the player who starts (black) are of varying strengths. The best moves (in order) are: 11–15, 9–14, 11–16 and 10–15 while 12–16, 10–14 and 9–13 are not so strong. Beginners are often told that their safest opening moves when playing black are: 11–15 . . . 8–11 . . . 4–8.

If you are playing white, the best responses are:
11–15, 23–19 or 11–15, 23–18 or 11–15, 22–18.
9–14, 22–17 or 9–14, 22–18
11–16, 22–18 or 11–16, 24–19
10–15, 21–17
12–16, 24–20
10–14, 22–17 or 10–14, 24–19
9–13, 22–18

Early in the game, you should line up your pieces one behind the other, closing up holes which will allow your pieces to be taken. This requires a gradual build-up of your position.

•

You should learn to avoid the beginner's trap of losing two men for one in exchanges such as this:
Black opens: 11–15 and white answers 22–17. Black plays 12–16 planning to go on to 20, but white plays 24–19, forcing 15–24, 28–12, and white has won a piece. Another way to do the same thing is 9–14, 22–17, 12–16, 23–18, 14–23, 26–12.
The loss of a single piece is normally enough to lose the game because your opponent can then go on to swap piece for piece and so end up with one to none, although there are some end positions where one piece can draw against two.

•

A piece can move only one square at a time, unless capturing. The capture is made by jumping over an opposing piece on an adjoining square into an empty square beyond. The captured piece is then removed from the board. Several pieces may be taken in this way in the one move, so long as each captured piece has an empty square beyond it.

If a player can make a capturing move, he must do so, even if it is to his disadvantage. Part of the skill of the game is manoeuvring an opponent into such a position. Where he has a choice of moves which will capture opposing pieces – a move which will capture two pieces, for example, or another which will capture three – then he may choose which move to take, but he must make all the captures that are possible for that move.

If a player fails to capture a piece which he could do so, then his opponent has three options before making his own move.

i) he can accept the offending move and do nothing

ii) the can insist that the move be taken back and replayed to make the possible capture

iii) he can 'huff' the other player by removing from the board the piece which made the offending move, although this option is less usual in modern draughts.

IT'S A FACT...
Andrew Knapp became the youngest winner of the English Amateur Draughts Championship when he won the event, at his first go, in 1986 aged 19 years and 322 days.

Avoid losing one of your draughts unless you are convinced that the loss is made up by gaining an equal or better position. Think any move through to ensure that the loss of one of your draughts is not repaid by the loss of two or more.

•

As you advance your draughts towards the king's row, try to avoid entering square 28 if you are black and white still occupies 32. If you are white avoid square 5 while black occupies 1. Unless your opponent is soon likely to be forced out of the square, it will render your draught immobile. Other weak squares may occur for black if he occupies 21 while white is on 30, or for white if he goes to 12 while black is on 3. There are some exceptions to this which will become more obvious as you develop experience in the game.

•

Initially the pieces may be moved forwards only – that is, away from the player making the move. However, when a piece reaches one of the four squares at the far edge of the board it becomes a king. It may then move either forwards or backwards. A king is recognised by being crowned – that is, another piece of the same colour (from among those previously taken and removed from the board) is placed on top of it to form a double-decker piece. A player's turn ends when a piece is crowned, even if the newly-made king is then in a position to take opposing pieces.

Once a draught has become a king, it should be brought into immediate use rather than being kept in reserve while you try to obtain more kings. He can capture uncrowned draughts or force your opponent's pieces into difficult positions.

•

A king is particularly powerful behind single men where it can attack without suffering counter-attack. Therefore in the opening, it is important not to let an avenue to your king row be opened up to the adverse pieces, unless you can also crown your pieces.

•

If kings can be arranged in triangular formations and brought boldly into battle, this will strengthen their position substantially.

Concentrate on taking as many of your opponent's pieces as possible and crowning kings. As soon as you gain an advantage of a single man increase it by exchanges.

•

Do not scatter your forces, back up advanced men, try to control the centre of the board and the double corner.

•

When surrounded and strongly attacked, it is sometimes better to sacrifice than to attempt defence.

•

There are two double corners, 1 and 5 and 28 and 32. These have special virtues as havens for a king because a king in a double corner cannot be captured by a lone pursuing king late in the game. However, a king in a single corner (squares 4 and 29), or in any border square other than a double corner, can be trapped there by an opposing king whose move it is.

As we have already mentioned, the game is won when all the opponent's pieces are taken, or are blocked so they cannot move. A tied game results when neither player is able to force a win. If a player is in a stronger position he may be required to win the game within his next 40 moves or else be able to show a clear advantage over his opponent. If he fails to do so the game is drawn.

GENERAL TIP

As a general rule, draughts in the centre of the board are better placed than those at the side. A piece at the side is less mobile, and there is a likelihood that it could be pinned there, putting the player in a weaker position for the end game. However, like most general rules, there will be occasions when moves to the side are preferable.

•

IT'S A FACT...

The Scot, James Wyllie, the son of a veteran of the Battle of Waterloo, has been described as the most original draughts player in the game's history. In the second half of the 19th century, he was world draughts champion for nearly 40 years, with occasional breaks.

DRAUGHTS VARIATIONS

Diagonal Draughts: This is an interesting variation of the standard game. It can be played with 12 pieces for each player, in which case the starting position is as shown in the board on the left.

If the game is played with nine pieces, this starting position is as on the right-hand board.

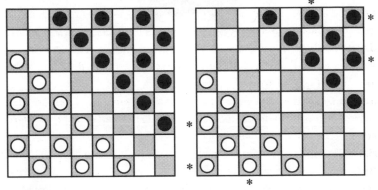

Pieces are crowned when they reach the opposite corner squares (marked * in the diagrams). The rules are exactly the same as for standard Draughts.

Italian Draughts: This is similar to standard Draughts, except that the board is placed so that each player has a white square at his left-hand corner, and there are different rules of capture. These are:

i) a king may not be captured by an uncrowned piece;

ii) a player who is able to make a capturing move must do so;

iii) if a player has a choice of capturing moves, he must choose the move which captures the greatest number of pieces. If a king may capture either another kind or an uncrowned piece, then it must capture the other king.

Spanish Draughts: In many respects this is similar to Italian Draughts. The difference is that the king is more powerful, having what is known as the 'long move'. This means that a king may be moved any number of squares along a diagonal, as long as it is not obstructed (rather like the bishop's move in chess).

A king may capture an opposing piece anywhere on the same diagonal provided that there are no pieces in between and there are one or more empty squares immediately beyond it. The jump may end in any of the empty squares beyond the captured piece. If the king, having made a capture, can then capture another piece on a different diagonal, he must do so. The move continues until the king has captured all the pieces it can. Only when the move is complete are the captured pieces removed from the board, but they may not be jumped over more than once.

German Draughts: This game is played in the same way as Spanish Draughts except that:

i) although uncrowned men can move only forwards, they can make capturing moves either forward or backward;

ii) a man is crowned only if its move ends on the far row. If its move takes it to the last row, and it is then in a position to capture other pieces by jumping backwards in the same move, it must do so. It therefore does not become a king on that move.

Russian Draughts: This is very similar to German Draughts, ie when a piece reaches the last row at the far side of the board it must jump backwards to capture other pieces if it may do so. In Russian Draughts however, it does become a king on that move. The other difference is that when a player has a choice of capturing moves there is no compulsion to make the move that captures the highest number of pieces.

Polish Draughts: This is played with the same rules as German Draughts, but is played on a square board with 100 squares. Each player starts the game with 20 pieces set out in the first four rows on opposite sides.

Canadian Draughts: This is also played with the same rules as German draughts, but uses an even larger square board of 144 squares, and each player starts with 30 pieces set out on the first five rows.

Turkish Draughts: This game can be played on a standard Chess board, although the traditional Turkish board has squares all the same colour. Each player has 16 pieces which are set out on both black and white squares on each player's second and third rows. The distinctive features of Turkish draughts are that pieces move forwards or sideways, but not diagonally, and move on both black and white squares.

A piece becomes a king when it reaches the last row at the far end of the board. It may then move any number of squares forwards, backwards or sideways. The method by which the king captures is similar to that in Spanish Draughts except, of course, that the jumps are not diagonal. The captured pieces are removed from the board immediately, not at the end of the move, and therefore do not block further captures in that move.

A player who is able to make a capturing move must do so. If he has a choice, he must choose the one which captures the greatest number of pieces.

The game is won by capturing all the opponent's pieces or by blocking them so they cannot be moved. The game is also won by a player with a king if his opponent is left with just a single uncrowned piece.

IT'S A FACT...

Asa Long has the unusual distinction of being both the youngest, and later the oldest, winner of the United States National Checkers Championship. He was just 18 years and 64 days old when he took the title in 1922, and was 79 years and 334 days old when he won his sixth title in 1984.

Go (Wei-Ch'i)

Go is a game of simple rules, but which is just as demanding and complex as Chess. There is little similarity between the two, apart from, the fact that they are both board games of pure skill played between two opponents. The leading exponents are Japanese and Go has an enormous following there.

COMPLEXITY RATING:	★ ★ ★ ★
NUMBER OF PLAYERS:	2
EQUIPMENT:	A board ruled with 19 horizontal lines and 19 vertical lines forming a total of 361 intersections or points; 181 black pieces called 'stones' and 180 white stones. The board is also marked with nine dots as shown on the top illustration overleaf. They are at the intersections of the fourth, tenth and sixteenth lines in each direction. These are for orientation, but are also relevant to the handicapping system which is part of the game.
TIME REQUIRED:	30 minutes to 1½ hours (although professional games can take much longer).

IT'S A FACT...

Go was first introduced to Japan, where it is now played professionally, in AD 754, when the Chinese Emperor Hinan Tsung sent a set of the game to his Japanese counterpart Koken Tenno. It was christened Igo, which phonetically became Go.

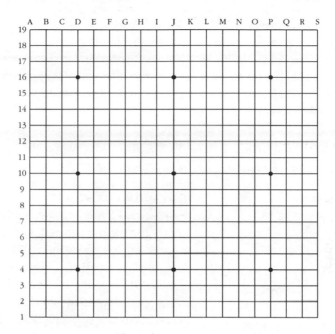

Origins: Go is believed to have originated in China about 4,000 years ago. It was later introduced to Japan, where the world's best players are now to be found. It is also popular in other Asian countries such as Korea and Taiwan, and has some following in the West.

Aim of the game: Each player attempts to form continuous lines or walls of his own stones to surround vacant areas of the board. He scores one point for every vacant intersection inside the territories he controls at the end of the game. Players also attempt to capture their opponent's stones during the game. Because the captured stone is removed it vacates a point of territory, and if it is still vacant at the end of the game, this counts towards the player's score. The game finishes when all vacant

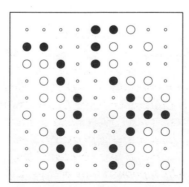

territory has been surrounded by one player. Both players need to agree that there are no more points to be gained. If only one player thinks the game is ended, he says 'pass', and is not allowed to make any further move. The other player continues playing until he agrees that he can secure no further points. Each player then counts up the number of points he has surrounded, and the number of his opponent's stones he has captured. The player with the highest total is the winner. The diagram at the foot of the previous page shows the end of a game on a small board.

A common mistake for beginners is trying to capture the opponent's stones all the time. It is more important to try to develop position on the board.

•

Basic rules: Play starts with an empty board. Black normally has first turn, and because this gives an advantage, the weaker player is usually allowed to play with the black stones. If players are about equal, they alternate in their use of black.

There is a further handicapping system so that if one player is considerably weaker than the other he may be allowed, on his first move, to place two or more stones on the board on the marked handicapped points. Go is one of the few games where a handicap system can compensate for different abilities and allow any two players to have a good game. Should the stronger player continue to win, the number of handicap stones may be increased as shown below:

Level of

Handicap	Handicap points used
2	P4, D16
3	P4, D16, P16
4	D4, P4, D16, P16
5	D4, P4, J10, D16, P16
6	D4, P4, D10, P10, D16, P16
7	D4, P4, D10, P10, D16, J16, P16
8	D4, J4, P4, D10, P10, D16, J16, P16
9	D4, J4, P4, D10, J10, P10, D16, J16, P16

Black starts by placing a stone on any unoccupied point or intersection on the board. White does the same, and players alternate until the game ends. Once they are played, stones cannot be moved about, but it is possible for stones to be captured and removed from the board. Since captures are comparatively infrequent, the board gradually fills up.

The corners are strategically the best areas on the board, and are usually strongly contested. There are many corner plays, but it is possible to become a good player by learning three or four dozen. Whether you are playing with handicap stones or

without, you should occupy the corners before the sides, and the sides before the centres. This is because fewer stones are needed to establish territory on the sides than in the middle of the board.

The first corner moves are usually at one of the points marked in the diagram below:

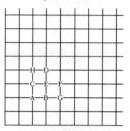

It is best to keep your stones linked, so you should develop from the corners you occupy to the side, rather than just play anywhere on the side. You should then move towards the centre by extending your side position.

•

It is better to stake out loose territories than to form solid walls around one corner. To illustrate this, it is worth realising that it takes 14 stones to seal off 30 points in a corner. With the same number of moves your opponent can virtually secure the rest of the board by staking out general territories.

•

Early stones placed on the third line are in the best position to make full use of the corners and edges of the board helping to surround territory.

•

TIP

Stones placed on the fourth line look towards the centre. If you are playing black with handicap stones, they are usually placed on the fourth line and are orientated towards the centre. A frequent mistake for those playing with black under these circumstances is to try to seal off the corners, which does not make best use of the handicap stones.

•

TIP

It is a waste of time to make territory on the second line.

•

Vacant points that are adjacent – horizontally or vertically – to a stone are known as its 'liberties'. Single stones normally have four liberties, but stones on the edge have only three, and in the corner, two (see diagram below). When all of a stone's liberties are occupied by enemy stones it is captured and removed from the board.

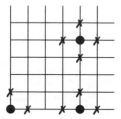

liberties marked with a ✗

In the following series, black has a group of three stones with one liberty, and in a position of capture. It is said to be in atari. If it is white's turn it can capture and remove them by placing a stone on the last liberty.

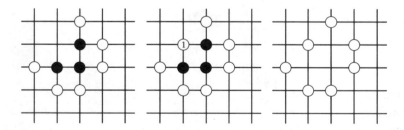

Two types of move are forbidden by the rules: the 'suicide rule' and the 'rule of ko'. Under the first, a player is not allowed to play himself into a position where he can be captured. In the following example, black is not allowed to play at A or B because his stone, or stones would have no liberties.

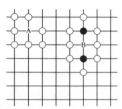

IT'S A FACT...
Today, Japan has about 10 million
Go players, and about 500
professionals, including a number
of women.

There is one exception to this: a player can place a stone where it has no liberties if, in doing so, it captures one or more of his opponent's stones. This is because such captures would create liberties. In the following example, black can place a stone on A if it is his turn, thereby capturing white stones 1, 2 and 3.

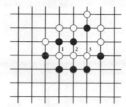

The rule of Ko prevents a move which would be continually repeated. In the next diagram, black can capture one white stone by placing his stone on A. Black's capturing stone would be in atari, and if white were now to play at B and capture this stone we would be back to the original position. This could be repeated, except for the rule which makes it illegal to capture straight back in a ko. White must make another move elsewhere on the board to allow black to overcome the ko situation.

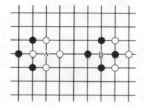

A deadlock, or seki, situation can develop on any part of the board where opposing groups are placed so that neither player can occupy an uncontrolled point without losing his own pieces. In the case of a seki, the stones are left untouched until the end of the game, and all free points in them are disregarded in scoring. In the diagram below, neither player can place his stone on point A without losing his formation.

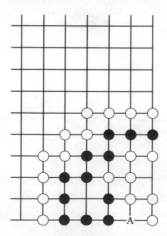

A group of stones of the same colour connected horizontally or vertically is known as an 'army'. Armies may be captured the same way as single stones. In the diagram below, white stones played on any of the points marked with a cross will capture black stones. Stones such as the black ones in this diagram which are liable to be captured on the next move are said to be in 'atari'. It is not necessary for the attacking stones to be connected horizontally or vertically.

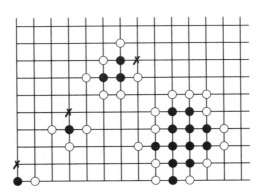

TIP

Stones on the very edge of the board tend to be rather short of liberties. It can be a positive area for development, but can also be a trap for the unwary. In the example on the right side of the diagram, the black army is captured by playing a white stone in an internal liberty – such an internal space is known as an 'eye'. This can be played only if the external liberties of the black army have been completely occupied by white stones. If they have not, a white stone cannot be played in the eye because it would itself be immediately captured.

•

TIP

An important principle which follows from this, is that whenever an army has two or more separate eyes it can never be captured.

•

TIP

It is important to understand how captures can be made, but it is more important to realise that surrounding vacant points is the primary objective and capturing stones is secondary to this. A general principle to follow is that stones should not be played inside territory which is securely held by the opponent as they are sure to be captured eventually.

•

---

*Since the scoring is based on the vacant points that have been surrounded,
stones should not be played unnecessarily within your own territory, as
they merely reduce your score.*

•

GENERAL TIP

*There is an increasing amount of literature available in English on the game,
analysing moves and tactics. It is worth following the games of the leading players,
and trying to imitate the way they seal off large territories. Amateur players find
this very difficult, but the best way to do it is to attack your opponent so that he
finds it difficult to invade the territory you are developing.*

•

GO VARIATIONS

Simplified Go: Go is often played on a smaller board, either 10 × 10 or 13 × 13, and
by partnerships of two players each. Partners take alternate turns using stones of the
same colour, but do not consult. A time limit is often fixed, of say one to five minutes
a move.

Go-Moku: This is a straightforward game for two using a Go board which originated
in Japan and is sometimes called Go-Bang or Spoil Five. Players divide 200 stones,
one set black and the other white. They then try to position five stones so that they
form a straight line (horizontally, vertically or diagonally) while trying to prevent the
opponent from doing so. The first to do so is the winner.

The board is empty at the start of the game, and each player in turn places one
of his stones on any vacant point or intersection on the board. If both players have
played all their stones without getting five in a row, the game can be declared drawn,
or continue with each player in turn moving one of his stones horizontally or vertically
to an adjacent vacant point until one player succeeds in forming a row of five.

IT'S A FACT...

*The first code of rules for Go was
drawn up in 1949, nearly 4,000
years after the game was first
developed. Before this, the absence
of definitive rules sometimes
caused heated disputes. In 1928, a
championship tournament in
Japan was suspended for a month
because of a dispute about the
rules.*

FIGHTING SERPENTS

The layout and moves have some similarities to fox and geese games, but this game is a contest between forces of equal strength.

COMPLEXITY RATING:	★ ★
NUMBER OF PLAYERS:	2
EQUIPMENT:	**The game is played with a board (which can vary in size) with three parallel lines which are intersected by short lines to produce a series of diamond patterns. The number of intersections may vary (the one here has 25 intersections, and the players have 12 pieces each.)**
TIME REQUIRED:	**10 to 20 minutes**

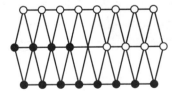

Origins: The game was probably taken to the Americas by the Spaniards 400 years ago, and today is played by the Zuni Indians of Central America.

Aim of the game: The player who succeeds in capturing all his opponent's pieces is the winner.

Basic rules: Pieces are placed on all intersections except the one in the middle.

Players draw lots to start, and the first player moves one of his pieces along a line to the vacant point. Players then take it in turns to move. Pieces are captured by jumping over them to empty points beyond. However, the jump has to be in a straight line, although for a double or multiple capture, the direction may be changed.

When a piece is captured, it is removed from the board. When a move does not involve the capture of an opponent's piece, a player can move any piece one space in any direction to a vacant intersection.

At the start of the game, the board is very cramped, and moves are confined. As the board opens up however, there is more scope for strategic play. You will need to look several moves ahead so that you can plan sacrifices of pieces to allow you to capture a greater number of pieces.

•

If you have the greater number of pieces towards the end you should be able to force a win, but you should not become over-confident because the game can turn quickly on a mistake.

•

If you have fewer pieces than your opponent, it is a good idea to play defensively, ie by keeping to the side lines and making him bring the game to you. If you keep just ahead of him at the sides, you should be able to take advantage of any errors he makes. It is therefore important to consider carefully any move before you make it, and when your opponent does so.

•

FOX AND GEESE

There are countless variations of this game, which is played all over the world. The distinctive feature of them all (unlike most other board games) is that the two players have unequal numbers of pieces, with different powers of movement, and they have different objectives.

COMPLEXITY RATING:	★ ★
NUMBER OF PLAYERS:	2
EQUIPMENT:	Draughts board; four white pieces and one black
TIME REQUIRED:	15

Origins: The game originated in Scandinavia in the Viking era, and has since spread widely throughout the world.

Aim of the game: The fox tries to pass through the line of geese, or the geese try to trap the fox so he cannot move.

Basic rules: The geese all start the game on the four black squares nearest to the white player. The fox can be placed on any black square on the board that black chooses. The geese move like men in draughts – one square forward diagonally, always on the black squares. The fox can move diagonally backwards or forwards, one black square at a time. It cannot jump over the geese as there is no taking in this game.

When black has been placed on the board, white moves one of his geese. The fox then moves, and play continues in turns.

The geese can always win if they keep together, and in as straight a line across the board as possible. If they leave a hole in their line, it is very easy for the fox to slip through and win.

•

FOX AND GEESE VARIATIONS

Wolf and goats: In this game white (the goats) has 12 pieces and black (the wolf) one. The white pieces start on the first three rows of black squares nearest to the white player while black starts in one of the black corner squares on the other side of the board. In this game the wolf and goats move the same way as the fox, but the wolf is able to jump over the goats and take them off the board. The goats however, cannot jump over the wolf.

The wolf tries to break through the goats, and the goats try to trap the fox so that it cannot move. As is the case in Fox and Geese, the goats should always win.

Fox and Geese is also played on special boards such as the one below shaped like a Greek cross. This game is played with 14 pieces, 13 of one colour (the geese) and 1 of another (the fox).

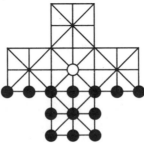

The players take it in turn to move, with the fox having the first move. The fox and geese move in the same way – one step in any direction along a line to an adjacent empty point. But the fox may capture geese – by jumping over a goose to an empty point beyond and removing it from the board.

The fox may make several such jumps in one move, capturing a goose with each jump. The geese, however, are not allowed to jump over the fox or one another.

The fox wins if it takes so many geese that they cannot trap it, while the geese win if they can trap the fox so it cannot move.

Again, in this version the geese should stick close together in moving, and with a little practice should win the game.

HALMA

Halma was the forerunner to Chinese Chequers, but is still popular in its own right.

COMPLEXITY RATING:	★ ★ ★
NUMBER OF PLAYERS:	**2, 3 or 4**
EQUIPMENT:	**Board and 64 pieces**
TIME REQUIRED:	**20 to 30 minutes**

Origins: Halma takes its name from a Greek word for a jump. It was invented in 1883 by George H Monks of Boston, Massachussetts.

Aim of the game: Players transfer their pieces for their corner or 'yard' to the corner diagonally opposite. The first to do so is the winner.

Basic rules: Halma is played on a chequered board with sixteen squares on each side.

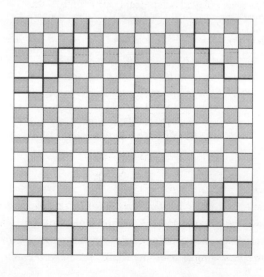

Each corner has a section, or yard, bounded with heavy lines and containing thirteen squares. Two opposite corners have an additional heavy line bounding an area with 19 squares. These areas are the starting and finishing positions.

There are four sets of pieces, each set being of a different colour. Two sets contain 13 pieces and the other two sets contain 19 pieces.

The game can be played by two, three or four players each playing separately, or by four people in two partnerships. Partnerships can be played in two ways: pairs are formed by players with pieces in adjoining yards, or they can be formed by players with pieces in yards that are diagonally opposite.

The second form provides more scope for partners to help each other.

•

If there are four players, each starts with 13 pieces, placed in the marked-off section in his corner of the board. If there are three players, one will move his pieces towards an empty compound which is a slight disadvantage. Each player can take a turn as odd. If there are two players, each starts with 19 pieces in one of the corners with the larger marked-off sections.

After drawing lots to start, each player moves one of his pieces in turn. There are two types of move – steps and hops. A piece may step one square in any direction to a vacant square. Alternatively, a piece may hop over any other piece (whether or not it is the same colour) if there is a vacant square immediately beyond it. In one move a piece may make several such hops, provided that each hop is over one piece into a vacant square. Steps and hops may not be combined in one move. There is no capturing and no pieces are removed from the board.

Opening and finishing moves are crucial in Halma. The first aim is to clear your own area; the second is to move all your pieces across the middle of the board before any other player; the third is to fill the outer squares of your opponent's area before fillin about 1600 BC. It was played in 16t

NTU

In a game for four players, the following is a useful, and solid, opening. Move 1: advance the central piece in your front line one square forward. Move 2: hop the piece which stands by itself in the rear corner of your compound directly forward over the two available heads, Move 3: hop the piece at the extreme left of your compound over the three available heads so that it moves along two sides of a triangle. Move 4: hop the piece at the extreme right of your compound along two sides of a triangle so that it is in a position alongside and corresponding to that of the last piece you moved. Move 5: bop the piece now at the left rear of your compound over the three available heads in a zigzag so that it takes up position one square in front of the last piece you moved. Move 6: bop the piece now at the right rear of your compound over the three available heads so that it is placed alongside and corresponding to that of the last piece you moved. Move 7: bop the piece now standing on the fifth square of the board's central path over two heads along two sides of a triangle so that it is now on the seventh square of the central path of squares. Move 8: push the last piece you moved one square forward and use the resulting ladder.

•

When only two are playing, an extra row of six pieces is used, and this opening game, although different in detail, is the same in principle and will give ideas for a solid start.

•

Do not neglect advancing your rear pieces in favour of your advance pieces because it is dangerous to leave pieces as stragglers.

•

Successful play consists of forming ladders, providing a series of hops for one's own pieces to take them a good distance across the board in one move – and blocking ladders formed by one's opponents.

•

Deliberate blocking, or placing one of your men between two prepared rungs of your opponent's ladder, is very satisfying, but while they hamper your opponent, they do not help you to win the game either.

HALMA VARIATION
Chinese Chequers:
Chinese Chequers is neither Chinese not Chequers (Draughts), but is a modern game based on the principles of Halma. It can be played by from 2 to 6 people, playing

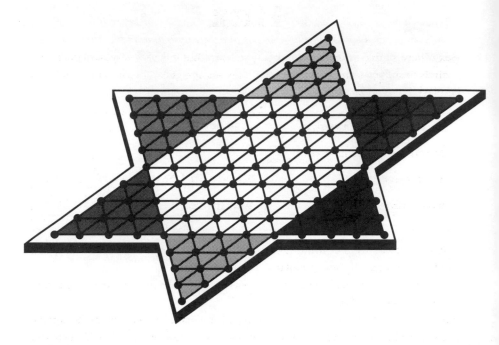

individually or with partners. A special Chinese Chequers board (shown above) is needed, together with 90 pieces in six different colours.

Like Halma, the aim of the game for each player is to be the first to transfer his pieces from one side of the board to the other. The board is shaped like a six-pointed star, with each point being a different colour.

If there are two players, each starts with 15 pieces. If there are two players, each starts with 15 pieces. If there are more than two players, each player has 10 pieces. The pieces are usually plastic pegs which fit into holes on the board, and there are six sets of 15 pieces – each set being of the same colour as one of the points of the star.

For a game between two players, each positions his 15 pieces in opposite points of the star. When there are more than two players, each one positions 10 pieces in a point. Partners usually take opposite points.

Players draw lots to start, and then move one piece in turn. Moves maybe in any direction, in steps or hops. A player can hop over his own or another player's pieces and may make several hops in one move. Steps and hops may not be combined in one move, and there is no compulsion to make a hop. Pieces are not removed from the board when they have been jumped.

GENERAL TIP

Because of its similarity to Halma, the tips for that game can generally be applied to Chinese Chequers.

HEX

Hex is very simple in principle and easy to learn. But it is also very intriguing, and analysis of strategy can be very complex. Hex sets are generally available, but it can be played with improvised equipment.

COMPLEXITY RATING:	★ ★
NUMBER OF PLAYERS:	2
EQUIPMENT:	**Board and 122 counters**
TIME REQUIRED:	**30 minutes**

Origins: Hex was invented in the 1940s by a Danish mathematician, inventor and poet, Piet Hein, and has become popular in many countries.

Aims of the game: Each player tries to form a continuous line of counters connecting his two sides of the board.

Basic rules: The Hex board is diamond-shaped and made up of adjoining hexagons. The standard board has eleven hexagons along each side, but boards with a greater or lesser number of hexagons may be used. Two opposite sides of the board belong to black and the other two belong to white. The four corner hexagons belong to both players.

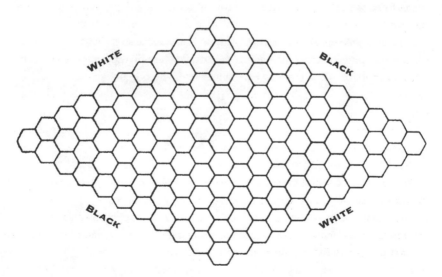

Two equal sets of counters are needed, one black and the other white. Using the standard board, the highest number of pieces a player will need for a game is 61, but normally he will need far fewer. In the first game, players draw for the choice of colour, and black plays first. The game begins with the board completely empty, and the players take turns in placing one of their counters in any vacant hexagon.

It is clear that black, having first move, has the advantage – especially if he places his first counter in the centre hexagon. However, no one has yet been able to work out how he should use this advantage to ensure a win. Nevertheless some players insist that black should be handicapped by not being allowed to place his first counter in the centre hexagon.

•

Turns then alternate, with each player placing one of his pieces on any unoccupied hexagon. Pieces may not be moved once they have been placed on the board.

In trying to make a line, do not just play on the hexagon next to the last man you put down. If your opponent sees that you are doing this, he will easily block you. Rather than trying to build a solid continuous line to begin with, you should place your counters in alternate hexagons. This will allow you move flexibility in reacting to moves by your opponent. You can then fill in the gaps as appropriate.

•

The winning line does not have to be straight – provided it has no gaps, it may twist and turn and may be of any length.

Alternative board: If you do not have the formal game, you can produce a home-made version by making a diamond-shaped board, and dividing each side into tenths. You then need to join up the points opposite one another across the board to create equilateral triangles. To play the game, the counters are placed on the intersections – not in the spaces. This is the exact equivalent of the original game.

LASCA

The excitement of Lasca comes from the sudden changes in the number of pieces held by each player.

Origins: Lasca was invented by Edward Lasker, an American chess master.

Aim of the game: Each player has 11 pieces, and the one which makes it impossible for his opponent to make any move is the winner.

Basic rules: The game is played on a square board which is divided into 49 smaller squares, alternating black and white with a white square at each corner. Play is on the white squares only.

At the beginning of the game, each player sets up his pieces on the white squares

COMPLEXITY RATING:	★ ★
NUMBER OF PLAYERS:	2
EQUIPMENT:	**Draughts-style board of 49 squares and 22 pieces, in equal numbers of black and white. Each piece is marked with a spot on one side. When the unmarked side is uppermost, the piece is known as a soldier, and when the marked side is uppermost, the piece is known as an officer.**
TIME REQUIRED:	**20 to 30 minutes**

of the three rows nearest to him. All the pieces start as soldiers.

White has the first move and after that the players move alternately. The moves and captures are similar to those of draughts, but Lasca's distinctive features are the columns and guides. A column may be a single piece or it may be a pile of pieces, one on top of another. The top piece of the column is the guide. The colour of the guide determines to which player the column belongs. The rank of the guide – soldier or officer – determines the way in which the column moves.

At the beginning of the game each piece is a single column with a soldier as a guide. A column guided by a soldier may move diagonally forward, one square at a time (just like an ordinary piece in draughts). When the column reaches the far end of the board, the guide is turned over to become an officer. A column guided by an officer may move one square in any direction, like the king in draughts.

Pieces are captured by one column jumping over an enemy column into an empty square beyond, again like the capture in draughts. In Lasca, however, no pieces are removed from the board, and only the guide is captured, not the whole column. The captured guide is added to the bottom of the column that captured it.

For example, if a column of two white pieces jumps over a column of two black pieces, the guide of the black column is added to the bottom of the white column. The other black piece which was on the bottom of its column remains on its original square. If the white column in this example was guided by an officer then it could jump back over the remaining black piece, adding it to the bottom of its column and ending up on its original square.

TIP

The best way to take your opponent's pieces is to let him jump over one of yours, and then jump over the new column yourself. In this way, he loses a piece and you do not lose any. You can determine how you are getting on in the game by seeing how many columns each player has. You can then work out how these numbers will change after a particular set of moves.

•

It is only the top piece of the column that is taken by a soldier and this means that the next piece becomes the guide of the column left behind. You should also try to remember which of your columns have got your opponent's officers in them. It is possible for you to capture one of his soldier columns and leave behind one of his officers, which would win the game for him. Of course, you might capture one of his columns and leave behind one of your own officers.

•

A player who is in a position to capture an enemy piece must do so, and if he can capture several enemy pieces one after the other in the same move, he must take them all. If he has a choice of capturing moves, he can choose the one he wants to take. A move ends when no more pieces can be captured or when a soldier reaches the far end of the board and becomes an officer.

The objective of the game, to make it impossible for one's opponent to move, is achieved either by having all the columns guided by a player's own pieces, or by blocking the remaining enemy columns so that they cannot move.

MAH-JONGG

Mah-Jongg is a tile game which is far simpler to play than its appearance suggests, but its subtleties make it a fascinating game to study in depth. Its name means 'the sparrows'.

COMPLEXITY RATING:	★ ★ ★
NUMBER OF PLAYERS:	4 is best, but the game can be played by 3

Equipment: A Mah-Jongg set is made up of 144 tiles (described below), four tile racks, tallies for scoring, a wind indicator and two dice. Among the 'playing tiles', there are 34 different designs, and since there are four identical tiles of each design, there is a total of 136 playing tiles. The other eight are 'bonus tiles' which are all different. The set is made up in this way:

The Circle Suit	Composed of tiles numbered from 1 to 9, with four tiles of each number	36 tiles

The Bamboo Suit	Composed of tiles numbered from 1 to 9 with four tiles of each number	36 tiles
The Character Suit	Composed of tiles numbered from 1 to 9, with four tiles of each number	36 tiles
The Winds	Four 'East' Four 'South' Four 'West' Four 'North'	16 tiles
The Dragons	Four 'White' Four 'Green' Four 'Red'	12 tiles
The Flowers	One 'Plum' One 'Orchid' One 'Chrysanthemum' One 'Bamboo'	4 tiles
The Seasons	One 'Spring' One 'Summer' One 'Autumn' One 'Winter'	4 tiles
	Total	144 tiles

The circles represent cash, the bamboos strings of cash, and the characters cash in multiples of 10,000. Each suit has nine values, usually marked 1 to 9 in arabic numerals. There are four tiles of each value, making 36 tiles in each suit or 108 in all three.

The suits are illustrated below:

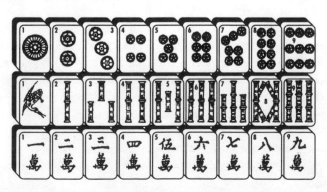

The 1 of the bamboos is a rice-bird, or sometimes a bamboo shoot, and the rest of the tiles are regular in appearance. The 1s and 9s of each suit are known as terminals and rank higher than other tiles in the suits, which are known as simples. Among the suit tiles, the 2, 3, 4, 6 and 8 are always green and this is important in the game.

The honour tiles are dragons and winds. There are three dragons, called Red, White and Green. The red and green dragons are shown in their respective colours, while the white dragon is a blank tile. Many sets have extra blank tiles which are replacements, not extra white dragons.

Of the four winds, East Wind takes precedence. The seven honour tiles are shown below:

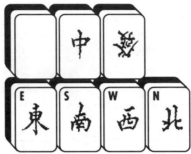

Honour tiles and terminals are often referred to as major tiles.

The eight bonus tiles represent flowers and the seasons, and display individual designs. They are also numbered consecutively in red (seasons) and in blue or green (flowers). They are not actually used in play, but represent a bonus for the holder. They are numbered consecutively in red for the seasons, and in blue or green for the flowers.

Seasons	Flowers
1 Spring	1 Plum
2 Summer	2 Orchid
3 Autumn	3 Chrysanthemum
4 Winter	4 Bamboo

While it is possible to record the scores with paper and pencil, it is traditional and convenient to use tallies, thin flat lengths of plastic. The normal practice is to use four denominations valued at 500, 100, 10 and 2 points, and to give each player two 500s, nine 100s, eight 10s and ten 2s, making 2,000 points in all. The 500s are marked with five red dots, the 100s with one red dot, the 10s with ten black dots and the 2s with two black dots.

Sets sometimes include four direction discs, showing the same symbols as the wind tiles.

Time required: A complete game, made up of a number of hands, may take from one to three hours for the Chinese, but among Westerners, they can last from four to five hours. Because of this, it is quite permissible to agree to play a fixed number of hands, or for a certain length of time rather than completing a game.

Origins: Mah-Jongg is of Chinese origins, and was brought to the West in the 1920s by an American, Joseph Babcock. He drew up a set of rules for western play retaining many of the features of the Chinese game, and added other ideas from western games. Mah-Jongg became enormously popular in the West, but became unnecessarily complicated when many of the Chinese practices not incorporated in Babcock's version were introduced as more research was carried out on the original Chinese game.

Aim of the game: Each player plays for himself, collecting sets of tiles with the object of completing their hand in a prescribed manner. The different types of sets each have a predetermined scoring value, and scores are determined after each hand.

The final winner is not necessarily the player who has won the greatest number of individual hands, but the one who has amassed the most points in the course of the settlements with his opponents after each hand. Some winning, and some losing, hands are much more valuable than others.

It is important that players should master the principles involved in the scoring of hands as early as possible. No grasp of the strategy and tactics of the game is possible unless a player has an idea of the potential scores of his hand, and those of his opponents.

•

Basic rules: Each player takes on the identity of a wind. For the first hand, this is decided after the players are seated, when each player takes it in turn to throw two dice. The player with the highest total becomes East. The other players' winds are decided by their position at the table relative to East which is the main wind, and the player of the East takes a dominating position in the first round. Each player in turn is East or Leader, and retains this title as long as he wins the hand (that is, obtains Mah-Jongg). Seating does not follow the compass points – the positions of East and West are reversed so that East has South on his right and North on his left. If the player who is the East wind wins a hand, the players retain the same winds for the next hand.

When one of the players other than East wins, the player on East's right (South) receives the title of East for the next hand. The player who was West becomes South, the former North becomes West, and the former East becomes North. When each of the four players has been East, and the fourth has given it up after losing a hand, one round has been completed. Each complete game usually consists of four rounds.

The first is named the East round when East prevails, the second is the South round and South prevails. Then comes the West round and then the North. The players need to remember which wind prevails because this affects the scoring.

To start the game, the tiles, including bonus tiles, are shuffled or washed, face down on the table, but East does not take part. Then, without looking at the tiles' faces, each player builds a wall that is 18 tiles long and two tiles high (with the long side of the tiles touching and the faces down). Each wall is then pushed towards the centre of the table so they form a hollow square like a Chinese city wall.

When the wall is built, it is breached. East throws two dice, and counts round the walls anti-clockwise, beginning with himself as one until he reaches the number shown. Therefore, a total of 2, 6 or 10 indicates South, 3, 7 or 11 is West, 4, 8 or 12 is North and 5 or 9 indicates East himself.

The player whose wall is to be breached then throws the two dice and adds his total to the total previously thrown by East. the player then counts clockwise along the top of his tiles beginning at the right hand corner. If the total is more than 18, he continues along the next wall. He breaches the wall by removing the stack of two tiles indicated by the total count, and places them on top of the wall to the right of the breach. These two tiles are known as the 'loose tiles', and it is normal to place one on top of the third stack to the right of the first breach, and the other on top of the fifth stack. The tile which was on the top is placed furthest away. When a player needs to draw a loose tile, he should take the tile further from the first breach.

If both loose tiles are drawn, they are replaced by taking the stack of tiles from the left-hand end of the box, the uppermost tile being placed furthest away. This can continue until the kong box is empty, but no tiles are taken from the live wall to replace them.

A broken wall, with the kong box separated, is shown below:

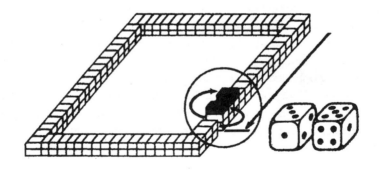

The order of play begins with East taking the first two stacks of tiles from the open end of the live wall, immediately to the left of the first breach. South, West and then North take two stacks each, until all players have 12 tiles. East then draws a pair of tiles and the other players one each in turn. The tiles are placed on racks so that they can be counted by opponents, but the faces are kept out of sight of other players.

The idea is to collect four sets, each of three or four tiles, and a pair. The first player to do this announces 'Mah-Jongg', and the game ends and scores are determined.

There are three types of sets: the pong, the kong and the chow. These are three tiles of the same kind, four of the same kind and a run of three such as 5, 6 and 7 of circles. Pongs and kongs can be suit or honour tiles, but a chow can only be made up of suit tiles. The sets are shown below:

North	North	North
	pong	

9 bamboo	9 bamboo	9 bamboo
	kong	

5 circles	6 circles	7 circles
	chow	

ACTUAL PLAY

Players begin by declaring their bonus tiles (starting with East) by placing them face-up on the table in front of them and drawing replacements from the kong box. If at any stage during play a bonus tile is drawn from the wall, it is declared and replaced with a loose tile. East may declare any kong he holds if he wishes. If he does, he places the tiles on the table, the two end tiles down to show that the kong was concealed from hand, and a loose tile is taken from the kong box for every kong declared.

The other players do the same, and East then discards any tile from his hand, placing it face up in the centre of the table and announcing it. Discarded tiles may be claimed by any other player to complete a pong or a kong, or for a Mah-Jongg. If so, he announces it and adds it to the set in front of him. The tiles must be face up to show that the set includes a discard, or is 'exposed'. The player then discards and the player on his right then has his turn.

If the discard is not wanted for a pong, kong or Mah-Jongg, then the next player can claim the tile to complete a chow which is then exposed, and the turn passes on to the next person on the right. A discard cannot be picked up to complete a set or to go Mah-Jongg. All discards, except the last, are deemed dead and cannot be claimed for any purpose.

With most hands, the tiles that should be discarded early in the game are determined by a number of considerations: you should throw out as soon as you can single tiles of winds (although not your own wind), single terminals, ones and nines.

At this time in the game the chance that they can be purged or chowed by your opponents is at its lowest; after terminals, you should discard twos and eights, while threes and sevens are borderline cases.

The best suit tiles to keep are the middle series, fours, fives and sixes because they are best placed for improvement (chow) from the draw.

•

You should also keep pairs, and two tiles of the same suit in sequence. With two-tile sequences you should also keep any tiles which are one or even two ranks away such as 3–4–6 or 3–4–7.

•

Every discard gives information about the state of the game, and as they are on display, they give more and more information about the game as it progresses. This should help to assess the chances of drawing a particular tile from the wall, and to get an idea of the make-up of the opponents' hands.

•

When a discard is not claimed, the next player takes the first tile from the live wall. A bonus tile, or one that completes a kong is declared, and a loose tile is taken from the kong box to replace it. This serves to balance the number of tiles held as Mah-Jongg requires four sets and a pair. Mah-Jongg could be achieved with a maximum of 18 tiles (4 kongs and a pair), and a minimum of 14, as the player who goes Mah-Jongg does not discard.

A player with an exposed pong can convert it to an exposed kong by drawing the fourth tile from the wall when a loose tile is drawn in the normal way, but not by claiming a discard. A player with a concealed pong does not declare it unless he converts it into a concealed or exposed kong.

A player who needs just one tile to complete his hand is said to be 'calling' or 'fishing'. If two players are calling, and both claim the same tile, precedence goes to the player whose turn would have come first.

If a player who has previously made an exposed pong, should draw the fourth identical tile from the wall and add it to the pong to convert it to a kong, and if another player should be calling that tile, that player may declare Mah-Jongg and 'rob the kong', taking the fourth tile as though it had been discarded, and adding it to his hand.

SPECIAL LIMIT HANDS

Certain Mah-Jongg hands are known as special limit hands, or full hands which, in a limited game are valued at the limit, irrespective of their actual score. In a game with no limit on the score, it is necessary for the players to agree in advance on a notional value for such special hands. The number of these hands has grown, and it is suggested that only an agreed number be allowed. They could include any of these:

1) Heaven's blessing If East finds that after taking any replacements for bonus tiles, and loose tiles for kongs, his original dealt hand is complete, he scores a full hand.

2) Earth's blessing If South, West or North hold a calling hand at the beginning of play, and Mah-Jonggs on East's first discard, he scores a full hand.

3) Gathering Plum Blossom from the Roof If a player completes his hand by drawing a five circle from the kong box, he scores a full hand.

4) Catching the Moon at the Bottom of the Sea If the last tile in the live wall is a one circle, and a player completes his hand in drawing it, he scores a full hand.

5) Scratching a Carrying Pole If a player completes his hand by robbing a kong of two bamboos, he scores a full hand.

6) Fourfold Plenty A hand which contains four kongs, exposed or concealed, and a pair of any tiles, is a full hand.

7) Buried Treasure A hand which contains four concealed pongs, and in which the last tile is drawn from the wall, is a full hand.

8) Three Great Scholars A hand which contains a set of each of the dragons, another pong or kong, and any pair, is a full hand.

9) Four Joys in Full or Four Blessings Hovering over the Door A hand which contains a set of each of the four winds, plus any pair, is a full hand.

10) All Symbols A complete hand composed entirely of honour tiles is a full hand

11) Heads and Tails A complete hand composed entirely of ones and nines is a full hand.

12) Imperial Jade A complete hand composed entirely of all-green tiles is a full hand. The all-green tiles are the 2, 3, 4, 6 and 8 bamboo and the Green Dragon.

13) The Wriggling Snake A clear suit hand which consists of a set of 1s, a set of 9s, a pair of 2s, 5s or 8s, and two sequences made up of the missing numbers is a full hand.

14) Thirteen Grades of Imperial Treasures or the Thirteen Unique Wonders A hand containing one of each of the thirteen major tiles (one of each 1 and one of each 9 from the suits, one of each wind and one of each dragon), plus a fourteenth tile which forms a pair with any one of them is a full hand.

SCORING

Scoring is carried out according to the table of values overleaf. The player who went Mah-Jongg is paid by the other players in turn, and they then settle between themselves according to the differences between their respective scores. At all times, East pays and receives double.

In calculating the score of a hand, points are first awarded in respect of the various sets and other elements which the hand may contain. These points are added together to give the basic score which may be doubled progressively for each of certain combinations which the hand may contain, and for each of certain conditions which it may satisfy. The final result is the total score.

Scoring table

Basic score		Doubles
Pairs		One double of basic score for each of the following:
Dragons	2 points	
Player's Wind	2 points	Mah-Jongg hand only
Prevailing wind	2 points	All chows
Player's wind		
if prevailing wind	4 points	No chows
		All sets concealed
Sets		One-suit hand (one suit and honour tiles only)
Pong (exposed):		Robbing the kong
Honours or terminals	16 points	
Simples	2 points	All hands
Kong (exposed):		Pong or kong of following:
Honours or terminals	16 points	Dragons
Simples	8 points	Player's wind
		Prevailing wind
Pong or kong	double	Player's flower and season
(concealed):	above	(pair)
	points	Set of flowers (4)
		Set of seasons (4)
Bonus tiles		Special hands
Flower or season	4 points	A limit
Players going Mah-Jongg		
Going Mah-Jongg	10 points	
Final tile from wall	2 points	
Mah-Jongg with only		
possible tile	2 points	

GENERAL TIPS

In playing Mah-Jongg, three things should be kept in mind: i) you should try to complete your hand as quickly as possible, ii) you should block your opponents by keeping tiles that they will find useful, and iii) you should try to build up a hand with a large count. However, do not concentrate on the third which is a trap many beginners fall into. The more expert you become, the more you will find that it pays to place greater emphasis on the first two elements.

•

MANCALA

Mancala has often been called the national game of Africa. It is the generic name for hundreds of games in which seeds are moved from cup to cup around a board in an attempt to capture opposing seeds. Names, rules and equipment vary from area to area, but the basic principles are much the same. One of the best known Mancala games is **Wari**. The strategy of these games is highly complex, and the best possible moves are determined by mathematical calculation.

COMPLEXITY RATING:	★ ★ ★
NUMBER OF PLAYERS:	2
EQUIPMENT:	**Board and 48 counters or seeds. The board may be a wooden dish with two rows of six shallow cups carved in it, or similar rows of depressions scooped out of the earth, or two rows of six 'holes' drawn on it. Boards have larger cups at each end to store capture seeds. The original counters were seeds or small stones, but coins, buttons or any other small objects may be used.**
TIME REQUIRED:	**20 to 45 minutes**

Origins: Mancala games are very old. There is some evidence from temple carvings that the games were played at least 3,000 years ago in Egypt. Today versions are played all over Asia and Africa, and throughout the Levant. They were also introduced to America by African slaves, and they have continued to be popular there.

Aim of the game: The simple object is to win all of your opponent's seeds by distributing your own, according to the rules, to capture and remove them.

Basic rules: At the start of the game, four seeds are placed in each cup. The players sit on either side of the board, and the six holes nearest to each player form his row. Players draw lots to start, and the first player begins by picking up the four seeds from any hole in his row, and 'sowing' them one by one, in a clockwise or anti-clockwise direction, in the next four holes. The direction of play is a matter of choice, but both players must continue in the same direction for the whole game.

The other player then takes the seeds from any hole in his row, and sows them one by one in the same direction. And so the game continues, each player in turn sowing the seeds from any one of the holes in his row.

If in any player's turn the last seed to be sown goes into one of his opponent's holes, and that hole now contains either two or three seeds, then he wins all the seeds in that hole, and removes them from the board. He also wins the seeds in any adjacent holes that contain either two or three seeds.

Right from the start, the trick of this game is to keep a constant watch on the number of seeds in your opponent's cups, to see which of your cups he threatens. You also need to check your own cups to see whether any has the correct number to capture your opponent's seeds. You will obviously need to prevent your opponent from capturing your seeds, and take advantage of any opportunities which are presented to you. On occasions you will have to make a choice between allowing him to capture some of your seeds, if it means being able to take some of his. If the result is an equal share out of seeds, whether you proceed with the move may be determined by whether you have already captured the most seeds.

If you have three cups in a row with one or two seeds in them, check your opponent's cups to see if he has sufficient seeds to endanger any of yours. If so, use your turn to move the threatened seeds, even if it means missing the opportunity to capture one of your opponent's seeds.

If any of the first few of your opponent's cups are empty, try to sow seeds in them to set up a possible capture in your next move.

If you have a single seed, try to move it into an adjoining cup if it already has three or more seeds. This will prevent it being captured.

If, during the course of a game, a hole contains twelve or more seeds, then a sowing from that hole will take more than one complete circuit of the board. When this happens, the original hole from which the twelve or more seeds were taken is left empty and it stays empty for the remainder of the game.

If a player has no seeds left in his row when it is his turn then the game is over, unless his opponent is able to sow further seeds on the empty side. He must do so if it is possible, leaving at least one seed in the empty row. If he cannot do so, the game is finished and he takes all the seeds left on the board and adds them to those he has already won.

If, towards the end of the game, the majority of seeds are on your side, avoid sowing seeds on your opponent's side. Skilfully done, this will reduce his options forcing him to sow on your side, gradually emptying his cups, and finally leaving him with no further moves.

•

If your opponent's row is empty and you have a choice of moves, make one which puts fewest seeds in his row.

•

Keep an eye on how many seeds you have captured. If you have 25, you have won and the game ends. The game may also end by agreement if the seeds are just being moved round the board with neither player being able to win any more. In that case, each player takes the seeds from his own row, and adds them to the seeds he has won, and the player with the greatest number is the winner.

MANCALA VARIATIONS

Ba-Awa: In this game, the first player lifts four seeds from one of his holes and sows them anti-clockwise. Where the last seed falls, he lifts and sows those seeds. This continues until the last bean falls in an empty hole when the turn ends.

The second player now starts from any of his holes. From now on, if any seed makes a hole up to four, the owner of the hole immediately transfers them to his store. If the last seed makes up a four, the turn then ends.

The last eight seeds are taken by the player who started. The beans are replaced four to a hole. The one with the most captures any holes he fills besides his own.

The second player now starts. The player who gets all the beans wins.

Lontu-holo: Each player owns the six holes in the half of the board to his left. Each has 24 seeds as shown in the diagram. The object for each player is to transfer all seeds to his opponent's half.

The first player lifts any of his cups and sows the beans round his half of the board. That cup is then missed out in the sowing. If the final seed makes up a four, the seeds are swapped to any opponent cup, along with other fours in an unbroken sequence, clockwise.

The player who gets rid of all his beans is the winner.

MU-TORERE

Mu-torere is a simple Maori game from New Zealand. It takes just a few minutes to learn, but can be quite a challenging and fascinating game.

COMPLEXITY RATING:	★ ★
NUMBER OF PLAYERS:	2
EQUIPMENT:	**Board and 8 counters**
TIME REQUIRED:	**10 to 15 minutes**

Origins: Mu-torere is the only known board game of Maori origin.

Aim of the game: The objective is to block your opponent so that he cannot move. The first player to do this is the winner.

Basic rules: The board consists of an eight-pointed star with a circle in the middle.

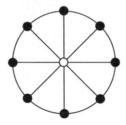

The eight points are known as the 'kewai', and the circle is called the 'putahi'. Each player starts with four counters, placed on four adjacent kewai. The players move alternately, with black having the first move.

There are three types of move:

i) a counter may be moved from one of the kewai to the putahi, but only if there is one of the opponent's counters on one (or both) of the kewai on either side of it.

ii) a counter may be moved from the putahi to any of the kewai.

iii) a counter may be moved from any of the kewai to the next on either side.

All the moves are subject to the rule that the point being moved to must be unoccupied – only one counter is allowed on each point.

For the first two moves each, you can move only to the centre a piece that is next to an enemy piece.

Try to work out the winning positions before you start. The scope for strategy might seem rather limited – a player's move is often forced and he has at other times a choice of only two moves.

NINE MEN'S MORRIS

Nine Men's Morris is one of the great old games of strategy.

COMPLEXITY RATING:	★ ★
NUMBER OF PLAYERS:	2
EQUIPMENT:	**Board; 18 counters**
TIME REQUIRED:	**20 to 30 minutes**

Origins: Nine Men's Morris is an ancient Egyptian game, found in a temple dating back to about 1400 BC. It has also been found as far away as Sri Lanka and Iceland. It has many other names, including Mill, Morelles, Merelles and Merels. It was very popular in Europe in the Middle Ages, and often played outdoors with the field of play marked on turf using stones. Shakespeare referred to this in 'A Midsummer Night's Dream':

> *The nine men's morris is fill'd up with mud*
> *And the quaint mazes in the wanton green*
> *For lack of tread are indistinguishable.*

Boards for the game have even been found carved into the medieval furniture of Westminster Abbey in London. Morris comes from Moorish, and was the name of a square dance which the game was said to resemble.

Aim of the game: Each player has nine counters of a different colour to those of his opponent, and attempts to capture or to block his opponent's pieces.

Basic rules: The game is played on a square board like this with lines forming 24 points of intersection:

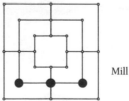

Mill

The board is empty to start with, and players draw lots with black usually starting. Each player in turn then places one of his men on any vacant point on the board. The objective is to get three men in a row along any line, to form a 'mill' – and to prevent your opponent from doing so. Each time a player forms a mill, he is able to pound or remove from the board any one of his opponent's pieces – except one which forms part of a mill, unless there is none other available.

After both players have placed all their men on the board they continue to play alternately, now moving one man at a time along a line to any adjacent point that is empty in an attempt to form further mills. As before, forming a mill entitles a player to remove one of his opponent's men from the board. A mill can be broken in one move by moving a man away, and reformed in the next to capture one of your opponent's men.

The diagram above shows an ideal position for this.

•

If as the game continues, a player is unable to move, the second player continues to do so until the first player is free to move again, at which point the turn alternates.

A further phase is reached when one player is reduced to three men. When this happens, these men become rovers, and can be moved to any vacant point, not just an adjacent one. The game is lost by the first player to be reduced to two men.

There is some argument about the merit of allowing the rover phase of the game. It does mean that the advantage of the game can change quite dramatically in favour of the player who had been losing up to that point, ie the one who has the rovers. It also means that the players will eventually face each other with three men each, and the advantage is then likely to rest with the player who was first reduced to three men. For these reasons, many players do not allow the rover rule.

There are two types of move: the attack which tries to make a mill, and the defence which tries to prevent the opponent from doing so. Sometimes a defensive move can prove to be an attacking one, thereby switching the initiative.

Gaining the initiative is important in this game, and black, which starts, can have a considerable initial advantage.

•

As a general rule, it is usually best to try to group your men rather than allow them to be scattered around the board.

•

In the rover game, it is a good idea not to reduce your opponent to three men (allowing them to become rovers, and to take on a decided advantage) unless

you are at least five men ahead, or are sure of making a mill and in a position to force a win.

•

NINE MEN'S MORRIS VARIATIONS

Three Men's Morris: This is a simpler game for two players, and the board is marked out like this:

Each player has four counters of his own colour, and they take it in turns to put one man on a point of intersection in an attempt to form a mill. The first player to achieve this is the winner.

Six Men's Morris: This game is played in much the same way as Nine Men's Morris, but using a board marked out like this:

Players each have six counters and take it in turns to place them, one at a time, on the board. The object is to form a mill along one of the sides of either of the squares. If a player succeeds in doing this, he may pound his opponent.

As in Nine Men's Morris, when all the men have been played onto the board, the game continues with players moving their men to form new mills. When a player is reduced to just two men, he has lost the game.

REVERSI

Reversi is a game of strategy in which fortunes can change frequently.

COMPLEXITY RATING:	★ ★ ★
NUMBER OF PLAYERS:	2
EQUIPMENT:	Board of 64 squares and 64 pieces (coloured white on one side and black on the other
TIME REQUIRED:	30 minutes to 1 hour

Origins: The game was invented in the 1880s, but was then the subject of a bitter dispute between two men who each claimed the royalties. After declining in popularity it has recently been revived.

Aim of the game: The game ends when there is a piece on every square, and the winner is the player who has most pieces of his colour face upwards.

Basic rules: One player takes 32 pieces and turns them white-side up. The other turns his pieces black-side up. Players draw lots to decide who has black, and he leads by putting one of his pieces on one of the four middle squares. White then follows by putting one of his pieces on a middle square. Turns alternate until all four middle squares are filled.

◆ TIP ▶

The best players start by placing their pieces in this way, but you do not necessarily need to do so.

•

After the central squares have been filled, the players continue to take it in turns to play. However each move has to be a taking move, and a player who cannot make a taking move loses his turn until he can take. A taking move is made by placing a piece so that:

i) it is in a square next to one containing an opposition piece; and

ii) it traps one or more opposition pieces between itself and another of the player's own pieces in a straight line – horizontally, vertically or diagonally – with no empty spaces in between. It is often possible in one move to take several pieces in different lines simultaneously.

In this example, blacks could be placed in any of the squares marked B, and whites in those marked W to take opposition pieces.

When a piece is taken, it is turned over to show the other player's colour. A piece may be turned over many times during a game as it is captured and recaptured. Pieces are not removed from the board at any time, nor do they move squares after being placed.

If a player captures more than one line of his opponent's pieces, and more than one piece they are all turned over.

For example, if black plays on the shaded square he will capture six pieces – a line of one, a line of two and a line of three.

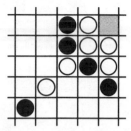

When pieces are turned over, they sometimes complete a line. No pieces are captured in this way because pieces can be captured only by a player putting down a piece in his turn.

In Reversi it is best to stay inside the central sixteen squares as long as possible, and the best squares to use are those on the long diagonals (the corner squares of the central block of sixteen). The first player to have to go outside the central squares is at a disadvantage in the rest of the game.

•

Outside the central block the most valuable squares are those at the corners, and the ones next but one along from them on the edge of the board. You should try to capture these squares yourself, or at least prevent your opponent from getting them.

•

You should avoid using the squares marked A in the diagram below.

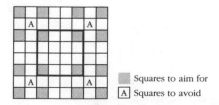

Squares to aim for
A Squares to avoid

REVERSI VARIATION

Players who find the normal board too big can play the game on a 4 × 4 or 6 × 6 board with 16 or 36 pieces. In both forms, players generally still place the first four pieces in the middle four squares.

SOLITAIRE BOARD GAMES

Solitaire board games are enjoyable and popular games for one person. There are a number of variations.

COMPLEXITY RATING:	★ ★
NUMBER OF PLAYERS:	1
TIME REQUIRED:	10–20 minutes

Equipment required: Solitaire is played with a special board and a set of pegs or marbles. The traditional French board is octagonal, and has 37 holes for the same number of marbles.

Traditional English boards are circular or square and have 33 holes for the same number of marbles. Some games need all the pieces, while others need only a certain number.

The boards are shown below, numbered to allow the solutions to be given.

English

```
        1   2   3
        o   o   o
        4   5   6
        o   o   o
7   8   9  10  11  12  13
o   o   o   o   o   o   o
14  15  16  17  18  19  20
o   o   o   o   o   o   o
21  22  23  24  25  26  27
o   o   o   o   o   o   o
        28  29  30
        o   o   o
        31  32  33
        o   o   o
```

French

```
        1   2   3
        o   o   o
    4   5   6   7   8
    o   o   o   o   o
9  10  11  12  13  14  15
o   o   o   o   o   o   o
16 17  18  19  20  21  22
o   o   o   o   o   o   o
23 24  25  26  27  28  29
o   o   o   o   o   o   o
    30  31  32  33  34
    o   o   o   o   o
        35  36  37
        o   o   o
```

Origins: Board Solitaire originated in France where it is said that it was devised by an imprisoned aristocrat in the 18th century. It was introduced to England soon after by French emigres, and has since spread to other parts of the world.

Aim of the game: In some Solitaire games, the idea is to clear the board of all but one piece, while in others the player tries to place the pieces in a certain pattern.

Basic rules: Pieces are moved in the same manner in all Solitaire games – either horizontally or vertically over an adjoining piece to an empty hole beyond. The piece which has been jumped is removed from the board. The game is won only if the final objective is achieved exactly. For example, the standard game is won only if the board has been completely cleared of all but one of the pieces, and with that piece in the centre or another specified hole decided at the start. Some games can be won by more than one method, but a player may have to make numerous attempts to work out the solution.

STANDARD SOLITAIRE

Played on an English board, the game starts from the centre after the middle piece has been removed.

To ensure that no piece is left isolated, try to ensure a methodical clearance working around the sections, and then towards the middle (or finishing point or points). Make a note of every move so that you can see how you went wrong when you come to look at the solution provided below.

Solution (English):
First clear the north section, except for 4.
5–17 (taking 10), 12–10. 3–11, 1–3, 18–6, 3–11.
Then clear the east section, leaving 19.
30–18, 27–25, 13–27, 24–26, 27–25.
Then south, leaving 29.
22–24, 31–23, 33–31, 16–28, 31–23.
Then west, leaving 15.
4–16, 7–9, 21–7, 10–8, 7–9.
Then move 24 six times to 22, 8, 10, 12, 26, 24.
Finally, clear the T you have left.
17–15, 29–17, 18–16, 15–17.

SOLITAIRE VARIATIONS

The game has a number of variations, particularly for the French board. Here are some of the better known versions which all begin with all pieces in position. The central piece is then removed and the player tries to end the game with these patterns:

The World:
Solution:
32–19,30–32, 17–30, 28–26, 25–27, 14–28, 43–21, 32–34, 4–17, 6–4, 18–5, 13–11, 5–18, 27–13, 7–20.

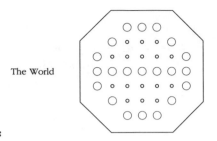

The World

The Apostles:

Solution:

32–19, 28–26, 37–27, 35–37, 25–35, 27–25, 24–26, 11–25, 25–27, 16–18, 19–17, 6–19, 4–6, 17–4, 2–12, 8–6, 2–7, 6–8, 22–20, 15–13, 12–14, 27–13, 13–15.

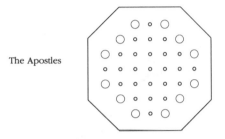

The Apostles

The Cross:

This can be played on either the English or French board with nine pieces, positioned as shown. The idea is to remove eight of the nine pieces, leaving one in the centre.

Solution:

English

10–4, 24–10, 15–17, 17–5, 19–17, 4–10, 10–24, 29–17.

French

12–2, 26–2, 17–19, 19–6, 21–19,2–12, 12–26, 32–19.

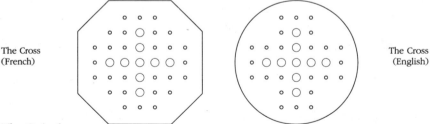

The Cross
(French)

The Cross
(English)

The Corsair:

At the start, the 37 holes of a French board are filled, and any one peg at the angle of the board is then removed (ie 1, 3, 15, 29, 37, 35, 23 or 9). The object is to remove all pieces except one, and that should end up in the hole diametrically opposite the empty hole at the start.

Solution: 35–37, 26–36, 25–35, 23–25, 34–32, 20–33, 37–27, 7–20, 20–33, 18–31, 35–25, 5–18, 18–31, 29–27, 22–20, 15–13, 16–18, 9–11, 20–7, 7–5, 4–6, 18–5, 1–11, 33–20, 20–18, 18–5, 5–7, 36–26, 30–32, 32–19, 19–6, 2–12, 8–6, 12–2, 3–1.

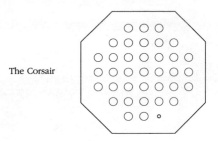

The Corsair

The Octagon:

Also played on a French board, all the holes are filled except those at the angle of the board (ie not 1, 3, 15, 29, 37, 35, 23 and 9). The player ends the game with only one piece left, in the centre of the board.

Solution: 27–37, 31–33, 37–27, 20–33, 22–20, 19–32, 33–31, 30–32, 36–26, 17–30, 26–24, 30–17, 34–21, 21–19, 18–20, 16–18, 8–21, 21–19, 7–20,11–25, 20–18, 25–11, 11–13, 2–12, 13–11, 10–12, 4–6, 6–19.

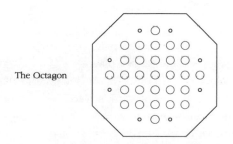

The Octagon

CLUEDO

Cluedo* is a game based on the popularity of murder mysteries, and involves a combination of questioning and deduction.

Origins: Cluedo was established in Britain in the great tradition of the British murder mystery story.

Aim of the game: Each player attempts to solve a murder which has taken place in a large house. Players move their pieces round the board from room to room, and by a process of questioning other players and deduction, they try to discover the murderer, the murder weapon and the scene of the crime. The first to do so is the winner.

Basic rules: The playing tokens are placed on the starting squares marked for them on the board. The colours indicate the name of the piece: yellow is Colonel Mustard, purple is Professor Plum, green is the Reverend Green, blue Mrs Peacock, red Miss

* *Cluedo® is the registered trade mark of Waddingtons Games Ltd.*

COMPLEXITY RATING:	★ ★
NUMBER OF PLAYERS:	**2 to 6**
EQUIPMENT:	**Board showing the ground floor plan of a house; six playing tokens; six tokens representing weapons; 21 playing cards representing six people in the house, six weapons and the nine rooms shown on the board; an envelope marked 'murder cards'; 'detective notes' cards to enable players to record the details of their investigations; and two dice.**
TIME REQUIRED:	**30 to 60 minutes**

Scarlett, and white is Mrs White. If fewer than six play, the spare pieces are still used, and placed in any room or rooms at the start of play.

The weapons are also each placed in a different room in no particular order. The nine room cards are then shuffled and one card is placed unseen in the 'murder envelope' in the centre of the board. The same process is repeated separately for the six weapon cards and the six person cards. The information on these cards remains a mystery until a player is able to make a correct deduction to win the game.

The remaining 18 cards are shuffled together and, without being shown to any player, are dealt to each person around the table. Some may receive more than others, according to how many are taking part. They will have a slight advantage, but not enough to distort the game.

Each player then adopts the playing piece nearest him, and for the rest of the game is that person irrespective of the cards he might hold. Miss Scarlett always moves first with that player shaking the dice and moving that number of squares along the passageway to any room the player chooses.

The next player on the left plays similarly, and is followed by all players in turn. When a player reaches a room, that person can then make a 'suggestion' by asking any other player, irrespective of where they are on the board, to come into the same room. In addition, the player whose turn it is can also bring into the room any weapon from anywhere on the board. For example, if the player with Miss Scarlet's token moves into the lounge, he might ask for Professor Plum's token to be moved there together with the dagger. 'Miss Scarlett' then says: 'I suggest the murder was committed in the lounge by Professor Plum with the dagger.' Any token can be called in, whether it is in the game as a playing piece or not.

TIP

Right from the start of the game, it is important to try to learn as much as possible by absorbing any information which you gain from your moves, or from what other players do. You can gradually eliminate from your suspicions people, weapons or possible murder sites, and finally come to the conclusion about the correct answers.

•

When a player makes a suggestion, the person on his left must look to see if he has one or more of those cards (in the example, Professor Plum, the lounge, or the dagger). If so, he must show one of them to the person who has made the suggestion. If the first player to the left does not have any of the cards, the enquiry passes on to the next person, and so on until someone has been able to show a card. When that happens, the first player's turn has ended, and play passes to the next person to the left. Each person plays in a similar manner until, by a process of elimination, someone eventually is able to name the three murder cards.

TIP

If you are the challenger (the person making the suggestion), and you are shown one of the cards you have named, that card is then eliminated from your enquiries, and you should note that on your detective notes cards. Remember though that the player who has revealed one card to you might well have another of the three, but does not have to reveal it in this turn. You can gradually build up a picture of what cards players do not have when they pass.

•

When a player is satisfied that he knows the three murder cards, he can in his turn make an accusation by writing the three names on his detective notes and checking his accusation by looking at the three murder cards in the envelope, making sure he does not show them to any other player.

TIP

You would normally do this after you have made a suggestion to each of the other players in turn, and none have shown you any one of the three cards you have named, and you do not hold them in your own hand.

•

If the accusation is correct, he turns the cards face up and shows his note to confirm his guess. He is the winner. If the accusation is not correct, the player replaces the three murder cards in the envelope without showing them to any other player. He has no further turns in the game, but remains to contradict any suggestions made by other players according to the cards in his hand.

If you are playing a series of games, and are behind in the total game score, you may feel you have nothing to lose in making an educated guess based on the information you already have to try to catch up.

One of the tactics of the game involves bluff suggestions by which a player can try to throw his opponents off the scent. You can suggest a person, weapon or room which you actually hold in your hand. In this way you may be able to satisfy yourself about the whereabouts of one card and at the same time mislead other players about a card you hold.

Players can enter rooms by the doors only, and cannot leave the room in the same move. In other words, entering the room ends the move. For example, if a player throws 6 and he needs just 3 to enter the room, he ignores the last 3 units after entering. No two players can occupy the same square, and a token cannot be moved through a square occupied by another piece.

A room, however, can be occupied by any number of pieces and weapons. A player can make a suggestion (which must always include three elements: room/person/weapon) on any of his turns to play, but his playing must be in the room involved in his suggestion. When playing tokens or weapons are moved to another room, they remain there and are not replaced in their original position afterwards. The next move will take place from the new room.

Secret passages on the board enable players to move their pieces in just one move from certain rooms to those shown on the board. This is done at a player's turn and represents a move without the need to throw the dice.

Take advantage of the secret passages as early in the game as you can, as this reduces the time you spend moving on the board, and the earlier you can start eliminating suspects from your list.

If it is discovered that a player has a card which he accidentally or otherwise failed to show to someone making a suggestion to him, he can have no further turns, and remains only to contradict suggestions.

Make very sure you do tell someone making a suggestion to you if you have one of the cards he names. If you do not you will eventually be found out, and will lose the game.

KENSINGTON

Kensington is a game of pure skill, but has a number of attractions for the casual player including the simplicity of its rules, and its appeal across wide age ranges.

COMPLEXITY RATING:	★ ★
NUMBER OF PLAYERS:	**2, 4 or 6 (but 2 is best for serious play, and this is the one described)**
EQUIPMENT:	**Board of interlocking hexagons and 30 pieces, 15 red and 15 blue.**
TIME REQUIRED:	**Games can last from 10 minutes to 3 hours, but a good average should be 20 to 30 minutes**

Origins: The game was created in the 1970s by two games inventors, Forbes and Taylor.

Aim of the game: Players place pieces on points of the board to try to take control of any of five hexagons. The first to do so is the winner.

Basic rules: The board is made up of seven interlocking hexagons shown in different colours. In the illustration overleaf, for ease of reference, the 72 points on the board are coded.

The first phase of the game starts with both players' pieces off the board, having drawn lots to start. Players then alternate in placing their pieces on the corner points of a triangle, square or hexagon until all the pieces are on the board.

At this stage, the majority of your moves should be constructive, rather than defensive. This means that you should be developing your pieces in your own or white squares with a view to forming triangles or squares. You also need to be defensive to some extent, or your opponent will begin forming triangles, squares and worse. However, too much effort spent on defensive placement will lead to a very negative game, and you will find it difficult to develop sufficiently to win.

•

A piece can only be placed on, or moved to, a corner point, and no point can be occupied by more than one piece. When a player occupies a point to take control

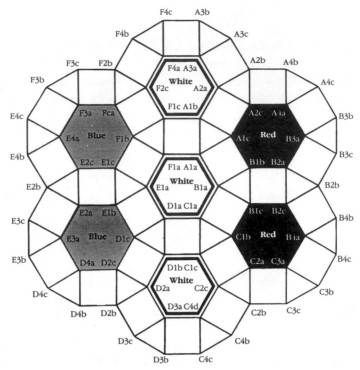

of all three points of a triangle, he can then move one of his opponent's pieces to any other unoccupied point.

When a player occupies a point to take control of all four points of a square, he can move two of his opponent's pieces to any two other unoccupied points. If a player occupies a point to take control of both a square and a triangle, he can still move only two of his opponent's pieces. The first player to take control of all six points of a white hexagon, or a hexagon of his own colour is the winner.

It is no great loss if your opponent does form an early triangle in the first phase, but you will need to take steps to block it before moving into the second or moving phase of the game.

•

Although it does not particularly matter if your opponent forms a triangle early in the game, you will need to watch for the threat of a 'fork'. For example, a game might start in this way:

	Blue	**Red**
1	D2a	C1b
2	D1c	

If red continues with his own plans (say B1b), then blue can play D1b (or D2a) which provides two threats – the opportunity to form a square by playing D2a or a triangle with D1a. In fact, red would probably play D2a, but blue would finish the triangle. The question to be asked is whether red should do everything possible to prevent blue forming both the square and the triangle. He would do this by making a second move to closely shadow red, but that would be at the expense of developing his own game.

•

―――――――――――――――― ◆ **TIP** ◆ ――――――――――――――――

When you form a triangle, move your opponent's most potentially dangerous piece to the furthest part of the board, ie well away from his other pieces. When you form a square, you can move two pieces, but make sure they are well separated when you place them.

•

―――――――――――――――― ◆ **TIP** ◆ ――――――――――――――――

When the placing of the pieces is nearing its end, it is important for you to avoid being in a position where it is easy for your opponent to reopen a triangle or square which he has formed earlier so he can remake it in the next move, and have the benefit of banishing one or two of your pieces to distant parts of the board. It is therefore important to do your best to 'block' such developments to prevent this. In the left-hand example below, where a square has been formed at 'A', your best move is to place pieces at points 1 and 2.

•

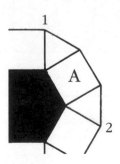 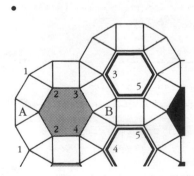

A triangle would need three pieces to block it and prevent it from being broken and reformed. Their placement depends on whether the triangle is on the edge of the hexagon, or on the inside. For the triangle marked A in the illustration on the right, you can block your opponent by placing pieces at either point marked 1 and both points marked 2. For the internal triangle marked B, you have more flexibility, and can block a triangle if it is reopened by having a piece on either of 3, 4 or 5.

In the second phase, each player takes it in turns to move one piece at a time along a line to an unoccupied adjacent point.

Once the moving phase starts, it is more dangerous to allow your opponent to make triangle or squares, because it is difficult to block the threatening triangle or square effectively. In addition, he has the immediate prospect of re-opening his completed figure with the next move with the idea of reforming it immediately, and sending another (or more) of your pieces to distant parts of the board. If you are the player to achieve this, it places you in a very strong position which can usually lead to a win.

•

While it is satisfying to scatter your opponent's pieces around the board, you must remember that the purpose of the game is to form a hexagon. One problem you may create for yourself by scattering your opponent's pieces is that you will soon run out of places to put his pieces because it is very easy for your opponent to start to run them together, like raindrops, forming triangles and possibly squares. If this happens, any progress you have made towards forming a hexagon may be reversed.

•

As you get close to forming a hexagon, you should generally try to consolidate your position by bringing pieces up in support, rather than forming triangles to move an opponent's piece.

•

If a player, in moving one or two of his opponent's pieces, completes a triangle or square for his opponent, the play goes ahead as though the opponent has made the square of triangle himself. Such a move would not be to the first player's advantage, but it may happen by accident, so it is worth keeping an eye open for such an eventuality.

•

If a player is not able to make a legal move, his opponent continues moving until the first player is able to do so again, or until the game is over.

KENSINGTON VARIATIONS

Kensington for four players The players form into two teams, with each team member having eight pieces in his team colour. Each member takes it in turns to play on each other's behalf, but may not consult during the game. The game is played to the rules for two players.

Kensington for six players The players form into two teams of three. Each member of the teams has a set of five pieces of his team colour. Each member takes it in turns to play on each other's behalf, but may not consult during the game. The game is played to the rules for two players.

MONOPOLY

Monopoly* is possibly the best-known and most popular board game of its kind in the world. It relies on luck in the throw of the dice, but is full of shrewd and amusing trading, and skill can often determine the final outcome.

COMPLEXITY RATING:	★ ★ ★
NUMBER OF PLAYERS:	**two or more, but best are four to six**
EQUIPMENT:	**Board, 2 dice, tokens, imitation bank notes, Chance and Community Chest cards, title deeds for each property, house and hotel tokens.**
TIME REQUIRED:	**Several hours, but can last much longer.**

Origins: During the past sixty years, a number of games have been invented to simulate life in a number of areas such as business or exploration. Monopoly is the best-known of these, having been invented in America in the mid-1930s. It has since become the highest-selling privately patented board game in history.

Aim of the game: Players buy and rent or sell property in order that they increase their assets. The wealthiest player becomes the eventual winner.

Basic rules: Monopoly is played on a board showing spaces indicating real estate properties (building sites), railway stations, public utilities such as water and electricity facilities, and rewards and penalties. At the beginning of the game, each

Monopoly® is the registered trade mark of Waddingtons Games for their Property Trading Game.

player is given £1,500, but the Banker (usually an elected player) holds all other equipment including money, property deeds and houses, not for his own use, but in trust for all the players.

Make sure you know all the rules of the game, because some players miss out on opportunities for making money by not doing so. Read the rules again from time to time to remind yourself of some of the more obscure benefits available.

•

The board produced in the United Kingdom looks like this, but property names vary in other countries:

Starting with the Banker, each player throws the dice, and the player with the highest total starts from the corner marked Go. Players follow the direction of the arrow, and move the number of spaces shown on the dice. A player may be entitled to buy the deeds for that site from the Banker, if it is still available, or gain any rewards or pay any penalties indicated. The object of owning property is to collect rent from opponents stopping there. If the site is owned already, the owner needs to claim the rent shown on the title deed. If the owner does not claim the rent before the next turn, he does not collect the rent. Rentals are greatly increased by the erection of houses and hotels. If a player throws double, he moves the appropriate number of squares, is subject to the penalties or privileges of that square, and then throws again. Each time a player passes Go, he collects £200 from the Banker, unless another instruction overrides this, eg a Community Chest instruction to 'go to jail without passing Go'.

Early in the game, you should consider carefully what property to acquire should the opportunity arise. A number of elements determine its real value to you: the probability of it being landed on by your opponents (there is a formula which determines this), the cost of the property, and the cost of building on it. By considering this information carefully, it is possible to grade the properties in order of desirability. The table below shows the most desirable at the top, and the least desirable at the bottom. It is worth memorising the following table to help you to choose which properties to acquire:

•

1. Light blue and orange groups
2. Crimson and red groups
3. Yellow and dark blue groups
4. Green and brown groups
5. Three or four railway stations
6. Two utilities

7. Two railway stations

8. One utility

9. One railway station

10. Single building sites (not in a complete group)

If a player lands on a square, and does not buy the property for whatever reason, the Banker must immediately offer the property for sale by auction, and must sell it to the highest bidder, and bidding may start at any price.

Try to acquire property you are interested in if you can, and start the bidding at a price much lower than shown on the board.

•

Watch each player's turn closely, checking where they land to see if you own the property so you can claim any rent due. Do not help other players to watch their properties.

•

Always keep an eye on your opponents' assets – how much cash they have, the properties they own, which ones they need to acquire to complete colour groups. You should be constantly aware of which player is in the strongest position, and who is the weakest.

•

The rules say you have to display your title deed cards so your opponents can see them. But they say nothing about displaying your money. So it is quite a good idea to keep some of your higher denomination notes out of sight (perhaps under a pile of £1 notes) so your opponents think you are less well off than you are. Beware though of your opponents doing this to you.

•

Try to calculate the probability of an opponent landing on your property. If there is a good chance that, in his next move, he could land on a property group you own, it might be a good time to erect a few extra buildings on the site. Similarly if you are heading for a high-rent group of properties owned by an opponent, it might be wise to defer any spending so you do not run short of cash to pay any rent.

If a player is unable to pay cash for rent due on one of your properties, try to negotiate the purchase of one of his properties, if it might be of value to you. If you have one of a set of three properties, and he has another, try to buy it perhaps at a discount. If you can complete a set with one that he has, it may be worth offering him more than the board price to acquire it.

•

When a player acquires a full collection of properties of one colour, he is initially entitled to build houses on those properties, although this must be done evenly among the properties, and for the full cost shown on the title deeds. Eventually, as shown on the title deed, he can build hotels on the properties in place of a full set of houses.

The advantage of owning houses and hotels rather than unimproved property is that rentals are very much higher, and the owner benefits enormously. It is therefore often a good idea to concentrate a good proportion of your finances on building whenever possible.

•

However, if you are unable to build immediately, remember that if you hold the title deeds of a complete colour group, you are entitled to charge double rent before any houses are built.

•

The biggest increase in rental always occurs when you erect the third house on each property. This is true for every colour group. To maximise your investment, always aim to build three houses on each site as quickly as possible.

•

If you own more than one colour group, it is nearly always better to develop the less expensive properties first. This is because you can buy more houses for the cheaper group than you can for an expensive group. The return on your investment is comparatively much better for several houses on a low-cost group than for fewer houses on a high-cost group.

•

If you are building on a number of sets of colour groups, and have already bought a number of houses, check to see if the bank is short of houses, and whether any other player is also building. If so, it is often a good idea to delay converting your own sites to hotels, because once the bank stock is exhausted, no other player can build until houses are returned to the bank.

•

If you have hotels on some sites, and your opponents are building houses, you can actually create a housing shortage by selling some of your hotels back to the bank in exchange for four houses. You will lose some rent, but this may be better than allowing your opponents to increase their rents by buying more houses.

•

A player goes to jail if his token lands on the space, 'Go to jail', or if he draws a card marked 'Go to jail', or if he throws doubles three times in succession. In the third case, he goes directly to jail, and does not land on the square indicated in the third throw. Unless he already has a Community Chest card which allows him to get out of jail immediately, a player usually stays in jail for three throws. He can, however, get out if he throws a double on any of the next three turns after landing in jail. If he does this, he immediately moves forward the number of spaces shown on the dice, carries out any transaction for that square, and then throws again as with any normal double throw. A player can also purchase a 'Get out of Jail Free' card from another player at a negotiated price, or he can pay a £50 fine before he throws the dice. After his third throw, a player must not remain in jail, and must pay a £50 fine.

Early in the game, a player loses valuable opportunities to buy property if he in jail, so it is worthwhile paying the fine as soon as possible. Later in the game, when all of the property has been bought, it does not matter if a player chooses to stay in jail because he can still buy and erect houses, buy and sell property, and collect rent. In fact, it could be an advantage because it means he is not landing on expensive property and having to pay rent.

•

IT'S A FACT...
*Since 1935 it is estimated that over
100 million Monopoly sets have
been sold.*

If a player is short of money he can mortgage property for the value printed on each title deed. To lift the mortgage, the player has to pay the original cost of the mortgage, plus 10 per cent interest. Houses and hotels cannot be mortgaged, but can be sold to the bank for half their price. To rebuild, a player has to buy the house back from the bank at full price after discharging any mortgage.

Later in the game, utilities and railway stations lose their value because they are not high rent properties. If you need to mortgage any property, look at any of these you own first.

•

A player who owes more than he can pay must turn over to his creditor all that he has of value and retire from the game. In making this settlement however, houses or hotels must be returned to the bank in exchange for half their cost, and this given to the creditor. If a bankrupt player turns over to his creditor property that has been mortgaged, the new owner must at once pay the bank the 10 per cent interest, and at his option lift the mortgage by paying the principal. The bank lends money only on mortgage security, and players may not borrow money or property from each other.

If a player cannot raise enough money to pay his taxes or penalties, even by selling his buildings and mortgaging his property, the bank will take over all his assets and, except for the buildings, sell by auction to the highest bidder. The player must then remove his token from the board. The last player left in the game wins.

There are three reasons for bidding for a property being sold by auction: you want the property; you want to prevent another player from getting it; you want to force up the bidding so that your opponent has to pay more than he would have without your intervention. In each case, be careful not to get carried away and end up bidding too much.

•

GENERAL TIP

It is always important to examine your financial situation before making any decisions such as buying property or buildings. You should always leave yourself enough cash to cover any expenses which might occur in the near future, including possible penalties from Chance and Community Chest. Take into account possible income, but never RELY on it. When assessing your cash reserve, you should consider cash you can raise by mortgaging such properties as single sites, single railway stations or utilities. Try to avoid being in the situation where you have to mortgage properties from complete colour groups, and above all, try to avoid having to sell buildings back to the bank.

•

IT'S A FACT...

*Apart from the relatively
commonplace underwater games,
Monopoly has been played upside
down, in tree houses,
underground, in the bath and in
a moving lift.*

MONOPOLY VARIATIONS

Short Monopoly: Before starting players decide the time the game will finish, and at the end the richest player wins.

At the start, the banker shuffles the title deed card and deals two to each player. The players then pay the bank the price of the property they receive.

The game then proceeds in the usual manner until the agreed finishing time is reached. Any player in the middle of a move when time is called is allowed to complete the move and any transactions.

Each player than adds up i) his cash in hand; ii) building sites, utilities or railway stations at the price shown on the board; iii) mortgaged property at half the price on the board; iv) houses owned valued at their respective cost prices; and v) hotels valued at the cost of five houses.

The player with the highest total wins.

The Free Parking Jackpot: At the start of the game, the banker places £500 under the Free Parking space. During the game, players who have to pay fines or taxes add that to the Free Parking jackpot instead of paying it to the bank. When a player lands on the space, he collects the money in the pot at the time. The first player landing there collects the £500 from the bank and any other penalty money. The bank does not contribute further, and players landing on Free Parking subsequently collect only the penalty money which has accrued.

Maximum Punishment: In the normal game, a player who is in jail can still collect rent, buy or sell property, and carry out normal trading. In this version, a player forfeits all these rights while he is in jail.

Best of three: In this version, players use three dice for each throw, but ignore one of the values in deciding where to move. This takes much longer to play than the normal game, and it is easier to avoid landing on hostile property. Successful players build up long stretches of properties next to one another to reduce the opponents' chances of avoiding them.

IT'S A FACT...

*Statistics show that, overall,
women competing in Monopoly
championships are more likely to
be successful than men.*

SCRABBLE

Scrabble* has become one of the world's most popular games, comparatively simple to learn, and just as enjoyable for beginners as for experts.

COMPLEXITY RATING:	★ ★
NUMBER OF PLAYERS:	**2 to 4**
EQUIPMENT:	**Board and 104 letter tiles**
TIME REQUIRED:	**Between 40 minutes and 1 hour**

Origins: Scrabble was invented in 1931 by Alfred M Butts, an architect forced out of work by the Great Depression. Butts was a lifelong devotee of anagrams and crosswords, and saw the potential for a game based on the principle of the crossword. Indeed in its earliest incarnations, Scrabble was named 'Crisscross Words'.

It was 17 years before Alfred Butts was able to find a company prepared to manufacture Scrabble commercially. But it took off immediately, and over 100 million Scrabble sets have now been sold around the world.

Aims of the game: The play in Scrabble consists of forming interlocking words, crossword fashion, on the playing board using letter tiles of various score values. Each player competes for the highest score by using his tiles in combinations and locations that take best advantage of letter values and premium squares on the board.

The tiles are selected at random, but Scrabble is not won by the luck of the draw. It is won by the player who has a sound vocabulary of everyday, and more obscure, words, and who develops a good knowledge of the many varied tactics which form an important part of the game. While the whole point of the game is to produce words with high scores, it is often the case that longer words can be outscored by the judicious use of one or two well-placed tiles.

Basic rules:

The letters, their points value, and number in the set are as follows:

A	1	9	G	2	3	M	3	2	S	1	4	Y	4	2
B	3	2	H	4	2	N	1	6	T	1	6	Z	10	1
C	3	2	I	1	9	O	1	8	U	1	4	Blank	0	2
D	2	4	J	8	1	P	3	2	V	4	2			
E	1	12	K	1	5	Q	10	1	W	4	2			
F	4	2	L	1	4	R	1	6	X	8	1			

A draw of tiles decides the start, with the letter nearest the beginning of the alphabet going first. Each player then draws seven lettered tiles, and the first player places a word on the board, across the centre square.

*Scrabble ® is the registered trade mark of J.W. Spear & Sons plc, Enfield, England.

Even at this stage, tactics can come into play. If you can start with a five-letter word or longer, you need to make sure that the highest possible value letter is placed on a double-letter square. By starting first, your word scores double points.

•

The second player adds one or more tiles to the word on the board, forming one or more new words. All tiles must be played in a row, either down or across the board, with all adjacent tiles forming legitimate words. Points are scored for each new or modified word formed.

Before putting down the first word that springs to mind, always look for possible alternatives, particularly those that use premium squares. Look out for triple-letter score squares, particularly when you can place high-value letters on them.

•

If a player uses all seven tiles in one move, he receives a bonus of 50 points.

Good players will often manage to use all seven tiles at once two or three times in a game, scoring the bonus each time. But they have to be worked out. Even though you may not be able to see a word on your tile rack, look for the opportunities presented by the letters already on the board. You should be thinking about the positions on the board where a seven-plus letter word could go, even before you have spotted the word on your rack.

•

The best way to develop those longer words is to hold on to the easy-to-use letters and blanks. Try to avoid having duplicates of letters, perhaps making exceptions of Es and Ss. If you have to choose between vowels when deciding what to discard, ditch the Os and Us in favour of As, Es and Is. Before getting rid of a U though, see if the Q is on the board, and check how many other Us have been used. When aiming for bonuses, try to have just two or three vowels on your rack, and get rid of the high-value letters as fast as you can.

Never start off with the idea of making one specific word, even though you have six of its seven letters. You may waste three or four turns hoping to pick up a solitary T or D, and you struggle along making insignificant scores as you are hoping.

Consider retaining combinations of leters that go together well (for example, -ERS, -ING, -EST, -TION). These can provide the key to bonus words.

As play continues, the players' scores are calculated after each move.

Rather than play a word, a player can choose to change one or more of the letters on his rack. Play then passes to the next player.

The game ends when all tiles have been drawn and one player has used up all the tiles on his rack, and no further plays are possible.

Most games of Scrabble in which the final scores are close are won or lost in the last few moves. If you have used all your tiles and the pool is exhausted, the scores of the other players are reduced by the sum of the point values of the tiles held by each player, and given to you. It is therefore most important to get out before your opponents, particularly if there are three or four. It helps to try to get rid of all high and medium-value tiles, by using them or returning them to the pool for replacement.

•

IT'S A FACT...

Enthusiastic players can compete in a Scrabble tournament somewhere in the country virtually every weekend.

SOME GENERAL TIPS

Scrabble players are generally of two types, defensive or offensive. If you aim only to win, regardless of the final scores, your best bet is a defensive game in which you would use a lot of short words, and lots of tightly-interlocking words. They open up very little of the board, preventing your opponent from scoring highly. An offensive player goes all out for 50-point bonuses, running risks and opening up premium score squares for his opponent. There is a skill in both styles, but defensive play is usually easier to achieve.

•

Be aware of the importance of two-letter words, particularly in the use of premium squares. If you can place, for example, the X on a triple-letter square so that it is scored both across and down, you can score over 50 points.

•

The two most valuable tiles in Scrabble are the S and the blank (which can be used as the letter of your choice). The S is useful because it can be used to pluralise many words. The blank is particularly useful in forming bonus words, where all seven tiles are used.

•

Try to increase your vocabulary using the dictionary of your choice. Concentrate in particular on two-letter words (good examples are AE, DA, EA, FY, IO, JO, OB,

UG and ZO) and three-letter words (AIN, DAS, GOY, LOX, NAE and YEX), and those using the awkward tiles (J, Q, X and Z).

•

Try to use the high value tiles (F, J, K, Q, V, X and Z) as soon as possible after picking them up, particularly as the game progresses, so you are not left with them at the end of the game. Otherwise their value could be deducted from your total score.

•

The official rules of Scrabble do not penalise a player who unsuccessfully challenges an opponent's word. If you do not recognise a word, challenge it immediately. If the word is not in the dictionary being used for the game, your opponent has to take back the tiles and lose his or her turn.

•

SCRABBLE VARIATIONS

Solitaire Scrabble: Use a single rack of letters, and try to score as many points as possible using all the tiles. This can be a useful aid in learning about 'set-up' plays and good tile retention.

Duplicate Scrabble: Invented by a Belgian, Hyppolite Wouters, this is widely played on the Continent, particularly in France. An arbitrator draws seven letters from a bag. All players then attempt to find the highest scoring move in a set time. The best move is then placed on the board, and all players who have found it score the appropriate number of points, the rest nothing. The arbitrator then draws a new set of tiles, and again all players attempt to find the highest scoring move on the board as it now stands. This continues until the tiles have been used up.

Back Scrabble: After a standard game of Scrabble has been completed, you can then play Back Scrabble. This consists of moving the letters, at least one, but not more than six, so that the remaining letters left on the board form complete words. The letters removed must be part of a single word. Points are scored for each letter removed.

IT'S A FACT...
The highest prize money in a Scrabble tournament was $10,000 awarded to the winner of the 1990 North American Scrabble Championships.

IT'S A FACT...
There are over 200 Scrabble clubs in Britain and almost 20 in America.

TRIVIAL PURSUIT

Trivial Pursuit* became particularly popular during the 1980s as a game based on tests of incidental knowledge.

COMPLEXITY RATING:	★ ★ ★
NUMBER OF PLAYERS:	**2 or more. It can be played in teams, with as many as 24 players taking part**
EQUIPMENT:	**Playing board; one die; box of question and answer cards; 24 colour category identification cards; six player tokens each with 6 niches which can contain scoring wedges; and 36 such wedges.**
TIME REQUIRED:	**1 to 2 hours**

Origins: Trivial Pursuit originated in the early 1980s, and became widely popular as a result of widespread interest in general knowledge and quiz competitions. A number of variations based on answering general knowledge questions have been produced subsequently.

Aim of the game: Players move their tokens around a board by answering questions in a variety of categories. The first to complete the circuit is the winner.

Basic rules: The board is illustrated with a wheel with hub, spokes and rim divided into squares, each showing one of six category symbols such as geography, entertainment, history, art & literature, science and nature, and sports & leisure.

Each player selects a token and receives six scoring wedges, one in each of six category colours. Players roll the die to determine who moves first. The leader rolls the die again, and starts from the hub at the centre of the board by moving his token the indicated number of spaces along any of the wheel spokes. The player is then asked a question from the category indicated by the space he lands on.

TIP

Your first throw will allow you to move to your choice of category in one spoke, so it is a good idea to start by going to your best category.

* *Trivial Pursuit: A Horn Abbot game licensed by Horn Abbot International Ltd, owners of the trademark 'Trivial Pursuit'.*

The question card is selected at random by another player from the box of questions. The answer is on the back, so it is important that the questioner should not reveal it. If the player correctly answers the question, his turn continues with another roll of the die. If the player answers incorrectly, the turn passes to the player on the left. A move may include a change of direction with each die roll, or at an intersection, but backtracking is not allowed. A player must always move the number of spaces shown on the die.

Try to answer every question, no matter what the category. Where the topic is obscure, the answer might actually be more obvious than you think. For example, a question about which company supplied the imperial Russian court with vodka from 1886 to 1917 might appear obscure, until you discover that the answer is 'Smirnoff'.

There is no time limit in answering questions, so if you feel you have a chance of doing so, do not hesitate to take your time.

Be careful in answering what appear to be obvious questions. For example, the southern-most state of the United States is Hawaii.

A category 'headquarters' is located at the junction of each spoke and the wheel rim, and when a player lands in the square and successfully answers a question, the appropriate colour scoring wedge is placed in his token. If the player answers incorrectly, he must move his token out of the square on the next turn and re-enter it later to attempt another question for credit.

A player landing on one of the 12 'roll again' spaces continues his turn by rolling the die again. A player whose token lands in the hub during the course of the game, treats the space as a wild-card space allowing him to choose the category for the subsequent question.

After a player has correctly answered a question in all category headquarters, that player must move his token towards the hub to attempt to win the game. He will need to throw the correct number to land on the hub. If he overshoots while attempting to enter the hub for a game-winning question, he can move to any spoke giving him a choice of five categories from which to choose the next question.

If you overshoot, you should choose the category you find easiest, because if you

answer the question correctly, you have another go, and a further chance to enter the hub.

•

When a player lands in the hub for a match-winning question, the opposing players select the category for the final question. The choice of category is made by simple agreement, or a vote, and the player must then answer it correctly to win the game.

You should take careful note during the game which categories your opponents do well on, and those they have more difficulty with. In that way, you can determine which he is least likely to be able to win.

•

Try to avoid giving any indication which categories you find easiest and most difficult. You should pretend to struggle with those questions you actually find easiest. For your most difficult categories, you should indicate that the answer is on the tip of your tongue, even if you have no idea. In this way, you might be lucky enough to persuade your opponents to give you an easier category when you reach the hub.

•

If the question is answered incorrectly, the player must leave the hub on the next turn, and re-enter it for another question. Because a correct answer always means another roll of the die, a player may meet the game winning requirements on the first

PENCIL AND PAPER GAMES

AGGRESSION

Aggression is both simple and complex in that it can be easily learned and played at a basic level by children, or it can be played with in-depth analysis of strategy and tactics.

COMPLEXITY RATING:	★ ★ ★
NUMBER OF PLAYERS:	**2 is ideal, but it can be played by three or more who may decide to form teams.**
EQUIPMENT:	**Paper and pencils**
TIME REQUIRED:	**15 minutes or more, depending on the number of countries played**

Aim of the game: In Aggression, players fight imaginary battles in a bid to occupy the maximum amount of territory.

Basic rules: A large sheet of paper is needed, and each player or team has different coloured pencils.

One player begins by drawing the boundaries of an imaginary country. Each player then in turn draws the outline of other imaginary countries adjoining one or more of the other countries. They may be any shape, but should not be too small. Any number may be drawn, but twenty will allow an interesting game. Each country should then be identified by letters.

Each player has 100 armies, and in the second stage of the game, players take it

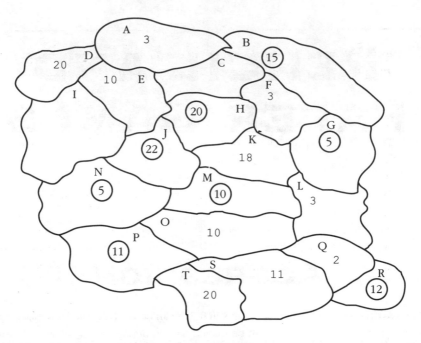

in turns to allocate any number of their armies to an unoccupied country, writing the number of the armies in the appropriate area in their chosen colour. The illustration above indicates how these might be distributed.

It is up to each player to decide whether to occupy a few countries with large numbers of armies, or to place a few armies in each of a large number of countries.

TIP

The greater the number of countries that are played, the smaller the armies need to be.

•

TIP

It is often a good idea to start by placing smaller contingents in a spread of countries to try to get a feel for how your opponent plans to place his armies.

•

TIP

If your opponent places a large contingent in one country, it is better to surround that country with a number of smaller armies which are bigger in total than his, than to try to defeat him with just one larger adjoining army. It may be possible for him to place other armies nearby which will then outflank your one large army.

Always watch out for isolated countries which do not have armies but which are totally surrounded by armies. There is a good chance you may be able to claim one.

In the third and final stage of the game comes the aggression. Beginning with the player who drew the first country, each player in turn uses the armies in one or more of the countries he occupies to conquer an adjacent country occupied by his opponent, wiping out his opponent's armies already stationed there. Adjacent countries are those with a common boundary. For example in the game illustrated, A, C, F and G are adjacent to B.

A player may conquer one of his opponent's countries only if he has more armies in adjacent countries than the opponent has in the country being attacked. The number of armies in the conquered country is crossed out, taking no further part in the game. The conquering armies, however, remain intact.

Look for your opponent's largest armies and try to defeat those first because of the threat they pose.

When looking to defeat an opposition army make sure you look all around the country because you can use the total of all the armies in countries which touch your target country.

A player conquering a country does not increase the number of countries he occupies – rather, the number of countries his opponent occupies is reduced. It should also be noted that countries not occupied by either player take no part in this stage of the game except as neutral zones.

There is little point in leaving a country as a neutral zone at the start because it does not count as anyone's country in deciding the winner. It is yours at the end if it has not been captured, but has just one army in it.

BATTLESHIPS

Battleships is a popular game in which skill and luck are equally blended.

COMPLEXITY RATING:	★ ★
NUMBER OF PLAYERS:	2
EQUIPMENT:	**Paper and pencil for each player, although Battleships has been produced as a commercial game with appropriate boards and pieces**
TIME REQUIRED:	**20 to 30 minutes a game**

Origins: It has been suggested that the game was invented by British prisoners-of-war in Germany during the Great War, but there is some doubt about this.

Aim of the game: Each player deploys his fleet on the board, and tries to determine where the other's vessels are and sink them. The first to do so is the winner.

Basic rules: Before the game starts, each player marks out on his sheet of paper two identical playing areas, each area consisting of 100 squares divided into 100 smaller squares, ten squares across by ten down. Each playing area is then lettered from A to J across the top, and 1 to 10 down one side so that each square can be identified by its number and letter. One area is marked Home Fleet and the other area Enemy Fleet.

Each player now places his fleet in the Home Fleet area without it being seen by his opponent. A fleet consists of the following ships:

1 battleship occupying 4 squares
2 cruisers occupying 3 squares each
3 destroyers occupying 2 squares each
4 submarines occupying 1 square each

A player may place his ships where he likes in the Home Fleet area, subject to these rules:

i) the squares forming each ship must be in a straight line, across or down.

ii) there must be at least one empty square between ships – in other words, no two ships may touch, even at a corner.

When both players have drawn their fleets then they can begin battle. The object is to sink the enemy fleet by naming the squares they occupy. To sink each ship, all the squares forming the ship must be hit.

Each player in turn fires a shot at the Enemy Fleet. The opponent examines his Home Fleet area to see whether that square is occupied by a ship. He must declare whether the shot was a hit or miss, and if it was a hit, he must identify the type of ship. The player firing the shot records a miss by marking the appropriate square in the Enemy Fleet area with a dot. Hits are recorded by marking the square with a letter identifying the type of ship.

In placing ships it is not advisable to place them all close together because when your opponent realises that, he will be able to reduce his field of fire considerably.

•

Do not place any of your ships in obvious squares such as the corners, and try for a mixture of vertical and horizontal placements.

•

If a battleship is hit, you should continue to fire at it by choosing adjoining squares until it is sunk. Once you have achieved that, because of the rules of placement, you should not fire at any of the adjoining squares. Remember the size of each ship so you do not continue firing needlessly at a ship you have sunk.

•

In the game illustrated below, for instance, it is clear that shots on squares B2 to B5 are required to sink the enemy battleship. It is also clear that, because of the rules about the placing of ships, squares such as B6, A2 and C4 must be unoccupied, so it would be pointless to waste shots on them.

	A	B	C	D	E	F	G	H	I	J
1									S	
2		B			C	C	C			
3		B								
4		B		C		D	D			
5		B		C						
6				C					S	
7		D								
8		D		D	D			S		
9										
10		S								

BATTLESHIPS VARIATION

Salvo: Salvo is a more complex version of battleships, also for two players. The aim, like Battleships, is to sink your opponent's fleet, but with the difference that instead of firing one shot in turn, a player fires a salvo of three shots. The opponent then declares whether any of the shots were direct hits and what type of ship was hit by the salvo. However, he does not have to declare the result of individual shots. For example, the first player may call out C5, D8 and H4, and the second player may reply: 'Two hits, one on a submarine and the other on a battleship.' The fact that a player does not know which of his shots were hits makes this a more complex game than battleships.

If a hit is recorded, you should continue to fire at adjoining squares in turn until you have sunk the vessels. Other tips for battleships also apply to salvo.

•

BOXES

Boxes is an extremely popular game among school children, and can be made as long or as short a game as the players wish.

COMPLEXITY RATING:	★
NUMBER OF PLAYERS:	**2 to 4 (but best with 2)**
EQUIPMENT:	**Pencil and paper**
TIME REQUIRED:	**From 10 minutes upwards (depending on how big the pattern of dots the players use)**

Aim of the game: Players try to complete with a fourth line as many boxes or squares as possible. The player making the most boxes wins.

Basic rules: A square pattern of any number of dots is drawn on a sheet of paper. A good number is ten rows by ten. Players then take it in turns to join any two of the dots that are next to one another by drawing horizontal or vertical lines. Whenever a player completes a box by drawing the fourth line, he initials it, and has another turn. He may continue his turn until he draws a line that does not complete a box. When there are no more dots to be joined, and all the boxes have been completed, the game ends, and the boxes are counted up for each player.

Early in the game, it is a good idea to create small groups of potential boxes with the open sides facing out from the edge of the pattern of dots. This means that when you are forced to concede boxes you can do so without doing major damage. Of course, the same opportunities will be available to your opponent with the boxes you have created.

Try to avoid linking up dots in strings as this could allow your opponent to make long lines of boxes later in the game.

As the game progresses and it is becoming harder to find a safe move, look for any pairs of dots which have not been connected with any other dots. These should allow you to make another move without giving away a box.

If you are looking for dots to connect, and are having difficulty finding a pair, check methodically along each line because this often helps you spot an opportunity which was not immediately obvious before.

When the only moves you have left are inevitably going to allow your opponent to make a number of boxes, and you have a choice of two or three groups, count up the numbers to make sure you are starting him off on the one with the least number.

NOUGHTS AND CROSSES

Noughts and crosses has been a popular children's pen and paper game for generations.

COMPLEXITY RATING:	★
NUMBER OF PLAYERS:	2
EQUIPMENT:	**Paper and two pencils**
TIME REQUIRED:	**5 minutes or less a game**

Origins: Noughts and crosses is derived from several ancient African board games such as Tic Tac Toe, Three in a Row and Achi. Versions have been found carved on the roofing slabs of the Temple of Kurna in Egypt from about 1400 BC.

Aim of the game: Players try to be the first to place their symbol, a nought or cross, in a straight line.

Basic rules: A framework is drawn consisting of two pairs of parallel lines crossing at right angles. Players draw lots to play first, and play alternately, the first drawing a nought and the second a cross, in any one of the nine squares which are vacant. Each player tries to block his opponent, while trying to complete a row horizontally, vertically, or diagonally.

TIP

Once you learn the simple strategy required for this game it is impossible to lose unless you make a major blunder. Between two experienced players, every game will end in a draw, with neither player being able to complete a row.

•

TIP

If you start first, and are playing a beginner you can sometimes win by playing this way, and if your opponent makes either of these two moves in reply:

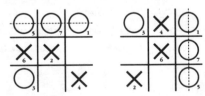

NOUGHTS AND CROSSES VARIATIONS

Tic Tac Toe: This is played on a square divided into nine smaller squares. Players alternate by placing noughts and crosses in squares trying to achieve three in a row. Like noughts and crosses, no one should win unless one player falls asleep.

Variation: Players have three counters each, and place them alternately. Play then continues with pieces being moved one square in any direction until one player gets three in a row.

Three in a Row: In this game, players start with three counters placed in a row on opposite sides of the board. The pieces are moved alternately one square in any direction until one person gets three in a row, but not the starting row.

Achi: In this game, which originated in Ghana, four pieces are used. They are placed in squares in turn, and then moved one square in any direction until one player achieves three in a row.

SPROUTS

Sprouts has some similarities with Boxes, but requires rather more ingenuity to win.

COMPLEXITY RATING:	★ ★
NUMBER OF PLAYERS:	2
EQUIPMENT:	Paper and pencils
TIME REQUIRED:	5 to 15 minutes (depending on the number of dots used to start)

Origins: Sprouts was invented in 1967 by two Cambridge mathematicians, and has become popular in many countries.

Aim of the game: Players join up a series of dots, and the last player to draw a legitimate line is the winner.

Basic rules: the game starts with any number of dots on a sheet of paper. Initially, it is probably best to use only three or four but this can be increased to six or so as experience of the game grows.

Players take it in turns to draw a line joining any two dots, or connecting a dot to itself. When he has done this the player puts a new dot on the line he has just drawn. It is then the other player's turn.

When drawing a line, a number of rules must be followed:

i) no line must cross itself, or cross a line that has already been drawn;

ii) no line may be drawn through a dot;

iii) a dot may have only three lines leaving it.

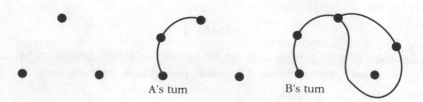

A's turn   B's turn

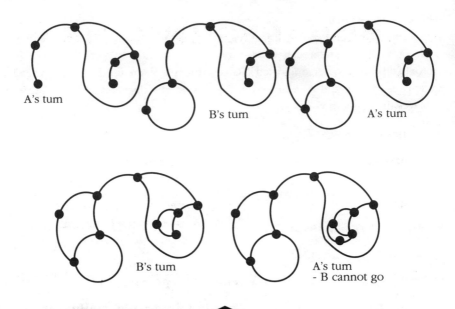

A's turn

B's turn

A's turn

B's turn

*A's turn
- B cannot go*

TIP

To win at Sprouts you need an ability to look two or three turns ahead. Beginners often fall into the trap of not taking into account the fact that each connecting line introduces a new dot to the game.

•

The game above shows how each turn being played produces a new dot:

TIP

Be very careful if you are trying to close up the game by connecting dots inside loops which have already been created, particularly if the game has started with just three or four dots.

•

TIP

Think carefully about the alternatives available to you, and to your opponent. It is very easy to be cut off from available dots by an unexpected move by your opponent.

•

GENERAL TIP

The simplicity of the game and the equipment means that you can practice easily by yourself taking both roles. In this way, you will soon develop a sense for available moves, and the potential traps.

SQUARES IN LINE

Squares in Line is very similar to Boxes.

COMPLEXITY RATING:	★
NUMBER OF PLAYERS:	**2**
EQUIPMENT:	**Pencil and paper (squared paper is helpful**
TIME REQUIRED:	**15 minutes, but longer if the pattern of squares is bigger**

Aim of the game: Points are scored for capturing the last square in each line. The winner is the player who has scored most points.

Basic rules: Players start with a piece of paper marked into squares. Beginners should start with a sheet of 6 × 6 or 7 × 7 squares, but as they improve, the number of squares can be increased.

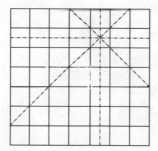

Players take it in turn to choose a square and put their initial in it. Whenever the square is the last one in a line, either from side to side, or up and down, or diagonally, he is given a score equal to the number of squares in the line. If more than one line is completed by a player he scores points for all the squares in all the lines.

The player who finishes a line is given an extra turn, and his turn ends when he cannot complete any more lines.

When playing Squares in Line, you should always remember that most squares have four lines running through them (one across, one up and down, and one running diagonally to the left and one diagonally to the right). Watch out for a chance score from more than one of these lines.

SQUARES IN LINE VARIATION

Marked Squares: This version of Squares in Line is played on a sheet of paper marked off into 81 small squares (9 × 9). The players take it in turns to mark squares, but in this game only the rows going across and the columns up and down count.

When you are able to secure the third square in a line, you score one point; for the sixth square in a line you score two points, while for the ninth and last you score three points.

If you get a score in more than one line by marking a square, you add both scores together.

At the end of the game, the winner is the player with most points.

PI

This simple but stimulating word game is perhaps more suited to adults than children. It has some similarities with Scrabble, but can be played anywhere there is a dictionary to hand.

COMPLEXITY RATING:	★ ★
NUMBER OF PLAYERS:	2
EQUIPMENT:	**Paper and pencils and a dictionary**
TIME REQUIRED:	**20 minutes**

Aim of the game: To complete words within a small grid.

Basic rules: The two players compete on a piece of graph paper divided into squares, perhaps 5 by 5 or 6 by 6. Each player takes it in turn to put a letter in a square, any square. The rules are that when there are three – or more – letters in a row they must form a word (read from either left to right or top to bottom, but not backwards). Also you cannot place a letter which makes it impossible later to form a word of two or more letters in that row. This is where challenges come in. Instead of playing a letter, a player can challenge the last move of his or her opponent, saying that either the word completed is not a real word, or that his or her last move has made it impossible to form a word later. To do this you need to know your words; a good dictionary will be the final referee. The loser is the first person who cannot meet his opponent's challenge, or who cannot make a move without creating a non-existent word. But beware: the challenge is a double-edged weapon, because if your opponent can justify the word you challenge he or she wins the game.

TIP

The game gives scope for skilful use of ploys. If your opponent is a little unsure on some words you may deliberately place a letter which cannot form a word. Your opponent will be too unsure to challenge and risk losing the game; but when he or she makes a move in the same spot you can successfully challenge them.

•

BEHEADINGS

Another game with a grim name, but don't worry, the beheading just refers to words. This game is quite a challenge for those who haven't played it before, but for experts it quickly loses its appeal as there is a 'perfect' answer which once known takes out the element of competition, unless a variation of the rules is applied.

COMPLEXITY RATING:	★ ★
NUMBER OF PLAYERS:	Unlimited
EQUIPMENT:	Pencils and paper
TIME REQUIRED:	25 minutes

Aim of the game: To compile words starting with the first letter from each of the 26 letters of the alphabet, which can nonetheless stand on their own.

Basic rules: Each player takes a piece of paper and writes out the letters of the alphabet vertically down one side of the page. The players then create a word from each letter in turn; but the words must be able to stand as complete words when the first letter is removed or 'beheaded'. So AFAR can be shorted to FAR, and CLOT can be altered to LOT, and so on. It's a good idea if you use different coloured pencils or pens for the 'head' and the 'body' of the words, so they are easier to distinguish. The round stops when one of the players completes all 26 letters. One point is awarded to each letter in the 'severed' part of the body. For instance AFAR would be given 3 points for the word FAR. So there is an incentive to come up with the longest possible examples. Another way of stopping the game is to have a time limit of say 20 or 25 minutes, otherwise the game can drag on if no one can complete the list. Other variations include rewarding players who come up with the shortest possible words rather than the longest.

TIP

Assuming that you are playing with the original rules, make sure you get as many words down as possible as quickly as possible. It is better to get the majority of letters filled in rather than lingering over one particular word.

STAIRWAY

This is a very simple listing game, suitable for children, which can be great fun nonetheless.

COMPLEXITY RATING:	★
NUMBER OF PLAYERS:	**2 or more, though it can be played as well by yourself**
EQUIPMENT:	**Paper and pencils**
TIME REQUIRED:	**It's best to set a time limit of 5 to 10 minutes**

Aim of the game: To think of as many words as possible of different lengths beginning with a particular letter.

Basic rules: The players choose a letter – any letter will do but avoid Z or X unless you want a low-scoring game – and the time limit is set. Then each player writes down, one below another, words beginning with that letter. Each word should be one letter longer than the previous one, and the effect on the paper is like a stairway of words, hence the game's name. Each word is given one point so the winner is the player with the longest stairway. You are not allowed gaps or missed stairs. If the game is a draw, the matter is decided by comparing the stairways word by word, and those made up of letters from earlier in the alphabet score an additional point. Again, the player with the most points wins.

There are no real strategies in this case, but don't forget the useful if rather lazy ploy of adding an S or sometimes later in the staircase an IES to the end of the word. You can also add other endings to a word already used, so that STRONG may become STRONGLY two words later. Purists might however argue that this ploy devalues the game as a test of word skills.

•

Another similar listing game is **Sequences**. The players have to list every word they can think of which has two consecutive letters of the alphabet appearing in order in it, ie AB in ABLE or ST in BEST. They get a point for each correct word. To make it much harder, players have to think of words where three consecutive letters of the alphabet appear in order, eg HIJ in HIJACK.

Write out the letters of the alphabet and look through them, trying to find groups or pairings which suggest the beginnings or ends of words.

•

CASCADE

This deceptively simple word game becomes much harder when played, as it should be, at speed. It is also suitable for playing on your own against the clock, and is a good test of vocabulary for adults and children alike.

COMPLEXITY RATING:	★
NUMBER OF PLAYERS:	**Any number**
EQUIPMENT:	**Paper and pencils**
TIME REQUIRED:	**Set a time limit of perhaps 5 or 10 minutes**

Aim of the game: To compile a list of words, where each one is just one letter different from the previous one.

Basic rules: The players agree beforehand on a word of perhaps four or five letters, and set the time limit. Then each writes beneath the original word a word with the same number of letters, and with just one different letter. The player is also free to re-arrange the order of the letters. By the end of the time limit, of course, the final word will almost certainly be unrecognisable from the first. So for example, you may start with BEST, move to WEST, then to EWES, then to SEEM and so on. No word may be used more than once. If the game is played against a set time limit then the winner is the person who has chosen the most words. An alternative method is to play to a set number of words, so the winner would be the first to reach, for example, 25 words. It is important that all the 'cascades' are checked thoroughly as one of the delights of the game is that as players hurry to extend their list they make mistakes, which then disallows every word made after the error. So just because someone finishes with more words does not always mean they end up as the winner.

Always check carefully that you have made a correct jump to the next word, otherwise most of your list could be compiled in vain.

•

TIP

Although the rules say you cannot use the same word twice, they do not prevent you from using the same combination of letters if you are stuck. So, after EWES, the player could go to STEW, the same letters as in WEST but clearly not the same word. (It is, however, open to the competitors to ban this 'sharp practice' from the start.)

•

MISSING WORDS

This is a simple word game played with pencil and paper which can be enjoyed by children and adults alike. Indeed parents might find it a useful way of improving their children's spelling and vocabulary.

COMPLEXITY RATING:	★ ★
NUMBER OF PLAYERS:	**2 or more**
EQUIPMENT:	**Pencil and paper**
TIME REQUIRED:	**No more than a few minutes**

Aim of the game: To fill in the missing letters and complete words as quickly as possible.

Basic rules: Each player has a sheet of paper on which a word is spelt out vertically down one side. Then, on the other side the same word is also spelt out vertically but this time backwards. So if the word was NAME, then the N in the first column would correspond with the E in the second. Each player then has to fill in the gaps between the letters to create a word. When one player has completed all the words the round ends, and for each missing word each player gives the winner of the round one point. The overall winner is the player with the most points after a set number of rounds. Here is an example:

B	ra	T
E	we	S
S	al	E
T	a	B

TIP

If you can't think of one word don't get stuck on it and waste valuable time. Move on to the next one. Otherwise you may find yourself losing more points than you should.

LOTTO

This simple number game can be played with many people and is one of the less demanding of numerical contests.

COMPLEXITY RATING:	★
NUMBER OF PLAYERS:	**2 or more plus a neutral 'compère' to draw the numbers. If there are only two of you, though, you can take it in turns to draw the numbers**
EQUIPMENT:	**Pencil and paper**
TIME REQUIRED:	**About 20 minutes**

Aim of the game: To place as many of the same numbers in a row as possible.

Basic rules: Each player is given paper divided into 5 squares by 5 squares. The compère has 48 small pieces of paper, and on each of these the numbers 1 to 12 are written, four times. These are then put into a hat or other suitable object and rather as in a bingo hall he or she calls them out one at a time. Each player writes down the number called out in whichever square they like. Their aim is to ensure that the same number appears in a column – either horizontal or vertical – as many times as possible. (The maximum clearly is four times.) There is only room on the 5 by 5 square for 25 numbers, so at the end of this each player counts up his or her score. The players can work out in advance how to do this. One system is to give 5 points for two like numbers in a row; 15 points for two pairs of like numbers; 30 for three like numbers; 40 for four like numbers; and 50 for a 'full house' – three like numbers and a pair of another. You can also award 10 points for five consecutive numbers eg 5, 6, 7, 8, 9. A row of different numbers would earn no points. The winner, naturally, is the player with most points.

If you start by putting your first number in the middle square this allows you some flexibility about where to 'move' your next number.

•

Don't spend too long looking to build up elaborate three and four numbers in a row. Keep your eyes open for any pairs just to make sure your score keeps ticking over.

ABSTRACTS

This interesting game has some similarities with the popular party game of charades, only it is written down. Children can play it at a basic level, but it has the scope to be very demanding and great fun if the players are prepared to use a lot of imagination.

COMPLEXITY RATING:	★ ★
NUMBER OF PLAYERS:	**It can be played with just two but is better with more.**
EQUIPMENT:	**Pencil and paper**
TIME REQUIRED:	**One round can be over in a few minutes.**

Aim of the game: The rules are very simple. One player selects an idea, thought, mood or concept of his or her choice and then draws an illustration of that. This is where the name Abstract comes in. There is no point in choosing something like a street and then drawing a picture of houses along a street with traffic in between; it's a little obvious. But it can be a great challenge for someone to try to draw a concept such as 'Monday morning blues' while the others try to guess it. You can introduce an element of competition if you like by awarding points to the first person to guess the concept.

INFLATION

This topically-named game looks very simple, but in fact players require careful thought to be successful at it.

COMPLEXITY RATING:	★ ★
NUMBER OF PLAYERS:	**2 or more**
EQUIPMENT:	**Pencil and paper**
TIME REQUIRED:	**5 minutes**

Aim of the game: Players have to think up words which continue a numerical sequence.

Basic rules: The player who starts writes down a three-letter word at the top of the paper. Each letter of the alphabet is given a number, 1 to 26, with A as 1 and Z as

26, and the total value of the first word must be less than 10. It may, for example, be the word CAB, whose value adds up to just 6. The number 6 is written next to the word. The next player has to think of another three-letter word which must start with a letter from the previous word (C, A or B) and whose numerical value is more than the first word's, ie here that would be more than 6. This could be, for example, BAN, which has a numerical value of 17. The next players must do the same and so on. The loser is the first player unable to find a three-letter word which has a numerical value greater than the previous word. No word can be used twice.

It is best to beat the previous word's score by using as low-scoring letters as possible, otherwise you allow the next player to start his word with a high-scoring letter – and make a score which you may have difficulty beating. For example, if you used the word BUY instead of BAN, this would allow the other player to use the word YAM, which scores 39.

•

A variation of this game is **Century**. In this game for two or more people the start is the same as Inflation. But this time the next word must begin with the last letter of the first word, and the combined numerical value of the new word and the original must be written down. In this example BAN could still be used, so adding 6 and 17 we get 23. This process goes on and the loser is the person whose word causes the *cumulative* total to reach 100 – hence Century.

HANGMAN

It's odd and a little macabre how such a popular children's (and adult) game as this can be based on such a grim subject. Despite that, it retains its favoured status with many youngsters, though it's best to keep strictly to fixed rules to gain the most enjoyment from it. In reality the game is based simply on word deduction.

COMPLEXITY RATING:	★
NUMBER OF PLAYERS:	2 or more
EQUIPMENT:	Pencil and paper
TIME REQUIRED:	5 minutes

Aim of the game: To guess the word your opponent has chosen before you are 'hanged'.

Basic rules: One of the players chooses a word in his mind which he then writes on the paper as a series of dashes representing the letters. The other player or players then have 13 – unlucky 13 – attempts to discover what the word is. Each opponent in turn suggests a letter. If the letter is in the word, the first player writes the letter or letters in the correct place. If not he or she draws the first part of the hangman and his hangman's stand – which is made up of 13 items in all including the victim's body. The other players are also allowed to guess outright what the word is, though in the strict rules of the game if they get it wrong that means they have lost the game. A softer version of the rules simply allows the hangman to draw another part of the apparatus. It is probably more interesting to use a points system to increase competition. So the successful hangman will get one point for each part of the drawing he makes. If the word has not been discovered that will be 13; if a correct guess is made it will be however many parts of the drawing have been made. The 'victim' will get 13 points if he or she guesses correctly or discovers the word, minus those parts of the drawing completed.

Although it might seem better for the hangman to choose a longer word, in fact it is often easier for other players to work out a longer word than it is a short one. So don't be afraid to choose three-letter words even if they seem quite easy. Your opponents may get lost in all the apparent choices of words they have.

•

When guessing it is best to discover the vowels first, as this will give you the shape and structure of the word. Try to look for patterns and remember that in English letters often go in pairs, for example GH, TH and QU.

•

JOTTO

This clever deductive game is more suitable for adults and older teenagers than young children.

COMPLEXITY RATING:	★ ★ ★
NUMBER OF PLAYERS:	2
EQUIPMENT:	**Pencils and paper**
TIME REQUIRED:	**20 minutes**

Aim of the game: To guess your opponent's secret word before he or she guesses yours.

Basic rules: Each player chooses a word which they write down and keep to themselves. The two words should be of the same length, perhaps four, five or six letters each. There is then a battle of wits as each player in turn calls out a word of the same length to test whether it is the same as his or her opponent's. If there is a letter in the test word which is in the secret word then the player acknowledges it, but does not say where in the word it comes. Gradually each player can work out the letters in his opponent's word and the winner is the one who correctly deduced the other's first. You should note that if there is, say, two As in your word and the other player suggests a test word with only one A in it, you only have to acknowledge one of the As.

Oddly, it is often the case that words with more than one of the same letter in them are harder to discover in this game than others.

•

If you choose a test word which has no letters in common with your opponent's this helps you to eliminate letters; and you can then use letters from that same test word in other test words to try out possible other letters.

•

GRID RUNNER

This is relatively simple game of cat and mouse that can be played by both children and adults with equal enjoyment. One of its pleasures is that in such a straightforward game there are a number of different strategies that can be employed to ensure some variety in contests.

COMPLEXITY RATING:	★ ★
NUMBER OF PLAYERS:	2
EQUIPMENT:	**A piece of graph paper and two pencils or pens of different colours.**
TIME REQUIRED:	**Skilful players can stretch the game out for some time but typically 10 to 15 minutes**

Aim of the game: The idea is to force your opponent's pencil line into a corner where he or she can only move by crossing your line – and thus losing them the game.

Basic rules: Take the graph paper which for example may be 30 squares by 30 squares in size. Find the spot where the sixteenth horizontal line crosses the sixteenth vertical line in the middle of the paper. The first player – it doesn't matter which – then marks the sides of two squares along this vertical line, one above and one below the sixteenth horizontal line. The other then does the same, except that he marks the sides of two squares along the horizontal line, one before and one after the vertical line. In this way you have a little cross in the middle of the paper. This is the only time in the game that the lines cross. The game now starts with the first player 'moving' his line by one square, followed by the other. By moving, the player has nominated which end of his line is the front and from then on the line can only move from that end, rather as if it was the front of a train. Each player, taking it in turns, then moves his train-like line around the paper one square at a time. A player is not allowed to go over the same square more than once but is otherwise free to go where he or she wants, including using the outer line of the graph paper. A player's line can *touch* his opponent's line in the corner of a square, but it *must not* cross it. A player wins when he boxes his opponent in so they cannot move without crossing the other's line.

This is a game where players can either be attacking or defensive in their tactics. One sound piece of advice is to block off as large an area as possible of the graph from your opponent – remember he cannot cross your line – so he has little room to move around in.

A high-risk but fun strategy is to attack your opponent by closely shadowing them around the paper. This can intimidate them and a quick-witted player will be able to capitalise on any mistakes they make. As Napoleon once said, always be bold!

FOG IN THE NIGHT

Fog in the Night is a complex game and more demanding than many other pen and paper games, having a wonderful element of uncertainty and risk built into it. Once mastered it can give hours of pleasure – or frustration!

Origin: Believed to have originated from Holland during the Second World War – which is appropriate given its cloak-and-dagger tactics and military terminology.

Aim of the game: Each player tries to eliminate the other's spy or to capture their home base.

COMPLEXITY RATING:	★ ★ ★ ★
NUMBER OF PLAYERS:	2
EQUIPMENT:	**Pencil and paper, divided into 7 squares by 7 squares**
TIME REQUIRED:	**30 minutes**

Basic rules: There is some preparation work to be done before the game is ready to start. First, the squares on the paper have to be made identifiable, which is done by treating them as if they are squares on a grip reference map (see page 248). Along the axis line in front of the players the squares are labelled A to G, while the squares along the side axis are numbered 1 top 7. This means that each square will have its own coordinates, eg B3 or F5. In addition the five middle squares in front of each player are numbered 1 to 5. These are the starting position of the players' troops or platoon. The middle three of these, ie 2 to 4, are then highlighted to represent the targets which the other player has to capture. Now each player has to keep a record of *all ten* players on the playing area, his five and the 'enemy' five. To do this each takes two pieces of paper and divides them each into columns 1 to 5 to represent first his or her soldiers and then the opposition. These columns, which must be kept secret from the other player, can then be used to keep track of all the soldiers by filling in the coordinates appropriate to each soldier. For example, soldier 4 may be in square D3, and so D3 is entered in the column under soldier 4.

Each platoon or troop, as we have seen, has five members. These are divided into four soldiers and one spy. The overall numerical value of the five members is 12, of whom the spy has zero value. Each player can give whatever value he wants to the four remaining soldiers in his troop, as long as they all add up to 12. A player could, for example, give one soldier the value of 6, another 4 and the other two 1 – though this may not be the best tactics. Again, each player should record the value he has given to the four soldiers in his own columns without revealing them to his of her opponent.

Now at last the game can begin. Each player takes it in turn to move one of his troops, one square at a time, forwards, sideways or diagonally. He or she records the square where his soldier lands, eg B4, in his column and also tells the other player for them to record. A crucial aspect of the game is that only one soldier can occupy a square at any one time. If a soldier lands – and of course this will be on purpose – on the square of an opponent then there is a 'fight'. Each player reveals the value of his soldier on that square. The winner of the fight is the player whose soldier has the highest value. So for example if a soldier has the value 5 he will defeat a soldier with the value 4 or less. The losing soldier becomes a casualty and removed. If they are equal in value, each is returned to their starting position. It will be seen from this that the spy, whose value is zero, will lose against any soldier. The game is over when either one player captures the other's spy or when one captures the other's three highlighted positions.

Player	1	2	3	4	5	1	2	3	4	5
Value	2	0	2	3	4				F2	
			D3	B1						

	A	B	C	D	E	F	G	
1		5	(4)	(3)	(2)	1		1
2								2
3								3
4								4
5								5
6								6
7		1	(2)	(3)	(4)	5		7
	A	B	C	D	E	F	G	

Player	1	2	3	4	5	1	2	3	4	5
Value	1	5	1	5	0			D3		B1
	F2									

It is best to balance the value of the soldiers fairly evenly otherwise this can limit the attacking power of your side, and at the same time make it more vulnerable to attack from your opponent.

•

Naturally your opponent does not know which of your team is the spy, your most vulnerable member, and so it is best not to isolate the spy by keeping him alone in the base position. Remember your opponent's main attacking soldier is likely to be his biggest value member, so either pit your most potent soldier against him or avoid altogether!

•

Try to break up your opponent's concentration by attacking on two flanks at once. One of these can be a 'decoy', a low-value soldier to sacrifice while another higher soldier is deployed elsewhere.

•

A high-risk but potentially good ploy is to double bluff your opponent by attacking with your spy. This is especially if you are playing a series of games and you normally attack with a high-value soldier. Your opponent may then get a nasty surprise when he attacks what he thinks is one of your less potent soldiers.

•

Another more sophisticated tactic is to have two very high value soldiers, 5 or even 6, and the others low; and then attack with one high-value and one low as a decoy. The other high-value soldier can be kept back as defence.

•

L.A.P. or Sectors

L.A.P.'s unusual name comes from its Polish inventor who was called L.A. Pijanowski. Its alternative name comes from the basic ingredient of the game – hidden 'sectors' to be discovered by your opponent.

COMPLEXITY RATING:	★ ★ ★
NUMBER OF PLAYERS:	Normally 2, but it can be adapted to 3 or more players and can be more fun with extra players.
EQUIPMENT:	Pencil and graph paper.
TIME REQUIRED:	25 to 30 minutes

Aim of the game: The main objective is for a player to discover the whereabouts of his opponent's hidden sectors on the graph through persistent and quick-witted questioning.

Basic rules: Each player has two pieces of graph paper eight squares by eight squares. The squares are then numbered and lettered down the respective axis to give each individual square its own co-ordinate eg F7 or A3. One graph is to keep a record of a player's own sectors, the other to check on his opponent's. A player then secretly divides his own graph into four different areas or 'sectors' of different shapes; but all covering roughly the same area. These are then numbered one to four – the Roman numerals I, II, III and IV can be used to avoid confusion. So how does a player discover his opponent's sectors? Each takes it in turn to call out a block of four squares, for example F–G, 6–7. The other player only replies by saying whether this block cuts across a boundary line between his sectors or not; but does not reveal which sectors are involved. This questioning takes place alternately and gradually each player builds up a picture of where his opponent's sectors lie. As an alternative, a player can suggest that a particular square is in a particular sector – eg D4 in section III – to which his opponent replies 'correct' if this is the case. Through this process the most sharp-witted player will ultimately discover where his opponent's sectors with their numbers are – and win the game.

Be careful not to over-use the question about whether a particular square is in a certain sector as this may limit the amount of concrete facts you are getting while your opponent builds up his picture. It is best to wait until you have at least a general idea of where the sectors are before asking a specific question.

•

Use the fact that a block does not cross a boundary as a positive factor, ie that you at least know the area of one individual sector, and then build from there.

If you have more than two players, then work out in advance in what turn you are going to ask opponents about which square is in which sector.

•

ALPHABET SOUP

This amusing little word game can be as flexible as the players like and is a good warm-up for quizzes and general knowledge tests, as well as a test of people's ingenuity. There is also room for some tactics for good players.

COMPLEXITY RATING:	★ ★
NUMBER OF PLAYERS:	2 or more
EQUIPMENT:	Paper and pencils
TIME REQUIRED:	No set limit, but it is better to restrict it to a certain number of rounds.

Aim of the game: To come up with the most unusual words starting with a given letter of the alphabet.

Basic rules: Each player takes a piece of paper and divides it into columns. How many columns depends on how demanding you want the game to be. Perhaps start off with five and then work upwards. Each column has a different heading or subject matter. These may be, for example, football teams, countries, tube stations, birds, pop stars. To start the game, one of the players silently repeats the alphabet (at any speed they like) and another shouts stop. Whichever letter the first player stopped on is the letter for that round – and then each player has to think of as many words as possible under each heading beginning with that letter. For example if the letter was P, then you might write penguin, pelican and parrot under the birds column, and Pimlico and Paddington under tube stations. (Note: only masochists would come up with Z or X!) When one player has at least one word in all the columns he shouts out and the round in ended. Scoring is done by crossing out all words which have been written by two or more players; each player scores one point for a word that he or she alone thought of, so unusual words are important. As an additional rule, you can deduct one point from a player for each column they failed to write any word in. The winner is the player with the most points after a set number of rounds.

It is better to fill in all the columns with just one unusual word than a number of different but fairly common ones. The best strategy of all is to get one unusual word in each column very quickly so that your opponents don't have a chance to come up with many choices. This is especially true if players are deducted a point for each empty column.

•

If there are a number of columns and you can't think of any word for one, don't stop and waste time thinking of one. It's far better to come up with good words for other columns that will score you points than agonise over just one column.

•

One delightful subtlety of the game when you are playing with (other) very bright and sophisticated people is the bluff tactic. They will all be thinking of the most original and unusual words possible. So after a few rounds why not slip in a few obvious ones they may not use – and score points with them!

•

GUGGENHEIM

This popular contest, sometimes called Categories, is a good family and party game and is a demanding test of a person's vocabulary and ingenuity against the clock. It's a slightly more complicated version of Alphabet Soup.

COMPLEXITY RATING:	★ ★
NUMBER OF PLAYERS:	2 or more
EQUIPMENT:	Pencils and paper
TIME REQUIRED:	A fixed time is set of say 10 or 15 minutes.

Aim of the game: To think of as many words as possible which begin with the same letter and conform to a particular category.

Basic rules: Each of the players chooses a category or subject matter, and these are then written down the left hand side of their piece of paper. The players also agree on a common word of perhaps five letters, which has no letters repeated and no Z's or X's in it. This word is then written horizontally across the top of the paper. The allotted time now starts. The object is for each player – it is also possible to play in teams – to think of a word which begins with the letter of the common word above it and fits in with the category in the vertical column to the side. Here is a simple example:

	S	H	O	W
Birds	Swallow	Heron	Osprey	Wren
Capitals	San Salvador	Helsinki	Ottawa	Washington
Trees	Sycamore	Horse Chestnut	Oak	Willow

When the set time is up the list of each player is examined. The aim is to get the most unusual word or example. If a player is the only one to have used a particular word he or she is given the best mark, which is the number of players minus One. thus if there are six players and someone has a word no one else has thought of, that person will get five marks. If one other person has thought of it they will receive the number of people taking part, here that would be six, minus two, ie four marks. If three got it they would receive three marks and so on. There are no marks if everyone uses the same word. Some rules also deduct a mark if a player has left a blank, though normally this simply counts as no mark. You can play as many different rounds as you want, altering the common word and also the categories if they become too boring or are too easy or too difficult. It's useful to have a dictionary and encyclopedia to hand to sort out disputes. Good players will want to use far more demanding categories and perhaps longer common words than the ones given in the example.

If you are playing the normal rule that blank spaces don't lost you any points, then you will score more heavily by taking your time to think up the most unusual words possible rather than filling in every gap.

However, if you are playing with experts who you know are likely to come up with unusual words it may be worth sometimes going for an obvious word – as they may consider it too obvious and leave you with a maximum score.

GARBAGE HEAPS

This odd pencil and paper game is suitable as a party activity, especially for children, and depends as much on manual dexterity as on deductive skills.

COMPLEXITY RATING:	★ ★
NUMBER OF PLAYERS:	2
EQUIPMENT:	**Paper and pencils or felt-tips**
TIME REQUIRED:	**15 minutes**

Aim of game: To negotiate your way around a course without crossing your or your opponent's path.

Basic rules: It is best if the different-coloured pencils or felt-tip pens used by the players are of the same type, to ensure fairness. The players then draw 16 points spaced out on the paper and numbered 1 to 16. These are the garbage heaps of the title. The players can toss a coin to see who goes first. The first to go then holds the pen or pencil by his or her thumb and finger tips, and at the end of the pencil, to make it harder to control. This player then draws a loop around the heap marked number 1, before drawing a random line around the course, eventually reaching the number 2 heap. This the player then encircles. It is now the other player's turn and he or she does the same. The two players alternate like this, scoring a point for each heap they circle. But they also lose a point each time they touch or cross an existing path, and as you are holding the pencil by your finger tips this is more likely than you might expect. Players are, however, allowed to pass through a garbage heap as often as they like without losing a point. The winner is the person with the most points at the end.

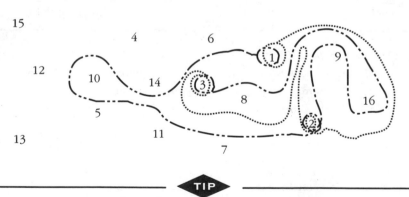

It is next to impossible not to cross a line at least once, so when you do, try to make sure that it at least enables you to reach other heaps without having to cross a line.

•

Drawing a line when you are only holding the pencil by your finger tips is quite difficult so if you want to win get some practice in first!

INDEX OF GAMES

A–Z listing: Where to find games and their variations